The A-Series Engine

ITS FIRST SIXTY YEARS

Recent Haynes books by the same author have included:

British Touring Car Racing in Camera
A photographic celebration of 50 years

Haynes Classic Makes Series
Bentley
A Legend Reborn

Haynes Classic Makes Series
BMW
Driven to Succeed

Haynes Great Car Series
Mini
A celebration of Britain's best-loved small car

Performance Fords

The A-Series Engine

ITS FIRST SIXTY YEARS

GRAHAM ROBSON

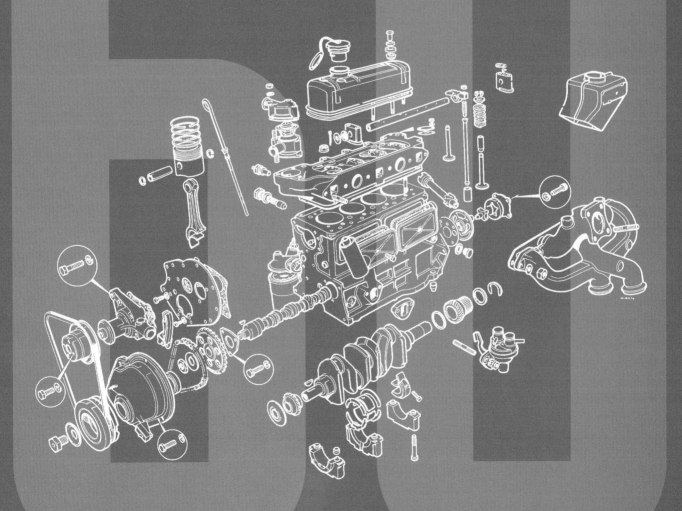

First published in November 2011

A catalogue record for this book is available from the British Library

ISBN 978 0 85733 083 3

Library of Congress catalog card no 2011930601

Published by Haynes Publishing,
Sparkford, Yeovil, Somerset BA22 7JJ, UK
Tel: 01963 442030 Fax: 01963 440001
Int.tel: +44 1963 442030 Int.fax: +44 1963 440001
E-mail: sales@haynes.co.uk
Website: www.haynes.co.uk

Haynes North America Inc.,
861 Lawrence Drive, Newbury Park, California 91320, USA

Designed and typeset by Dominic Stickland

Printed in the USA by Odcombe Press LP,
1299 Bridgestone Parkway, La Vergne, TN 37086

Contents

Introduction

It isn't often that an engine gets a history book all to itself. Even so, BMC's famous A-Series power unit deserves that honour – not only because it was launched 60 years ago, in 1951, but also because it kept BMC, then British Leyland, alive for many years. The engine, which Austin's chairman Len Lord had originally commissioned to use in a series of small Austins, went on to power the legendary Mini, then the 1100, then the Sprite and Midget sports cars – and a series of other family machines. In the end, around 14 million of them were produced for nearly 50 years – and the many survivors are enthusiastically being tuned, modified and improved by specialist concerns to this day.

This is a story that I have wanted to relate for some years – but not just as a 'cast-iron versus aluminium', bores, strokes and power outputs tale. I wanted to make clear that the A-Series, in its own important way, was absolutely central to the growth of BMC, to the very survival of British Leyland, and to the product-planning of almost every one of the cars built by those corporations in the last 50 years.

Accordingly, this book not only covers the life of the engine itself, but also the story of the corporations that embraced it. It's a story, too, which tells us who the dominant bosses, engineers and sporting personalities actually were – and also tells the reader how an A-Series could turn up in unlikely places, doing unlikely jobs.

It took a long time for me to research all the threads, but even I – a gnarled old hand who over the years has often been in and out of Longbridge, the 'home of the A-Series' for so long – was surprised by what was unearthed.

How many people, for instance, realise that the A-Series – or AS3, as it was originally coded – might have been a side-valve unit? That at one time in later life it might have been converted to a neat overhead camshaft unit? That there was once a thought of it being used as an auxiliary engine in a tank? That there was a diesel derivative, which never found its way into private cars? And that one of the serious proposals for its replacement would have been a three-cylinder unit?

As any reader, motoring enthusiast, author or researcher will surely realise, when writing this book I found it difficult to compress all the information into a package which covers every aspect without hiding behind a pile of statistics. At this point, therefore, I'll merely point out that without the A-Series there would simply never have been a Mini, that without the A-Series BMC would never have got back into the small sports car market which they covered so well, and that they would surely never have been able to make up to 10,000 cars a week at Longbridge and Cowley.

Over the years, for sure, the A-Series has had rivals, but I submit that none of them has ever had such a following. This book, I hope, proves why.

GRAHAM ROBSON
Autumn 2011

Acknowledgements

How do you keep a list of 'thank yous' to a manageable length? It's not easy, especially where such a famous and universal product as the BMC A-Series engine is concerned, one which was in production for so long. The fact is that the number of people who have helped me over the years is enormous.

To put this into perspective, I personally bought my first A-Series car (an Austin A35) in 1959, I started writing about cars in 1960, and I have been a full-time motoring historian for 40 years. I seem to have been involved in A-Series-powered projects – mainstream or motorsport, modern or historical, corporate and personal – throughout that time.

During that period, distinguished Austin, BMC and British Leyland directors and engineers – as various as Sir George Harriman, Alec Issigonis, Harry Webster and Spen King – along with motorsport luminaries such as John Cooper, Geoff Healey and Stuart Turner, have all shared their knowledge and their opinions with me. They, along with a multitude of helpful, enthusiastic, knowledgeable and patient colleagues and consultants, have all come to my aid.

Accordingly, what follows may look impressive, but it does not even approach the total of all those who have helped me to provide something like the full story of the life and times of this remarkable power unit, of which around 14 million were built. Here, therefore, are the principal characters – along with a sweeping apology to those I have not mentioned:

The British Motor Industry Heritage Trust, centred at Gaydon in Warwickshire, which is not only the repository of all things historical concerning BMC (and much of British Leyland), but also has an impressive number of researchers and historians on site who sometimes make my efforts look puny in the extreme.

Am I allowed to name names? Good, for apart from MD Julie Tew, who understands my whims, I have also been helped enormously by Gillian Bardsley, Richard Bacchus and Jan Valentino in my search for facts, figures and images.

Then there was the Modern Records Centre, at the University of Warwick, where a vital resource of Austin (and later) BMC records is available, by appointment, for scrutiny by serious students. At an early stage they realised that I wanted to dig deep, and encouraged me to do so.

I must not forget the Reference Library at the National Motor Museum, at Beaulieu in Hampshire, which really does have references, carefully annotated and easy to locate – and helpful staff to mop fevered brows. Their only requirement, which I pass on readily, is that everyone, even seasoned researchers, should call first, before turning up, to make sure that the space and expertise one needs is on hand.

Finally, there was also the Institution of Mechanical Engineers, who provided invaluable copies of the learned papers concerning the A-Series, which were read to the Institution in the 1960s.

Those were the main corporate sources I consulted, but the following individuals also made my work easier to complete:

John Baker – whose 'Austin Memories' website is at once authoritative, entertaining and complete.
John Barnett – who was BMC's, then Austin-Morris', chief engine development engineer in the 1960s and 1970s, for giving me a most illuminating interview.
Ray Bates – my long-term friend, acquaintance and engineering expert from Standard-Triumph days, who eventually became technical director at British Leyland in the 1970s, and who gave me a great insight to the comings and goings of management at that time.
Peter Browning and his colleague/deputy **Bill Price** – for helping me so much with the story of A-Series cars in 'works' motorsport.

Keith Calver – a true A-Series restoration/tuning expert, who not only builds some of the most powerful A-Series engines today, but writes so persuasively about them too.

Anders Clausager – for sharing some of his mountainous expertise on BMC, British Leyland and Rover Group cars.

John Davenport, Roger Dowson and **Richard Hurdwell** – who were heavily involved in specifying and preparing the Group A MG Metro Turbo racing cars which surprised so many observers in the 1980s.

Ian Elliott – ex-Austin apprentice, then distinguished BMC/British Leyland PR man, who knows more about the history of Longbridge than anyone else I know, and could so easily have written a better book than I have – but realised that he simply did not have the time.

Charles Griffin – one-time British Leyland technical chief, for his insight into the company during his later years at the helm, and in retirement.

Geoffrey Healey – a man I greatly admired, and always listened to, when he could find time to tell me about the Austin-Healey Sprite racing car programme.

Geoff Johnson – who led the Austin-Morris engine design through the 1970s, for relating the complex story of how his team tried to replace the A-Series, but was frustrated at every (financial) turn. Like me, he is a total dog lover, and he knows just how completely I fell for Yogi when I visited him.

Karl Ludvigsen – the distinguished author, who provided me with Harry Weslake/patent details which I never thought I would have a chance to see.

Rob Lyall – although originally a Rover engineer, Rob went on to manage the BL Technology facility at Gaydon during the Harry Sheron/Spen King development phase, and regularly kept me on the straight and narrow when it came to historical research.

Brian Moylan – king mechanic turned author, who provided valuable images of the racing engine.

Jon Pressnell – fellow author/historian – he knows why.

Mark Robinson – the editor of *Mini Magazine*, who not only helped me with names, places, numbers and references, but sometimes indulges me by allowing me to write about the Minis which I admire so much.

Barney Sharratt – an Austin expert, whose book *Men & Motors of 'The Austin'*, also published by Haynes, was an inspiration to me.

Stuart Turner – the distinguished BMC Competitions manager of the 1960s, who later became an author too, for his many insights into the use of A-Series-engined cars in motorsport.

David Walsh – of the Austin A30–A35 Owners' Club, for sharing his expertise, that of his club, and for loaning invaluable images and providing technical details.

John Wheatley – avid Austin-Healey owner and BMC enthusiast, who provided a great many notes on the company of whose engineering team he was such an important member.

And for helping me to find images which tell a proper story: **Bill Piggott, John Colley, David Knowles, Ryno Verster** and **Paul Woolmer**.

There are, of course, others who should also receive recognition, but – as any fellow author will understand – where does research and fact finding ever end . . . ?

Timeline

1922 Introduction of Austin Seven. From 1923, always sold with 747cc engine.

1938 Len Lord joined Austin as works director.

1939 Austin Seven finally dropped, after 17 years.

1941 Len Lord appointed technical director.

1945 Len Lord appointed chairman and managing director.

1947 Austin introduces first post-war small/medium car – the A40 Devon.

1949 Work starts on a new very small engine, the 'AS3', soon renamed A-Series.

1951 Introduction of the new A30 family car, using the 803cc A-Series engine.

1951–52 Austin merged with Nuffield, to form the British Motor Corporation (BMC).

1952 The A-Series fitted to the Morris Minor S2 – its first use in a non-Austin car.

1956 Introduction of the Austin A35/Morris Minor 1000, with 948cc A-Series engine.

1957–58 Progressive build-up of A-Series manufacture at 'Morris Engines', at Courthouse Green, Coventry.

1958 Introduction of the Austin-Healey Sprite, the first sports car to use the A-Series engine. The MG Midget, a sister car, would follow in 1961.

1959 Introduction of the new Mini (officially the Austin Se7en, and Morris Mini-Minor), with transversely-mounted 848cc A-Series engine and front-wheel drive.

1961 Introduction of the first Mini-Cooper with a 997cc engine. Engines built at Courthouse Green.

1962 Introduction of the Morris 1100, complete with 1,098cc A-Series engine. Other badge-engineered models followed. A-Series engine manufacture progressively moved from North Works to East Works at Longbridge.

1963 First use of 998cc engines in front-wheel-drive Mini derivatives. Introduction of 1,071cc S-Type engine – the first of three S-Type engines.

1964 Introduction of 970cc and 1,275cc S-Type engines for Mini-Cooper S.

1965 Introduction of BMC Mini Tractor, complete with 948cc diesel derivative of A-Series engine.

1966 Introduction of Midget/Sprite sports cars with quantity-production 1,275cc engines.

1968 Design of 9X-type engine for new-generation Mini completed. Later cancelled.

1971 Introduction of Morris Marina, with A-Series engine. A-Series usage now at its height.

1973 Introduction of A-Series-engined Austin Allegro.

1980 Introduction of A-Series-engined Mini Metro.

1982 Introduction of A-Series-engined Austin Maestro (similar but larger Montego followed in 1984).

1990–91 Last use of A-Series in Metro models.

2000 Last use of A-Series engine in private cars ('classic' Mini, October 2000).

Profile: Leonard Lord, Father of the A-Series

The comic-strip definition of a tycoon is of someone who swans around in a huge stretch limo, smoking huge cigars, and doing shady financial deals behind the backs of organised labour. He looks rich, dresses accordingly, and spends shareholders' money on yachts and private planes for his own use. He dresses well, gorgeous secretaries scurry around to satisfy his every whim, and he acts like the millionaire that he is.

Leonard Lord (he became Sir Leonard in 1954) was not like that, for by any standards he was a rough diamond. Often to be seen around his factories, he usually looked dishevelled, his hawk-like face was often scowling, his manner was combative, his hat was usually on the back of his head, and a smoking cigarette was ever-present.

At his peak as chairman of BMC, he controlled 40% of British car production, and he did it in his own inimitable way. He was, in fact, a classic case of the WYSIWYG syndrome – What You See Is What You Get. He looked rough and tough – and he was. He could sound crude and uncaring – and he was. No one doing business with Len Lord ever got the benefit of the doubt, and it showed. To receive the rough edge of Lord's tongue was an experience not to be wished for. Yet, under the skin and behind the veneer, he could also be unexpectedly kind.

People usually reacted to him in the same way. Even after he was knighted, Sir Leonard Lord was still 'Len Lord' to his acquaintances, and there was widespread incredulity among his contemporaries when he accepted a peerage in 1961. But even that came on his own terms, for he took a quite unexpected title, snorting that: 'I'm going to be Lord Lambury. No, not Lord Lord – that would sound bloody stupid . . .'

Yet here was Britain's most effective motoring tycoon. He ran Austin for a decade in the 1940s and was the master of BMC in its ten formative years. He was, by any reckoning, the Father of the A-Series engine. It was Len Lord's vision which also brought the Austin-Healey marque into existence, and which recognised the genius of Alec Issigonis' design for the new Mini. Other major announcements, such as the MG MGA and the tie-in with Pininfarina, were only possible because of his vision, and his ambition.

Len Lord was also unique – as the only major personality to walk out on Lord Nuffield before he was sacked, then to come back with a takeover of the Nuffield Organisation 15 years later. He might have been a brutal, aggressive, unlikeable operator, but he could always deliver. After his work at Cowley in the 1930s, Morris Motors had been transformed – and after he had retired from BMC in 1961 the gradual slide towards a merger with Leyland began.

Coventry Kid

Once, long ago, Coventry was a famous motoring city – the hub of the British motor industry. Its managers and its workforce were a special breed, cocky enough to think that they were the world's best. As someone who started his working life in Coventry, I met lots of them.

Those were the days in which a young man was always proud enough to be called a 'Coventry Kid'. Leonard Percy Lord was certainly one of them. Born in the city in 1896 and educated at the prestigious local Bablake school, he started working at Courtaulds (a large textile concern), and did not join the motor industry until 1922.

Starting from that point at the Hotchkiss company (which was building Continental-copy engines for Morris Motors, and would soon be swept into Morris' grasp), Lord specialised in production engineering. Working under Frank Woollard, he made sense of Hotchkiss' ramshackle facilities, so when William Morris took over the Wolseley car concern in 1927 Lord was speedily despatched to Birmingham to repeat the trick.

By that time his reputation – and personality – was well established. In whatever he did, his manner was always abrupt, his tolerance level extremely low, and his temper legendary. If he had been less than brilliant at everything he tackled, he would surely have been thrown out of job after job.

Although he could be charming, for short periods, such moods didn't last long. Lord never wasted time being nice to people, and if there were rules to be accepted, or niceties to be observed, they were invariably flouted. Callers rarely found Lord at his desk until the final years, for he was usually out and about in the factories, often dabbling with the design of new cars, invariably setting up instant deals, and generally galvanising action from otherwise sedate departments and offices.

Production genius

Above all, though, we will remember Len Lord for his organising genius. Throughout his working life, he positively fizzed with energy, inspiring everyone around him to make things better, easier, faster – and in greater numbers. Those who worked with him – or for him – fell into two categories. Either they idolised him, sweated blood for him, and glowed in the promotions which followed; or they left, disillusioned by the tornado surrounding him, the hostility which was never hidden far away, and the refusal to consider anyone's feelings.

His record, though, spoke for itself. Hotchkiss of Coventry had started making Morris engines in a multi-floor building quite unsuited for engineering: Lord and Woollard sorted out the mess, installed early examples of transfer line machinery, and boosted production to match Morris' sales at Cowley. Wolseley of Birmingham was bankrupt when Morris took over, but after five years Lord's booming personality had transformed its prospects.

Then there was the miracle he worked for Lord Nuffield at Cowley. Arriving there in 1932 to rationalise the business, he found factory buildings which had been added, piece-meal, to existing blocks, assembly lines which needed men to push cars from station to station, and far too many models in the range. Three years later the place had been modernised, the model range simplified, and sales had boomed. In 1933 Morris had built 44,000 cars; two years later more than 96,000 left the same premises. Demands for a big pay rise from Lord Nuffield were then refused, the eruption was inevitable, and Lord stormed out.

Wealthy enough not to go crawling around for other, less important, work, Lord bided his time. Job offers, in any

case, came only slowly (his volcanic temperament was well known, and many concerns would not consider hiring him).

Less than two years later, in 1938, Lord Austin hired him to transform the Austin business, which he duly did. Starting by rescinding the factory's smoking ban (as a nicotine addict he was not about to obey it anyway!), he went through the business like a whirlwind. A replacement for the Seven was readied in little more than a year, Austin successfully started building trucks to compete with Bedford (which was owned by GM), boosted the building of military aircraft and aircraft engines for the RAF, and laid down a new range of overhead-valve engines, the first ever to be designed by the conservative Austin business.

Post-war ambitions

Until 1945 Austin was totally submerged in the war effort – not even Len Lord could fight against the exigencies of war, but it was typical of the man that Austin was the first to announce post-war cars, first to start selling cars in big numbers to the USA, and soon became Britain's largest car maker. Within five years he had inspired the building of a vast new assembly hall at Longbridge, and more new buildings were on the way.

Len Lord's demons drove him, not only to be first and best, but to keep on taking his revenge on Lord Nuffield, who had never been forgiven for his snub in 1936. Although there can't have been enough hours in the day, Lord not only ran his empire with an iron hand, but also visited the Austin styling studios every day.

The expert production engineer was also a compulsive designer who thought he knew more about engineering and styling than those he paid to do those jobs – and often he was right. Much of what went into the post-war Austins originated from Lord's office in 'The Kremlin' at Longbridge, though some of it, like the dreadful A90 Atlantic style, was nothing to be proud of!

By the late 1940s, though, this barely-controlled volcano of a man was looking round for more. Convinced that the Austin business, on its own, would not be big enough in a few years, he set his sights on annexing the Nuffield Organisation. Not surprisingly, Lord Nuffield resisted being taken over, and did not even want an amicable merger.

In the end, though, the merger was inevitable. Lord was still in his 50s, vigorous and ambitious, easily defeating the will of Lord Nuffield, tired, lonely and well into his 70s.

The British Motor Corporation (BMC) which resulted was Len Lord's greatest achievement.

Soon after it was formalised, Lord, who had once vowed to dismantle Cowley, 'brick by bloody brick', swept back into overall power, persuaded Lord Nuffield to retire from the business only a year after he had ceded control, and rapidly built up a major empire.

In the 1950s, when Britain was still making more cars than any other nation except the USA, and when cars were still being supplied in big numbers to the old 'Empire' countries like Canada, Australia and South Africa, Len Lord was in his element. Shrugging off his knighthood as merely something which meant reprinting all the company notepaper, he flew all round the world, nosing inquisitively into subsidiary companies, sizing up export markets, and generally acting like the Emperor of an independent nation.

BMC might have had shareholders, thousands of them, but Len Lord rarely seemed to consider their interests. More interested in making and selling a lot of cars (which, in strike-hit Britain of the period, meant placating the trade unions) than making big profits, he embraced 'badge-engineering' as if General Motors had never invented it, and unleashed a flood of new models.

It was Len Lord, rather than his lieutenants, who set about the rationalisation programme, reducing BMC's original quiver of 11 different engine families to four within five years, and making sure that Austin and Morris shared the same new body platforms by the end of the same period – yet maintaining different Austin and Morris dealer networks in most British and overseas cities.

His vision, though, was bigger and more wide-ranging than that. Above all, he was pragmatic, realised that his staff were not always clever enough, and became the first British boss to turn to an Italian styling house – Pininfarina – for a series of new models for the 1960s.

Not only did he encourage his team to dabble with the development of gas-turbine-engined cars and to fight Ford head-to-head with new tractors and new delivery (panel) vans, but he also invented the new Austin-Healey marque, and gave almost immediate approval for the Mini when it was shown to him.

It was as a dictator, rather than a manager, that he spotted the Healey-designed Healey 100 prototype of 1952, and swept it into the BMC family. Donald Healey, having agreed to buy A90 engines and running gear from Longbridge, was looking to build only 20 cars a week, but Lord, having inspected the first car, offered to rename it the Austin-Healey 100, to produce ten times that number at Longbridge, and to take on the Healey business as design consultants. All this, please note, was done without involving his colleagues: as ever, they followed up breathlessly, administering what Len Lord had proposed, turning his dreams into reality.

There was more sports car vision as the decade progressed. First of all he approved the production of the MGA at Abingdon – this being by far the largest investment the sports car maker had ever tackled – and followed it up by asking Donald Healey to design a new small sports car for BMC (this became the Austin-Healey Sprite, and eventually the MG Midget too). Lord, and only Lord, had enough faith in BMC's sports cars – and, particularly, in their sales potential in North America – for him to designate and expand Abingdon as BMC's sports car production centre.

His biggest triumph came towards the end of the 1950s, when even he must have been thinking about retirement. When the time came for BMC to develop a range of new small cars, Lord allowed technical chief Alec Issigonis to develop a superficially bizarre concept, that of a tiny and boxy four-seater saloon only ten feet long, yet using an existing four-cylinder engine.

The trick, which nonplussed almost everyone else, was to place this engine sideways, and to drive the front wheels. All this, along with rubber cone suspension and all-independent suspension, was so new that there *must* have been corporate nervousness.

Yet Lord never hesitated. For once he had not interfered at the design *or* the styling stage, he had not insisted on playing safe with conventional engineering, and he backed his gut feeling with millions of tooling capital. The Mini, and cars like the BMC 1100 which followed, underpinned BMC for the next decade – the decade *after* Lord had gone.

Although he had announced a move into 'partial retirement' in 1956, when he was only 60 years old, few people believed him at first, especially his long-time deputy George Harriman. Yet it was true enough, and five years later Sir Leonard stood down, allowing the smooth, urbane, always dapper and likeable Harriman to take his place.

The change of atmosphere at BMC was immediate, with many readily admitting that Longbridge was a quieter place when he had gone, and that the smack of firm leadership had evaporated. In retirement, though, as in his working life, the newly-ennobled Lord Lambury was always predictable. Although he stayed on the board until 1966, and everyone knew he was there, there were no explosions. When he died in 1967, he was genuinely mourned by thousands.

Biography

1896	Born in Coventry	**1945**	Became chairman and managing director of Austin.
1910	Started an apprenticeship at Courtaulds (textile factory) in Coventry. Later worked for Coventry Ordnance factory, then Daimler. Became a production specialist.	**1951/1952**	Inspired and masterminded formation of BMC – the fusion of Austin and the Nuffield Organisation. Became managing director, adding the chairmanship a year later.
1922	Joined Hotchkiss & Cie of Coventry, which built engines for Morris cars.	**1954**	Knighted by HM Queen Elizabeth II, to become Sir Leonard.
1927	Joined Wolseley Motors of Birmingham.		
1932	Appointed managing director of Morris, working at Cowley: helped found Nuffield Organisation.	**1961**	Retired from day-to-day management, becoming honorary president in 1963 after Lord Nuffield's death. Raised to the peerage, as Lord Lambury, in 1962.
1936	Resigned abruptly from Nuffield.		
1938	Joined Austin Motor Co as works director.	**1967**	Death of Lord Lambury.
1942	Became joint managing director of Austin.		

When Sir Leonard Lord became Lord Lambury, and finally retired from BMC in the 1960s, a glittering retirement party was held to celebrate his career. Among those present were Sir George Harriman (on the left of this picture) and Sir Alec Issigonis (on Lord Lambury's left). (*BMIHT*)

CHAPTER 1

Longbridge in 1945: the post-war scene

Who knows when, and where, the first thoughts about a new car – and a tiny new engine to power it – came along at Austin in the mid-1940s? In theory, of course, that was a period when every one of Austin's staff, from Leonard Lord to the tea ladies, was supposed to be occupied in a massive war effort, with Longbridge building everything from Lancaster bombers to 'jerry cans', and from soldiers' helmets to Churchill tank suspension units.

Well, yes – except that this was not the way that Leonard Lord, that human dynamo who had arrived like a thunderclap at Longbridge in 1938 as the company's newly-appointed works director, wanted to run the business. Since the company's founder, Lord Austin, had died in May 1941, Lord had effectively become the master of all he surveyed. Officially technical director since 1941, joint managing director (with financial specialist Ernest Payton) and deputy chairman (also to Payton) from 1942, he became Austin's chairman and managing director in November 1945. Throughout the war, in any case, Lord had been running the company in his own very personal way, and intended to carry on like that in the future.

So, what next? The hard-working staff at Austin had their own fears. When the war was over, military contracts would end abruptly, existing tooling for private cars and trucks would have to be dug out of store, re-installed, re-commissioned, and repaired where necessary, and all the time there would be very little actually going out of the factory gates. To use that famous Bette Davis one-liner from a Hollywood film of the period: 'Fasten your seat belts, it's gonna be a bumpy ride . . .'.

The fact was, however, that Lord, the rough and tough-talking tycoon, a dynamic manager with the compulsion

(and the right) to interfere at all levels of the design and development process, already had a post-war 'master plan' in his head, and was ready to bulldoze it through in the next few years: no one at Austin, in any case, was likely to oppose what he had in mind. He had, after all, arrived at Longbridge from a position of high office at Nuffield, in 1938, found that Austin's product lines were old-fashioned, boring and staid, and had been intent on changing all of that very rapidly. He had not got very far when Hitler's armies marched into Poland on 1 September 1939, and changed the world – for ever.

As forecast, no sooner had the Second World War been won than government orders for the type of material which Austin had provided began to dry up or – worse – be cancelled. Even before then, the pace of military orders, and the frantic reorganisation of needs and aspirations, had eased considerably. The entire factory complex, which was considerably larger in 1945 that it had been just a decade earlier, and which had been incredibly busy for years, now looked as if it might suddenly become empty, deserted and bereft of new work.

Dozens of different types of military hardware had been produced by Austin in six years of war, which varied from machines as massive as the four-engined Lancaster and Stirling bombers, Fairey Battle light bombers, Hurricane Mk II fighter aircraft, wings for Beaufighter fighter-bombers (Standard built the rest and assembled the complete planes), to items as small as steel helmets for the troops, as heavy as Churchill tank suspension units, and as disposable as jerry cans for carrying fuel. In some cases, of course, the numbers produced were absolutely colossal – such as 1.35 million large calibre shells, 3.35 million ammunition boxes and magazines, 2.5 million steel helmets and 300,000 Vickers and Hispano machine-gun magazines. (In 1939, by the way, Austin was also asked if it would consider making Merlin aero engines – the type which powered legendary aircraft like the Spitfire and the Lancaster – but that contract eventually went to Ford in the UK, and to Packard in the USA.)

To do all this – and particularly to manufacture complete aircraft – Austin, at Longbridge, had expanded considerably in recent years, and, for good military reasons (in case of bombing), a variety of contracts were widely dispersed over the rambling estate. Amazingly, although the German war machine seemed to know what Austin was doing, and knew where the factories were located (it is extremely difficult to hide a factory that big, and detailed aerial photographs were available), Longbridge was bombed only once in six years, and then not seriously.

As is made clear in Chapter 12, the ageing complex of what was then known as North Works, South Works and West Works had been large enough (though looking increasingly old-fashioned) to produce private cars and,

from 1939, trucks, and there was also a compact flying ground, with several criss-crossing runways, in the same estate. The whole was closely surrounded (and further growth thus rendered impossible) by main and branch-line railways, and by main and less significant public roads.

From 1936, however, as Britain's military rearmament programme got under way with a vengeance, an entirely new – and vast – 'shadow factory' was erected on behalf of the government on 23 acres of land at Grovesley Lane, Cofton Hackett, and another 15 acres were added later. This area was close to, but unconnected with, the rest of the Longbridge factory, the two sites being delineated by the flying ground itself.

Although colloquially known as the 'Cofton Hackett' plant, it soon became officially known as 'East Works' – even though it was south of any other part of the existing Austin complex! Along with a new 500ft x 190ft flight shed (closer to the airfield, and where aircraft were tested and hidden away from curious gazes from above) these buildings were first used to manufacture thousands of Bristol Mercury radial engines and, later, Bristol Pegasus

Longbridge – the original factory

The very first Austin car was conceived in a factory at Longbridge, on the south-western outskirts of Birmingham, in 1905/6, and it was there that the legendary A-Series power unit would be designed, developed and ultimately manufactured.

Originally set up in 1893, as a copper-plate printing works, White and Pike Ltd turned it into a tin printing factory, but the business failed in 1901 and the plant closed down for four years. Newly free of his commitment to Wolseley, where he had been general manager and effectively the technical supremo too, Herbert Austin then bought the Longbridge site in November 1905, for £7,500, and immediately set up a business called the Austin Motor Company.

This original site eventually became better known as Austin's South Works, but as expansion followed expansion new factory

blocks were added and became, respectively, the North, West and (with government help) East Works. Expansion influenced by the need to accommodate facilities to manufacture military projects – which included what was, by the standards of the day, a sizeable airfield (or 'flying ground') – was a major factor, the result being that the Longbridge site which emerged from the Second World War in 1945 was vastly bigger than that which had been built up only gradually before 1914.

In the 1950s and 1960s further vast expansion took place, including the building of two massive new car assembly buildings (CAB1 and CAB2) and the multi-storey car park, the final touch being in 1979–80 when West Works was more than doubled in size to accommodate body press and assembly tooling for the new Austin Metro.

The A-Series engine was originally manufactured in North Works, but as demand for this power unit continued to increase the facilities were mainly moved to East Works in 1962–63, where the final engines were built in 2000.

Before the A-Series engine came along, Austin cast around for anything – anything at all – to keep their vast factory busy. In the late 1940s, for instance, the now redundant East Works was used to manufacture the 'Austin Champ' 4x4 for the British Army, and the Rolls-Royce engines needed to power it.

engines. From 1938/9 the same complex was used to begin the building of complete military aircraft. By any standard, unless the entire Cofton Hackett complex and flight shed were to be handed back to the state (which had financed, and still owned, it), Austin would find itself with enormous empty spaces to fill in peacetime.

Len Lord – who, for his part, was above all a go-getting entrepreneur – had no qualms about all this. He was convinced that he could soon find enough business to keep all of 'his' empire running profitably in peacetime, and wanted to get the civil side of Austin up and running again as soon as possible: in particular, he had an eye on selling huge numbers of cars to North America, a part of the world market which Austin had never previously attacked. Even so, for purely practical reasons it was not going to be possible to introduce new models straight away, and in 1945/6 Austin made it clear to its

shareholders that it would have to spend up to a million pounds to re-equip and modernise Longbridge.

Design of new models would take months, tooling (if the materials and the priorities were favourable) might take another 18 months, which meant that nothing was likely to go on sale until 1947. Each and every one of the Austin range would need to be renewed in the early post-war period, and it could not all be tackled at once. As far as ground-up new designs were concerned, we now know that it was the vast A125/A135 Sheerline/Princess types, along with the export-intended A40 Devon/Dorset range, which got priority. It was a measure of what Lord then thought of as small cars, that he publicly referred to the 'new small 8hp and 10hp' models, though these were the 1.2-litre A40 types.

The immediate implication was that in 1945/6, the Austin cars which could be put into production first – to get the show on the road, as it were – for the civilian market, would have to be modified versions of those which had filled up the plant in 1939, and that most of these would be destined for export markets. Unhappily for Len Lord, and for the Austin dealer chain, the old Seven was well and truly obsolete, and the relatively new Eight was a 900cc-engined car, so that the original post-war line-up would not contain a truly small car, and it would be years before the gap could be filled. On the other hand, it was fortunate for Austin (and some rival concerns were not so lucky) that all the existing tooling which had been stored away throughout the war years had survived unscathed, undamaged by enemy bombing, and could be re-commissioned at short notice.

Not that this was all good news. Under the pre-Lord management – where Sir Herbert Austin had been the master of all he surveyed, and where the long-serving A.J. Hancock (who had joined Austin from Wolseley when the new business was set up in 1905/6) had been chief engineer for most of the 1920s and 1930s – the Austin product line had been undistinguished and unadventurous in the extreme. Reliable, maybe, and offering good value for money, of course, yet they offered no technological excitement. It is worth noting that by 1938, when Len Lord arrived on the scene like a tornado in a calm sea, every Austin had a side-valve engine, all of them still had beam axle front suspension, and every one used the traditional girder chassis/separate bodyshell layout. Nor were there any signs of impending change.

It is also significant, and worth recalling, just how old some of the 'building blocks' – the engines, gearboxes and chassis designs, for instance – actually were when Len Lord arrived in 1938. Of the company's three current bestsellers, the basic layout of the Austin Seven (chassis, and engine) still dated from 1922, the 10/4 (and its 1,125cc engine) from 1932, while the Light 12/4 (and its 1,525cc engine) had arrived in 1933. By any measure, therefore, Austin seemed to have been stuck in the same groove for a decade.

Not only did Len Lord set out to change all that, but he also got the company back into the commercial vehicle market (see the panel 'Birmingham Bedfords' – success with trucks' on page 23, and elsewhere in Chapter 2), and if the Second World War had not erupted in 1939 he might have succeeded quite briskly. A master plan, for sure, was schemed up within weeks of his arrival – a copy of this ambitious document is in the company's board minute books. But it was not to be. In 1945, as in 1939, there was still so much to do, and he had to set priorities.

One of Austin's (and Lord's) most pressing needs was to find a new small engine, for there had been no innovation, at almost any level, since the start of the

This was the venerable old Austin 7 engine, introduced in 1923, which was finally discontinued in 1939. The new A-Series engine would have to replace it, by being lighter, more powerful and more modern in outlook. (*BMIHT*)

1930s. The brutal fact is that before work on a brand-new power unit (what became the A-Series engine, first conceived in 1949), Austin had not launched a new ultra-small engine since the Austin Seven had been introduced in 1922 – 27 years earlier. In spite of what the romantics might think, this should prove, quite conclusively, that there was no design relationship, of any sort, between the two engines!

The heritage of that Austin Seven engine, however, tells us a lot about Austin, and about Longbridge. When first revealed, it was originally shown to the public as a simple side-valve 696cc engine with two crankshaft main bearings: it was then speedily enlarged to 747cc, in 1923, after the first hundred cars had been assembled. It then retained that size until the end of its life at Austin, and it is highly significant (if only to establish a tradition), that the cylinder stroke was 76.2mm/3.00in. We would see a lot more of that dimension during the next 50 years!

In every respect – design, looks and architecture – it was a 'vintage' type of engine, which would survive until 1939. After that, Reliant (of Tamworth) would buy the special tooling and the design rights, and carried on manufacturing the same engine in considerable numbers (for its own three-wheelers) until 1962.

That legendary engine, and the Austin Seven car which it was to power, had not originally been designed at Longbridge itself by a big team, but was originally schemed up at Herbert Austin's own home, Lickey Grange, just a short distance from the factory. Austin's then chief engineer, A.J. Hancock, had nothing to do with it at first. It was there, in the autumn of 1921, that Herbert Austin installed young Stanley Edge, who had joined Austin in 1917 as an apprentice when he was only 14 years old, and was just 18 when he started work on the most legendary of all old Austin power units. Herbert Austin set him up with a drawing board in the billiard room of the Grange.

Herbert Austin apparently provided the ideas, and some sketches, but Edge did the rest. Once the initial Austin Seven prototype cars and engines were produced in the first months of 1922, Edge was moved back to Longbridge, took up residence in a boarded-off section of the engineering offices, and work then progressed in a more predictable manner. The existence of the project 'went public' early in 1922 (though cars were not shown at that time), the car was launched in the autumn, and the first deliveries took place in the winter of 1922/3.

Tooling, modern for the period, but of course archaic by post-Second World War standards, was installed in North Works at Longbridge, and the new power unit thus became Austin's 'default' small-car engine for the next 30 years. In the early 'vintage' years, the Seven engine had only a two-bearing crankshaft, a side-valve cylinder head, and produced all of 10.5bhp at 2,400rpm. Thus equipped, an Austin Seven struggled to reach 50mph, which was probably just as well for it only had rear-wheel brakes and rudimentary chassis engineering.

Although the figures and layout seem truly prehistoric by modern standards – even by the standards under which the A-Series was to be designed – they were competitive by the standards of the day. And although the engine was neither modern nor outdated, it was at least reliable, and experience showed that it was also capable of being tuned to remarkably high levels.

The Austin Seven, and all its derivatives, immediately became Austin's best-selling model, and little basic change was made to the sturdy little side-valve engine until the late 1930s, though peak horsepower eventually reached 13. Then, at last, in June 1936 the engine was thoroughly updated; although the same basic side-valve layout was retained, for the very first time it was given a three-bearing crankshaft (a new centre bearing was added to the cylinder block), and at the same time the peak bhp rose to 16 (21bhp on the Nippy 'sports' model).

A new Austin model, rather confusingly named 'Big Seven' (which in engineers' terms it most assuredly was not), was then introduced in the autumn of 1937, this being a somewhat larger car running on a lengthened Seven-type chassis frame and suspension which was intended to fill the gap between the ageing Seven and the equally middle-aged Ten. However, the confusion is that the Big Seven's engine itself measured 900cc, and was definitely *not* an evolution of the three-bearing Seven. Instead it had bore and stroke dimensions of 56.77 x 88.9mm, and was actually a smaller version of the existing side-valve Ten engine, which itself dated from 1932.

Even in the depths of the Second World War, Len Lord was thinking ahead, and had made sure that the old side-valve Seven engine would not be resurrected. Even so, in September 1941 he announced publicly that the first post-war Austin cars would be a continuation of the 1939 models. He and Austin, in any case, were fortunate that one private-car production line was kept open at Longbridge during the war, for the production of a variety of Austin Eights and Tens (many with special utilitarian military body work) for use by the Allied military forces. From 1940 to 1945 inclusive nearly 39,000 such machines were produced, which at least kept the engineers and managers within the company in touch with automotive as opposed to purely military activities. Even so, although some experimental work carried on little was done to find a modern replacement for the Austin Seven.

That, then, was the situation in 1945, when Austin needed to get new cars – *any* cars – back on the market as soon as possible. In fact Lord and his colleagues had already taken the decision to drop the truly obsolete 1930s models such as the Big Seven, the 14, 18 and 28, and to concentrate on the new models which had been rushed on to the market in 1939. Even so, and even in 1945, one could see why a new engine – which became the A-Series – was needed, for the following were the only machines which were ready to be revived:

Austin Eight	*900cc*	*Announced 1939, approx 48,000 produced so far;*
Austin Ten	*1,125cc*	*Announced 1939, approx 45,000 produced so far;*
Austin Twelve	*1,535cc*	*Announced on the brink of war in 1939, approx 250 produced so far;*

– which would immediately be joined by a new derivative:

Austin Sixteen	*2,199cc*	*Previewed in 1944, a larger-engined Twelve with the very first overhead-valve Austin engine.*

So, what now would be Austin's strategy for the next few years?

CHAPTER 2

Len Lord and the late 1940s: 'Design me a new engine'

So it was that, as the Second World War neared its close, Austin could finally lift its gaze from the military machines which it had been building in such numbers since 1939 – the last of these being the mighty four-engined Lancaster heavy bombers which had brought so much devastation to German towns and cities – and optimistically start to develop private cars once again.

Since the mid-1930s, when Lord Austin's company was at its pre-war peak but stagnating, Austin had made two major steps forward, although Lord Austin himself had sadly died in 1941. On the one hand, the factories had been much-expanded and much-modernised to help produce all the military equipment, while on the other, that formidable businessman Leonard Lord was now the company's chairman and CEO. Not only was Lord, the rough and tough-talking tycoon, a dynamic manager with a compulsion to interfere at all levels of the design and development process, but he already had a post-war 'master plan' in his head.

The fact is, that if Len Lord had not arrived at Longbridge in 1938 the little A-Series engine programme might never have evolved in the way that it did. The first new Lord-inspired Austins were trucks, designed in 1938, which were put on sale just as soon as they could be tooled up and new buildings erected to house them; but there was a linear ancestry between them and what would follow elsewhere in the Austin empire in the next decade or so.

Too many historians have stated that it was Lord himself who brought the truck ethic to Austin, but the fact is that a modest truck design and development programme (independent of any other company, and including diesel engines) had been ongoing at Longbridge since 1935. Lord, however, wanted to start over, apparently not believing in diesels for this size of machine, and being willing to emulate (if not actually copy) what other companies were already doing, rather than make all the same mistakes himself. To power the new Lord-type trucks, therefore, there was to be a new overhead-valve six-cylinder engine, followed by a four-cylinder derivative in the early 1940s, for a military project which was then stalled, and it was evolutions of these which became the very first overhead-valve engines to be fitted to Austin private cars.

So why is this important? Simply because these new engines broke a long sequence of side-valve engines from Longbridge; the all-new four-cylinder engine set a precedent, the A40 Devon engine (another overhead-valve power unit) followed on in 1947, and the A-Series eventually evolved as a smaller, entirely different but definitely related family descendant of both of them: the common DNA is achingly obvious.

Philosophically, therefore, the A-Series story really began in 1938, when Len Lord arrived at Austin as the newly-appointed works director (though, effectively, it is

Leonard Lord joined Austin as works director in 1938, and immediately set about modernising the company's products. He would be chairman and managing director of Austin, later of BMC, from the 1940s to the 1960s. (*BMIHT*)

now clear that he was the managing-director-in-waiting). He took over, incidentally, from the long-serving C.R.F. Englebach, who had been works director since 1922, and whose eyesight was finally failing. The change came abruptly in February 1938 when, according to the Austin board minutes:

'Mr Englebach informed the board that he was willing to resign his position of Works Director . . . if the Board would appoint Mr L.P. Lord in his place . . .'

– which was accepted, the result being that Len Lord joined the board forthwith. It was the start of a lengthy tenure at Longbridge, which would last for 23 eventful years.

Right from the start, Lord embarked on a whirlwind examination of Longbridge, the Austin company, and its business, one result being that he was rarely to be found at his desk. He was soon identified as a ruthless firebrand, who *always* got his own way, who was usually seen with a cigarette dangling from his lips, and who demanded the same dedication to the job as he himself

was demonstrably willing to give. Within 30 days he had worked up the 'Lord master plan' for the rejuvenation of the Austin business, one which was going to cost a fortune in capital investment, but which would also result in a completely different Austin company from the one which existed when he arrived.

The original plan foresaw new 8, 10, 12, 14, 18 and 25hp cars (effectively, therefore, the rejuvenation of the entire range), with four- and six-cylinder engines, and he also suggested the introduction of three new trucks. Overhead-valve engines were mentioned for the first time: except for the unique twin-cam Austin racing cars, which were still reaching maturity on British race tracks, no other Austin had ever used overhead-mounted valves, and none were even under development at Longbridge at this time.

For the time being Lord was happy that in order to get the new 8, 10 and 12hp models (all of which would, indeed, appear in 1939) into production, all

Well before Len Lord (right) set his sights on joining forces with Nuffield, he had spent years working for Lord Nuffield (left) at Cowley. That connection had ended in a big argument, so in 1951 Lord was determined that he would be the boss.

would have to use existing side-valve engines, while the body platforms of the 8 and 10 models would come from Pressed Steel (rather than being constructed at Longbridge itself), that company being urged to meet near-impossible schedules to get the job.

In the meantime, Lord wanted his engineers to spend much of their time on the evolution of three new and closely-related trucks. Not only were these intended to face up to competition from an existing range of successful Bedfords (Bedford was owned by General Motors), but they would also ape (or improve on) many of the features of those machines.

The pundits soon realised this. Because some of the Austin truck design was clearly copied from Bedford (this saved a great deal of time), the new Austins were almost inevitably christened as 'Birmingham Bedfords' and had a very similar style. Initially the Bedford engine had been

supplied to Bedford by its parent company, General Motors of the USA, and was eventually 'Vauxhallised' and put into production in the UK as a version of the legendary 'Stovebolt Six' for which the American GM cars and light trucks were already famous. Although there were major differences in layout between the two, it was therefore easy to see where the main influences for Austin's first overhead-valve 'six' came from. I emphasise this heritage because, in the next few years, it would also have a bearing on the way the little A-Series engine would be designed.

Although the original Lord 'master plan' had mentioned proposed new ohv 'sixes' for cars (of 1,810cc, 2,510cc and 3,512cc), and 3,178cc engines for the trucks, these were merely 'paper' engines which had not even had time to get beyond the 'why don't we . . .?' stage. The original overhead-valve Austin 'truck' six to be finalised was to be a 3,460cc power unit (which would eventually be enlarged to 3,993cc for post-war usage, which included a 'High Speed' evolution for use in Sheerline and Princess models), but by 1943 further complications had set in.

As the pressures of war increased, the British government dabbled with the idea of producing its own

'Birmingham Bedfords' – success with trucks

It was the new range of Austin trucks, announced in 1939, that inspired much of the tiny A-Series engine that was to follow. More details are included in the main text, but it is worth noting that during the Second World War these trucks and their newfangled overhead-valve engines played an absolutely vital role in keeping the armed forces moving.

Between March 1939 and July 1945, the following were produced:

1½-tonners	4,625
2-tonners	27,787
3-tonners	42,656
5-tonners	7,415
Morris and Bedford trucks also assembled	10, 059
Grand total	*92,542*

version of a 'Jeep'-like 4x4 vehicle, and approached Austin to see if they were interested in getting involved, in a joint project with Nuffield. Although this project was indefinitely postponed within months, the engine that would have powered it was not. This, in fact, was an overhead-valve four-cylinder power unit of 2,199cc, a closely-related derivative of the 3,460cc 'six', these two engines always being intended to be machined on much of the same new tooling at Longbridge.

These were both simple and robust power units, with cast iron cylinder blocks and cylinder heads, and should be considered as the true ancestors of the A-Series, though they were much larger and not nearly as sophisticated in detail. The 2.2-litre engine was rated at 58bhp at first, with

all the electrical components – starter motor, dynamo, distributor and spark plugs – on the right (off) side, and with the Zenith carburettor, petrol pump, inlet and exhaust manifolds on the left. The combustion chambers, by the way, were simple lozenge shapes in the cast iron head, the inlet ports being siamesed. Does all that sound familiar? It should, because the A-Series would follow the same architecture.

Adapted very rapidly for use in Austin's own cars, the new four-cylinder engine would be used in models like the Austin 16hp, the A70 Hampshire, the A70 Hereford, in the Austin taxi cab of the period (and other periods to follow!), along with light commercial applications. With a cylinder bore increase, we now know that this

Lord Austin (left) and Len Lord (centre) had the honour of conducting HM King George VI and the Queen around the new 'shadow factory' building at Longbridge in 1940, where hundreds of Fairey Battle fighter-bombers were being assembled. In later years this factory became Longbridge's 'East Works', and was where millions of A-Series engines would be manufactured.

Len Lord (in hat) was a decisive and successful picker of consultants. Here, in 1953, he is at Longbridge as Donald Healey sets off to the USA on a sales tour with the brand-new Austin-Healey 100 sports car.

engine could be enlarged to 2,660cc for the A90 model and other Austin and BMC uses, where it proved to be very successful. Eventually, too, it was used to great effect in the first-generation Austin-Healey 100 BN1 and BN2 sports cars. In fact it set a whole variety of standards against which smaller and more modern Austin engines would subsequently try to measure up.

Next up, therefore, was the second overhead-valve four-cylinder engine which Austin had ever designed – and the reason that I mention this in some detail is that it all had great relevance to the A-Series which was to follow. Even so, in the late 1940s there was great disappointment in Austin's dealer chain (and, probably, in Austin's own management ranks, though this was never allowed to show) regarding what happened next.

Maybe now was the time that the development of a new small Austin car should have begun. But it did not, and that decision was put off again. The reason was not one of being over-cautious, but was instead because of a diktat from Britain's government, which could see that the country needed to export a majority of its products in order to start paying off its wartime debts – and that one of the most logical ways was to encourage the development of cars which would sell strongly overseas. The way that this policy could be made to work was by allocating sufficient sheet steel supplies only to manufacturers who toed the line, and to withhold them from those who did not.

Whatever, this was going to involve major changes in Austin's policy, and as early as 1946/7 Len Lord took the opportunity of explaining, to his shareholders, his vision of what Austin would be doing in the immediate post-war period. He had concluded, he said, that although there should be a new 'baby' Austin one day, it could not figure in his top priorities. This was because he could not guarantee to sell a high enough proportion of such new cars on the export market.

On the other hand, he had concluded that for the time being Austin's best strategy was to make a big effort at conquering the American market – not, of course, with what we might call American-sized cars, but with cars of a size that the Americans did not produce themselves.

Before the Second World War, Austin had exported far more medium-sized cars than small models, and was convinced that it could do so again, though not necessarily in the same markets. This perhaps explains why Len Lord set his hat at breaking into the North American market with the cars that we now know as the A40 Devon (1.2 litres), the A70 Hampshire (2.2 litres) and the A90 Atlantic (2.6 litres). In his mind there was no place, as yet, for anything smaller than them.

When they appeared in 1948 the A70 and A90 models both used the civilian version of the 'Jeep' engine already mentioned, but between 1945 and 1947 most of Austin's engine design efforts went into producing another engine, in a family which would also stay in production at

The very first new model that Len Lord influenced at Longbridge was the platform-chassised Austin 8 of 1939. This would be the last small Austin ever to be fitted with a side-valve engine. The A-Series-engined A30 would replace it in 1951. (*Barney Sharratt*)

Longbridge for an enormously long time – for 43 years, no less. Bill Appleby, who later became chief engine designer, takes most of the credit for the layout of this power unit.

That engine, looking in so many ways like the 'Jeep' engine, but being entirely different from it in every nut, bolt, component and casting, was the overhead-valve Austin power unit that powered the original A40 Devon and Dorset models, and was revealed in 1947. In so many ways – it would officially became the B-Series when redesigned in early BMC days – this became the true father of the A-Series which followed it, for its 'architecture', if not any of the actual detail components used, was very similar indeed.

In motor industry 'architectural' terms, the resemblance to the 'Jeep'/A70/A90 Series which had already appeared, to the A-Series, which would follow four years later, was uncanny – or, rather, it would have been uncanny if one did not know that the same team of engineers had been responsible for all of them. All three relied on siamesed-porting for the cylinder heads, with the pushrods somehow threading their paths around the ports; all three located all their electrical accessories on one side of the engine; and all three were simple, robust, long-stroke designs, with cast iron cylinder heads and cylinder blocks.

A-Series, B-Series and A70 engines: kissing cousins

It is important to stress that although Austin's new post-war overhead-valve engines looked the same, and shared the same basic architecture, they were completely and utterly different in detail. To emphasise: although all the main components were machined in the same massive workshops at Longbridge (principally at North Works, at first) none of them was a smaller or larger version of the other.

Purely for interest, therefore, I quote the very basic bore, stroke and capacity details of each engine:

Engine	Year launched	Bore (mm)	Stroke (mm)	Capacity (cc)
A-Series	1951	58	76.2	803
A40/B-Series	1947	65.48	88.9	1,200
A70/16hp	1944	79.4	111.1	2,199

Incidentally, to demonstrate how deeply the Olde Worlde British attitude was entrenched at Longbridge, I should point out that in Imperial measure the strokes of the three engines were 3in, 3½in and 4³/₈in respectively.

In its description of the A40 in October 1947, it was perhaps *The Autocar* which best summed up the important advance bestowed by overhead-valve engines:

'The A40 engine is 1,200cc, which would be 36bhp on the old [side-valve] assumption: but the actual figure is 40bhp, showing an advance. The 900cc engine of the 8hp Austin produced 23bhp, and the 1,125cc engine of the Austin Ten gave 35bhp.'

Compared with the 'Jeep'/16hp engine, however, there was one major advance. This was the shaping of the cylinder combustion chamber, where Harry Weslake, for some time a consultant to Austin, had been working his magic. As *The Motor*'s erudite technical team commented in their description of the new engine, 'The combustion spaces viewed from below are kidney-shaped, with the valve heads occupying the "bumps" of the kidney. This arrangement allows the provision of adequate water passages immediately adjacent to the valve seats, and also directs the mixture to one side of the head, therefore promoting swirl and improving scavenging.'

Do not, for a single moment, dismiss this as a mere detail, for in many ways it was central to the top-end design of a whole new generation of Austin engines. It worked well on the A40 (eventually to be known as 'B-Series') engine, and it would also work very well indeed on the little A-Series that was to follow. Modern tuners have described it as incredibly good in its aim, which was for improved economy – marked by the fact that little change is needed to the ignition timing for a full racing engine. They also make the point that all the principles, down to small details, were carried forward, and replicated, for the smaller A-Series power unit.

It all stemmed, apparently, from experimental work that Weslake had been carrying out during the Second World War. Weslake actually received UK approval of a patent for his newfangled combustion chamber in 1943: the time frame probably explains why such a layout was not adopted for the original 2.2-litre engine, which must surely have been committed to series production before his work became known. (We also know that Weslake went on to apply for a patent in the USA in 1948, which was granted in 1952.)

As expected, the UK patent goes into considerable detail (including drawings of a typical overhead-valve cylinder head), and makes clear that the justifiable 'invention' centred around the shaping of the head casting around the valve heads themselves, and the judicious placing of the sparking plug to make the most of this. According to my esteemed contemporary historian Paul Skilleter, who wrote the definitive history of the Morris Minor:

'Having visited his patent agents, the West Country cylinder head expert then showed his results to Len

Lord – with whom he'd worked in his usual fiercely independent freelance manner back in the 'Thirties . . . Lord wanted to adopt the head, but first there was negotiating to be done, and Harry recounted his conversation with Len Lord to me in 1977 . . . "I said, 'Look, I'm not going to do any more work for you people to the benefit of your shareholders and not some benefit to me.' So he said 'That's all right, Weslake, we'll pay you royalties': it must have been 1947 to 1960".'

A-Series: getting started

So now the scene was set, and finally Austin's engine designers, led by the long-serving Bill Appleby along with his deputy (and eventual successor) Eric Bareham, were unleashed on Austin's third major engine design programme of the 1940s, which was to result in the A-Series, one of the most successful automotive engines of all time.

Bill Appleby was the long-serving Austin chief engine designer who led the team that produced the post-war series of engines – A-Series, B-Series and C-Series – though it was actually his deputy, Eric Bareham, who was effectively chief designer on the A-Series project. (*BMIHT*)

Although serious detail work on the engine we think we know so well began in 1949, all manner of project work, dabbling, and 'why-don't-we . . .?' studies had been ongoing before then. Looking back at the original Len Lord 'master plan' which he presented to the board in March 1938, there was no settled mention of a new small engine – though it was clear that if the finance was made available to him, his overall intention was to replace the entire range of Austin cars, engines and transmissions.

Production of one long-established engine family – the side-valve 900cc and closely related 1,125cc units – was to carry on throughout the war, the same engines being used to power the relatively young Austin Eight and Austin Ten models from 1945 onwards. This, though, was only a stopgap. Even in the darkest depths of the war, and at Len Lord's direction, Austin somehow found time to dabble with the design of a tiny three-cylinder two-stroke engine. The thinking behind this power unit, no question, was influenced by the late-1930s success of the German two-stroke-engined DKWs, for there were no British rivals of the period from which to take any inspiration. However, even though prototype units were built, and tested in otherwise undistinguished Austin Eights, that project was swiftly abandoned when development of the larger-engined Austins demanded priority.

Other reliable sources (notably Barney Sharratt's magisterial survey of the A30/A35/A40 models) confirm that Eric Bareham started concept work – paper studies – on the layout of a new ultra-small-car engine as early as mid-1942. Not only did Bareham start sketching up details of a brand-new overhead-valve engine (to bowdlerise Jaguar engineer Bill Heynes' famous statement: 'Drawing lines on paper is cheap – it's only when you start cutting metal that the costs mount up . . .'), but he also considered doing an overhead-valve conversion of the existing 900cc side-valve engine.

Not only that, but there was thought of developing a three-cylinder version of the Eight's 'four', which was actually built, though soon cancelled when the problems of balancing its forces became evident. In all cases, the availability of existing machine tooling, which could possibly be modified for a new purpose, was taken into consideration, as it was already clear that there could be supply logjams in the immediate post-war years. Bareham then left Austin in 1945, to work at Lagonda, returning to Austin in 1947 before any real work on the A-Series began.

The waters were then muddied in 1948 when a

Inspired by Joe Ehrlich, this water-cooled 670cc engine with a simple side-valve layout had some merit in the late 1940s/early 1950s, but was neither refined enough nor powerful enough to do the job in the A30. Now, on the other hand, if there had been an A20 . . .

This air-cooled 500cc twin-cylinder engine, as used in the intriguing 'Dragonfly' prototype, was just one of the projected engines which fought for approval against the new A-Series.

remarkable character called Ian Duncan (of Duncan Industries in Norfolk) sold himself and his front-wheel-drive prototype, the Dragonfly, to Len Lord and Austin. This, Duncan thought, should become the basis of Austin's next small car, but the evidence is that Len Lord was more interested in buying up the prototype and its designers to stop them falling into the hands of any of his rivals, than in having the Dragonfly built in quantity at Longbridge. The cost to Austin was £10,000 and a three-year development contract for Ian Duncan.

Which is as may be – but the fact that the only completed Dragonfly prototype used a 500cc overhead-valve air-cooled BSA A7 motorcycle-type twin-cylinder engine must have confused many logical minds at Longbridge for months. Unhappily for the romantics, however, the fact is that every important feature of the Dragonfly – not only the engine, but the Moulton-type rubber suspension and the front-wheel-drive – was fairly briskly abandoned, which left Bill Appleby and Eric Bareham with an open challenge in which to develop a more conventional new power unit.

Even by 1949, however, the idea of developing a brand-new side-valve design had not been abandoned completely. Although Len Lord had virtually concluded that all future Austin engines should have overhead valve gear, he was still attracted to the idea of the simplicity and the low potential cost of producing a side-valve unit. But not for long, and by mid-1949 the team was homing in on AS3 (the project code at this point) as an 800cc overhead-valve engine.

Because those were the days before computers were available, and when most other mechanical aids to an engineer's skill and experience were either bulky, expensive or both, the initial design stage involved much sketching, scribbling, note-making and eyeball-to-eyeball discussion. Although by this time Bill Appleby carried the official title of 'chief designer – power units', he left much of the detail design work to his deputy Eric Bareham, and Bareham's own team.

Even though it was not read before the Institution of Mechanical Engineers (IMechE) until 1963 – a full decade after the A-Series went into production – many elements

AS3 or A-Series – what's in a name?

Purists will want me to make it clear that the original engine was known internally as the AS3, and that the 'A-Series' name was not adopted until after the formation of BMC (the British Motor Corporation). The first Austin car destined to use the new little engine was the new-generation Austin A30/Austin 'Seven'; this carried the project code AS3, and the new engine picked up the same code from the beginning.

of Bill Appleby's extremely closely reasoned paper entitled 'The BMC A-Series Engine' tell us much about the way that the engine came to be what it was. In this paper, incidentally, Appleby confirms that this engine 'was re-classified as the "A-Series" unit at the time of the formation of the British Motor Corporation. It was then decided that this unit and its derivatives would power all the smaller range of BMC cars.' I have no hesitation, therefore, in using that title for the engine from the very beginning, even at the very start of its public life.

Way back in 1949, it seems, two decisions were made

which would define the engine for life, at least one of which would come to limit its potential in later life when a lot more power was sought for use in sporty and heavier cars. Both were strongly influenced by what had already gone before in the design and development of the A40 (soon to be B-Series) power unit. One was that the new engine would have a small bore/long stroke layout; the other was that it would group all its components/accessories on one side of the cylinder block, but *not* the pushrods, so that a cylinder head with siamesed inlet and exhaust ports became almost inevitable. Not only that,

Eric Bareham, by then happily retired, inspects an A-Series engine rebuild – the unit which he had designed in the late 1940s . . .

. . . no doubt wondering how he could have improved the details if only he had had the time.

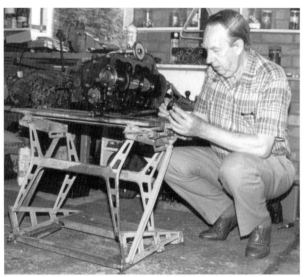

Engine layouts – you choose

In his seminal paper on the design of the original 803cc A-Series engine, Bill Appleby stated that 'the camshaft and pushrods are on the right-hand side of the engine looking from the front, and are on the same side as the inlet and exhaust ports. This construction was adopted to avoid the fitting of tubes in the cylinder head to enable the pushrods to pass the spark plugs.' Because of a lack of space, siamesed inlet and exhaust ports were therefore essential.

Two years later, when Standard designed their new 803cc 'SC' engine for the Standard Eight (both bore and stroke dimensions were identical with the A-Series, by the way), the camshaft was placed on the other side of the engine from the inlet and exhaust ports, and tubes were fitted in the cylinder head, for Standard thought they could deal with any oil leaks that developed. Siamesed inlet and exhaust ports were therefore not essential (though siamesed inlet ports were chosen, and used until 1964, when the first of the racing Spitfire cylinder heads was revealed).

For all these reasons, it is quite untrue to suggest that the Standard engine was a clone of the A-Series – and, in fact, for machinery utilisation reasons it was based around the cylinder centres of the old Triumph Mayflower side-valve power unit. This meant that it was slightly larger, could finally be enlarged to 1,493cc, and would eventually take over from the A-Series in the MG Midget of 1974–79.

Who was right and who was wrong? You choose.

---

but in production form there would be conventional cast iron cylinder blocks and heads, though light alloy heads were also tried at an early experimental stage. (The alloy head was soon abandoned, not only on cost grounds, but because valve seat inserts would have been needed, and Longbridge had no experience, or equipment, to deal with such details.)

For interest, I remind the reader that the earlier A40 engine had a bore of 65.48mm and a stroke of 88.9mm, which equated to stroke/bore ratio of 1.36:1, making it considerably 'under-square'. It was, in other words, altogether typical of an engine which might also have been designed in the 1930s. As far as this particular engine was concerned, the narrow bore had been chosen at the design stage in 1944/5, when British automotive licensing and taxation still leaned heavily against any engine which had a large piston area – which meant that most engines were laid out accordingly. When the A-Series came to be designed, however, it was four or five years later, and that long-standing law had been scrapped in favour of a licensing 'flat rate', and there was therefore no longer any marketing need for it to ape the A40 engine – though it did!

These were the days, however, when there was still a great deal of conservative thinking within the Austin organisation (it had become ingrained by Lord Austin's own philosophy, and though Len Lord had already done his best to shake things up, there were limits), and this certainly explains why Appleby's opening remarks in his IMechE paper included:

> 'The first decision to be made when designing a new engine is the stroke/bore ratio. The engine designed prior to the proposed new one was the 1,200cc four-cylinder engine, which had . . . a ratio of 1.3:1. This engine had been a great success, over half a million cars having been sold. We could see no point, therefore, in changing this ratio, which was maintained on the new engine . . .
>
> 'In any case, since the stroke was shorter [compared with the A40 engine], piston speed would be reduced by about 14 per cent for the same number of revolutions, and it is really the actual piston speed which matters, not the stroke/bore ratio, providing the latter is not extreme.'

This, on its own, was very interesting and very significant, for it went against the thinking of other concerns that were designing engines at the same time, and it must also have been influenced by the availability of certain machine tools which Len Lord was set on using again. The fact is that Ford's new medium-sized units (for the Consul/Zephyr range) and Vauxhall's E-Class engines (Wyvern/Velox) were both absolute contemporaries with the A-Series, but *both* of them had over-square (big bore/short stroke) layouts.

To make this puzzle yet more perplexing, I now refer to a long and erudite analysis of the Nuffield Organisation's new XP four-cylinder engine (which would be used in several Nuffield models in the 1940s and 1950s, including the famous MG TB/TC/TD/TF range), which had appeared in *The Autocar* in November 1939. Although it was penned by technical editor Montague Tombs, it was decidedly influenced and 'censored' by Nuffield's own engineers. Two of Tombs' comments make their own point:

> '*I could not resist the temptation to ask what was the starting point in laying out a new design. The answer was extremely interesting – the starting point is the inlet valve . . .*'

And elsewhere, when the general layout of the engine was discussed and the point was made that the ratio of the stroke to the bore was smaller than before, Nuffield's own response was:

> '*When this engine was requested, a major point was that weight must be saved – a lot of weight. To save real weight is a big problem: something drastic has to be done. And one obvious way to do it is to shorten the stroke, for a short stroke means shorter cylinder barrels, a smaller crank chamber and shorter throws of the crankshaft . . .*'

This, of course, is diametrically opposed to the approach taken by Appleby, Bareham and his colleagues in laying out the A-Series engine a decade later. In spite of the high-minded protestations of Appleby in his IMechE paper, and of other Austin/BMC publicists over the years, there must have been a strong traditional element in the process too. As has already been mentioned, it cannot be pure coincidence that the cylinder stroke of the obsolete Austin Seven engine and that chosen for the new A-Series were precisely the same – 76.2mm, or, in traditional Brummie-measure, exactly three inches. It was not as if any ancient but still operating crankshaft grinding machines had survived, but there was surely an element of 'well, it worked once, it ought to work again' in this decision.

Those were the days when little attempt was made to build in a great deal of capacity 'stretch' to a new engine

Tiny British engines – the marketplace in 1949

When Austin set out to design a new engine for its next 'baby' car, the existing competition from rival British concerns was feeble indeed. Here, in simple tabular form, is what was on offer from Austin's major rivals in 1949, when A-Series work began:

Make	Engine size (cc)	Peak power @ rpm	Comment (engine family announced)
Austin	900	23 @ 4,000	Side valve, launched 1932
Ford	933	23 @ 4,000	Side-valve, launched 1932
Hillman			No small engine on sale – none would appear until 1963
Morris	918	30 @ 4,400	Side-valve, launched 1934
Standard	1,009	28 @ 4,000	Side-valve, launched 1933
Vauxhall			No small engine on sale – none would appear until 1963

It was, in other words, high time that one of Britain's 'Big Six' produced an overhead-valve small engine of some type. As it transpired, Austin would be first in 1951, and Standard would not be far behind, but did not follow suit until 1953.

Incidentally, it is absolutely and categorically *not* true that Standard copied the A-Series for their new small 'SC' (Standard Eight/Ten) power unit, as the architecture of the two engines was entirely different.

at the design stage. As originally drawn up, the new power unit was to have a 58mm cylinder bore (which meant that the power unit would measure 803cc), and although the block was arranged to have a modicum of cooling water around each of the cylinder barrels this was really as small as Austin's casting suppliers could guarantee. The cross-sectional engine drawing (see page 38) shows a very slim water jacket surrounding cylinders 1/2 and 3/4, though there was more at each end of the block.

Appleby and Bareham, in fact, were encouraged to design the engine so that it could eventually be enlarged a little – to 948cc, with a cylinder bore of 63mm – but certainly no more, and even then this dimension was not adopted until five production years had passed. As we shall see, when the time came to consider making the engine larger and more robust for motor racing purposes, and eventually to submit to marketing department requests to enlarge the engine to suit the new front-wheel-drive ADO16 (Austin/Morris 1100) range, this

The ever-modest Bill Appleby was an extremely capable designer, and led the whole department that produced the A-Series in the late 1940s/early 1950s.

caused real headaches. (As is made clear in the panel on page 30, 'Engine layouts – you choose', Standard went through a series of similar traumas with their contemporary SC unit in the 1960s and 1970s, but had a little more space of which to take advantage.)

The most important decision, or series of decisions, regarded the location of all the components which had to be used. As time progressed, independent observers and analysts came to agree that what was done at the design stage eventually had an adverse effect on what could be done to develop the engine in future life. This was to group every single electrical 'hang-on' on one side of the engine, and to find space for the camshaft, the pushrods, the inlet and exhaust manifolds and the carburettor (later fuel injection) on the other. (This, in fact, is what had already been done on the larger A40 engine, on which design work was complete and which was now in series production.)

Once again, to quote from Bill Appleby's learned paper: 'In the first place, the camshaft and push rods are on the right-hand side of the engine looking from the front [of the engine] and are on the same side as the inlet and exhaust ports. This construction was adopted to avoid the fitting of tubes in the cylinder head to enable the push

This was the layout of the A-Series cylinder head as laid down by Eric Bareham in 1949, which went on to persist for half a century. Maybe it was not ideal for peak power production, but two inlet ports (circular section) and three exhaust ports (rectangular section) were adequate except for very high output needs.

rods to pass the spark plugs, which would have been necessary if the camshaft had been on the other side of the engine.

'It was considered that the tubes could be a source of oil and water leaks, and as production of the engine was likely to be several thousand per week, a small percentage of leaks would create a serious service problem.

'This construction does, however, compel one to use siamesed inlet ports and a centre siamesed exhaust port. We have never found any disadvantage from using a siamesed inlet port; in fact it appears to have an advantage in that the volume of the induction system, is less than that of separate ports and therefore there can be a quicker response to any demand from the accelerator. A siamesed exhaust port, however, is not desirable, and its disadvantages can only be overcome by using first-class exhaust valve materials. We now use 21-4N as our standard exhaust valve material.

'Another feature of BMC engine design is to put all the electrical equipment on the side of the engine away from the carburettor and the inlet and exhaust manifold. This is done to prevent any petrol drip from the carburettor or heat from the exhaust manifold affecting the electrical components. This meant that the drive from the camshaft to the distributor had to be taken across the engine . . .'

Because the original AS3/A-Series was not, by any means, intended as an ultra-powerful, or even a sporty, power unit, it was equipped with conventional, not to say conservative, carburation, manifolding and camshaft profile details. As Bill Appleby noted:

'. . . We insist on engine flexibility over a wide speed range, including good pulling power at low rev/min. This we secure by using large valves, a low valve lift, a conservative valve timing, and a comparatively heavy flywheel. Our standard valve timing is: inlet opens 5deg BTDC, inlet closes 45deg PBDC, exhaust opens 40deg BBDC, exhaust closes 10deg PTDC, the valve opening period being only 230deg. A study of the power curve shows that maximum torque is developed at 2,200rev/min.'

A consequence of the chosen valve gear/camshaft layout was that one side of the cylinder head casting looked quite crowded. Looking at it from the machined face/junction of head and manifolding, the sequence was: exhaust port, space for pushrods, inlet port, space for pushrods, exhaust port, space for pushrods, inlet port, space for pushrods, and exhaust port. In those early days the inlet ports were circular in section, the exhaust ports oblong, but a good deal of development and evolution would follow in the years to come. Both inlet ports, but only the central exhaust port, were siamesed and, whether Appleby and team were likely to admit it or not, a great deal of compromise had had to be made.

One other oddity featured – not one which was likely to exercise the engine designers, but one which would come to irritate Alec Issigonis and his cohorts in years to come when he proposed to mount the engine across the structure of his new cars, instead of in the conventional 'north-south' alignment. This was that the electrical distributor stuck out like a sore thumb; it was even more of an excrescence than the dynamo and starter which lived close alongside.

What this would mean – and I will be covering the events in a later chapter – is that the distributor would be facing squarely into the flow of dirt, water and generation detritus which entered the Mini's engine bay. Not only that, but Issigonis always used to complain that it took up several inches of useful car length which might otherwise be devoted to the passenger cabin.

Working under the guidance of Bill Appleby, Eric Bareham was the Austin engineer who led the design team that produced the A-Series engine between 1949 and 1951.

When the engine was originally designed there was lively debate as to which carburettor should be used. Then, as later, it was clear that the constant-vacuum type SIU instrument was technically superior to conventional fixed-jet types like those on offer from Zenith and Solex (which were both brands owned by the same company in any case), but although the engineers preferred to use SU, when the new engine was being designed there was a commercial and 'political' problem. Simply, and brutally, SU was owned by the Nuffield organisation, who were deadly rivals of Austin, and although they were willing to supply carburettors to Austin it was apparently to be at an unacceptably high unit price.

Test work, therefore, was concentrated on a fixed-jet carburettor, and in the end the downdraught Zenith 26JS instrument was chosen. This, in conjunction with a modest 7.2:1 compression ratio (which was as high as could be used because of the still rather doubtful quality of 'Pool' petrol supplies in the late 1940s) resulted in a reliable power unit.

Although a listing of original 'target' horsepower figures and estimates does not seem to have survived, there is little doubt that the project team was quietly pleased with the results that they achieved in prototype testing. By the time the Zenith-equipped AS3/A-Series was ready to meet its public it was rated at a claimed 30bhp at 4,800rpm – which might have been just a tad over-optimistic, as years later the official power/torque graphs showed it to be 28bhp.

No matter. Already it compared very well with the obsolete 900cc side-valve engine recently used in the Austin Eight (23bhp at 4,000rpm), with the 27bhp at 4,400rpm which was claimed for the original 918cc side-valve Morris Minor, and with the 23bhp at 4,000rpm claimed for the 933cc side-valve Ford Anglia engine.

Once detail design was well under way – there would be many detail changes in the last few months before launch, but the majority of the job was completed by the end of 1949 – prototype testing could begin. The first engine fired up on a Longbridge test bed in the spring of 1950, and the first road car to use the AS3/A-Series engine was completed by the end of the year.

Now it really was Big Breath time, for a brand new family car – the Austin A30 (or the 'New Seven', as Austin publicists would have liked to call it) – would be launched in October 1951. Would the new engine do the job for which it was intended?

CHAPTER 3

Out with the old, in with the new

Designing an engine is one thing, but building it in quantity is quite another. By any standards, producing the all-new A-Series was going to be a colossal job – especially as it became the third all-new range of Austin engines to be launched since the end of the Second World War. Not only that, but Longbridge was also arranging to produce Rolls-Royce four-cylinder B40 engines for fitment to the Champ military 4x4 vehicle (and eight-cylinder B80s for other non-Austin military vehicles), these being totally unrelated to any Austin product.

Nor was that all, for as originally planned the A-Series had been intended only for use in the Austin A30. However, within months of the setting up of BMC (the British Motor Corporation), in the spring of 1952 it was also earmarked for use in the Morris Minor range (which was being assembled at Cowley), and plans to ramp up the rate of production had to be made, even before first deliveries of A30s had got under way.

First, though, development work on the new small saloon car, and on the engine installation, had to be completed. Well, before an AS3/A-Series engine was even ready to go into a car for road-proving purposes, the design of the new car itself had to be carried out. As already mentioned in the previous chapter, a new car might well have been produced more speedily if management had not been drawn into purchasing Ian Duncan's technically-advanced Dragonfly, and into the long and sometimes contentious evolution of the style of the new conventional car which replaced it.

In the end it was chief designer Johnnie Rix who got the go-ahead for a new model from Len Lord, for a project which was to be a small four-seater four-door saloon, and was to have an all-steel monocoque structure. Although

there was always the romantic idea that this was to be a 'new Austin Seven', there was absolutely no mechanical or technical link to that wonderful old, but thoroughly obsolete, machine. Although the 'footprint' of the new car was rather like that of the old, it had a slightly shorter wheelbase, but a similar cabin package, and shared not a single component. Even so, until the style and (by definition) the packaging of the car could be concluded, there was little that the engine and transmission engineers could finish off in their own fields of expertise.

At about the same time that Eric Bareham started work on the little four-cylinder engine, work began on the shaping of the car itself. First of all chief stylist Dick Burzi inspired the shaping of a neat two-door shape, one in which the lines and proportions were already beginning to settle down. In the meantime, however, Len Lord had fallen for the charms (and the no-doubt persuasive salesmanship) of the Loewy Studio. Not only had Raymond Loewy's team built up a fine reputation for styling cars, locomotives, buses, the Coca-Cola bottle and many non-automotive industrial products in the USA, but it had also forged a so-far very fruitful link with Britain's Rootes Group, for which they had inspired the new-generation Minx and new-generation Humber Hawk, both of which had been launched at the Earls Court Motor Show in October 1948.

Lord did not seem to be worried about any clash of interests, however, and arranged for Loewy's Bob Koto to fly over to Longbridge in mid-1950, where he was provided with the packaging details required and all the facilities he needed. Within months, and with great help from Kenneth Howes, he worked up a full-sized clay model of which Lord and his trusty deputy George

This was the architecture of the A30 of 1951, Austin's very first chassisless (monocoque) private car, and the very first to use the A-Series engine. In this guise the engine was a 28bhp 803cc unit. (*BMIHT*)

Harriman thoroughly approved. However, this deal was only ever intended to be a short-term contract, so Koto left Longbridge assuming that what he had finally produced would be accepted – only to discover, a year later, that it had been altered in almost every way! In particular, and at Len Lord's request, the tail had been shortened by several inches, the position 'in space' of the rear seat raised, and the roof line raised to suit.

The final car (which was, let us not forget, Austin's very first monocoque design) featured a structure worked up between Ian Duncan and ex-aircraft industry stressed-skin expert Ken Garrett, but the detail styling was carried out during the winter of 1950/1 by Dick Burzi's team at Longbridge (with, need one emphasise, much advice – for which read 'interference' – from Len Lord himself). Burzi, Argentinean by birth, had originally worked in Italy for Lancia before he moved to the UK, where he became Lord Austin's chief stylist in the mid-1930s. It was Lord's wish, and not Burzi's responsibility, that the new 'Austin Seven' (this was a name which could not, and did not, persist, so henceforth I will only refer to it as the A30) should be visually conventional in style. In fact it was the first of a family of cars which included the new-generation Austin A40 Cambridge of 1954 and the A90 Westminster, and all came unmistakeably from the same studio and the same team of styling/design engineers.

It would probably be fair to suggest that the car itself, and its structure, really went ahead without reference to the brand-new engine. The entire front end of the car could certainly have been lowered by some inches, this

being obvious when the bonnet of an A30 is raised to inspect the engine and the observer finds that the little power unit is almost lost. The engine itself, that is, for in order to take advantage of the relatively large engine bay volume the engineers chose to use a down-draught carburettor with a cylindrical air cleaner/air filter on top of that.

Similarly, there was a new-generation four-speed synchromesh gearbox tucked away under the steel floor pan immediately behind the A-Series engine. This was extremely compact, as it was never intended to deal with much more torque than the new 803cc engine could provide.

The very first of a handful of A30 prototypes took to the road before the end of 1950 – chief designer Johnnie Rix pulled rank to make sure that he was the first to get any impressions of a journey to and from Wales – and by this time the entire Austin organisation was gearing itself up towards a public announcement at the Earls Court (London) Motor Show in October 1951.

Although high-speed Continental testing of prototypes eventually became normal for Austin (and, indeed, all other companies in Great Britain's 'Big Six'), it is a fact that no work in Europe was carried out on A30s until the end of 1951, immediately *after* the car had been shown to the public. This at least meant that the prototypes did not have to be kept away from prying eyes by being camouflaged, nor did they have to be tested at night.

In the meantime Austin, which still had no proving ground facilities of its own, used public roads and the new MIRA facility (near Nuneaton) instead. Like all its rivals, Austin had its own open-road favourite routes, challenges and locations, so it was no surprise that the rest of the industry knew a lot about the A30 and its A-Series engine within weeks of road testing starting. Testing was often carried out in North Wales, particularly on the Bwlch-y-Groes pass.

Not that this was ever a routine process. As John Barnett (who eventually took charge of all engine development at Longbridge, but joined Austin in 1951) recalled:

'The durability mileage was done on what was known as the Welsh route, where a batch of A30s – about four of them, I think – would go out on the night shift, and would get back in the morning. One night, I remember, there was consternation, because four set out, and only three came back! The leading cars hadn't spotted that the fourth car was missing – so they had to have a search for it, and found that it had actually gone off the road somewhere in the Welsh hills.'

Engine development, of course, was initially carried out on one of the banks of test beds that had been installed in the Experimental block at Longbridge, but much in-car work was also needed. A lot of work was carried out at MIRA (the Motor Industry Research Association) at Lindley, near Nuneaton, which was a converted ex-RAF aerodrome close to the A5 main road. Because every rival used MIRA from time to time, inter-company security and secrecy was almost impossible to maintain – especially as the beer garden in a nearby village pub gave an unrivalled view of each and every one of MIRA's special sections.

MIRA, however, offered much that Austin needed: not only a high-speed circuit whose limits were way above the A30's 60+ top speed, but a wet-weather skid pan, water splashes, a dust tunnel and a lethally damaging stretch of Belgian pavé track.

Building up the empire

While all this testing was going on, Austin management had been grappling with a sizeable problem: where and how to manufacture the engine and transmissions themselves, and where to assemble the A30 motor cars which they would power.

First there was the location of engine and gearbox manufacture and assembly to be settled, this being only the most recent of a series of upheavals which had taken place at Longbridge. It is worth recalling that in 1939, when civilian car and truck assembly had closed down to

aid the war effort, Austin was making a series of old-style, old-fashioned side-valve engines, along with the new large overhead-valve six-cylinder 'Birmingham Bedford' truck power units. All these were made, somehow, in the rush, crush and amazingly old-fashioned-looking North Works.

Starting in 1944, and during the first few years after the war, facilities and tooling to make the larger and oldest-type side-valve engines were swept away, though the 900cc/1,125cc Austin Eight/Ten engines were continued. Then, of course, two massive investments followed up – the plant to make new-type 2,199cc petrol engines (for the Austin 16 and, soon, the A70 range), closely followed by huge investment in the 1,200cc/A40 engine which would be introduced at the end of 1947.

Starting in 1949, when the first 'long-lead' machine tools were ordered from Archdale, an increasing amount of time was devoted to getting ready to produce AS3/A-Series power units and the related gearboxes. At that time, of course, Austin had still not got together with the Nuffield Organisation, so only one immediate use for the new small engine was envisaged.

This was all carried out in 1950 and 1951, and it is a

The A-Series was a very compact little unit that fitted easily into the engine bay of the all-new A30 family car's bodyshell. *(BMIHT)*

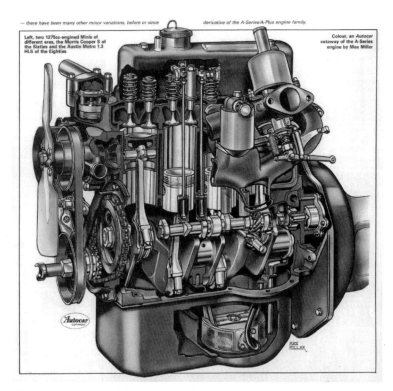

— there have been many other minor variations, before or since   derivative of the A-Series/A-Plus engine family.

Left, two 1275cc-engined Minis of different eras, the Morris Cooper S of the Sixties and the Austin Metro 1.3 HLS of the Eighties

Colour, an *Autocar* cutaway of the A-Series engine by Max Millar

This was the anatomy of the SU-equipped version of the A-Series engine of the 1950s, showing the simple but rugged layout of this three-main-bearing power unit.

measure of the complexity of the process that deliveries of the A30, which had first been shown to the world in October 1951, did not actually begin until May/ June 1952. Clearly it was a colossal enterprise, with a massive upheaval of North Works involved in order to manufacture the new engine and the new gearbox that would be fitted behind it. Indeed, so great was the project that in 1953 Britain's *Automobile Engineer* devoted no fewer than 12 pages to a description of A-Series engine tooling, followed up by a further 12 pages about the gearbox itself. (Purely as an aside, *Automobile Engineer* quoted three significant figures for the hardware: that a complete A30 weighed 1,475lb, the engine itself weighed 219lb, and the new gearbox weighed a mere 43lb.)

Amazingly, Len Lord does not seem to have subjected this big capital investment and management upheaval to any detailed scrutiny by his less senior colleagues on the Austin board of directors, where the minutes of meetings held in the 1948–52 period are both subdued and terse on the subject. On the other hand, and purely as a comparison, much more time seems to have been devoted to discussing the new Champ 4x4 contract (and the preparation for the manufacture of the new

Rolls-Royce engines which would go with it), and the implications of the changes needed to East Works.

While all this was going on Austin was also preparing itself for the cataclysmic upheaval which would soon lead to the foundation of the British Motor Corporation and finally, in 1968, to the setting up of the fundamentally flawed British Leyland colossus.

Even in 1948, when the AS3/A-Series engine had been no more than a gleam in Len Lord's eye, he had begun to look ahead strategically, into Austin's possible future. Although Austin was a market leader, both in terms of British and export car sales, Lord concluded that it would have to grow considerably more to be economically stable in the 1950s and beyond. In round figures, he concluded that Austin would need to become at least twice as large – maybe three times as large – as it already was.

This, Lord also decided, was probably not something that Austin could tackle on its own. Although there would be great personal and commercial obstacles to be overcome, Lord concluded that there ought to be a series of mergers in the British industry. The 'Big Six', in other words, needed to become the 'Big Five' as soon as possible, and Austin needed to get involved in a merger.

But with whom? Not with Ford, nor with Vauxhall, for both were already controlled by vast USA-based parent companies (Vauxhall was a General Motors subsidiary). With Standard? Maybe, but Lord did not get on with the arrogant, irascible Sir John Black, who ran it. How about the Rootes Group? Once again there was a personal problem, for trying to 'mate' Len Lord with William Rootes would have been like introducing a lighted match to a pile of explosives.

Which left the Nuffield Organisation, which Lord had re-created for Sir William Morris (but definitely in his own, rather than in that tycoon's image) in the early 1930s, an enterprise from which he had left in high dudgeon in 1936. Surely a rapprochement was not possible? Yet it was, for Nuffield's founder/chairman/dictator (who had become Lord Nuffield) was ageing rapidly; and because Miles Thomas had quite recently left the business there was no obvious successor in sight. Not only that, but the new Morris Minor (designed by Alec Issigonis, and just released) looked promising, and Len Lord was already jealous of it.

Amazingly, therefore, when Len Lord once again approached Nuffield in 1948 he was received civilly, if rather formally. Before the end of that year exploratory talks had made some progress. A personal announcement followed, to the effect that they would proceed with

the merger of certain interests. For the time being such co-operation would be limited, though the statement pointed out that 'there would be a constant interchange of information on production methods, costs, purchases, design and research, patents and all other items which would be likely to result in manufacturing economies'.

All this was done very thoughtfully, and very carefully, so that neither company could be accused of trying to carve out an increased sector of the market, and to work against the public interest, yet questions were asked in the House of Commons, and several hostile (left wing, anti-business, need I add?) articles were published in the ensuing months.

Before too long, in fact, this rather tentative project was seen to have been an abortive exercise, for neither company seemed to want to go too far in confidential discussions in case it harmed its own interests before those of such an arm's-length merger became apparent. Even though more than a decade had passed, there must, in any case, still have been residual animosity between Len Lord and Lord Nuffield. We must remember that Lord had suddenly and abruptly stormed out of Cowley in 1936 after a dispute with Nuffield over payment, and that he was later heard to say that he intended 'to take that business at Cowley apart, brick by bloody brick'.

Accordingly, by mid-1949 it was clear that these

This display unit of the original 803cc A-Series engine showed neatness and purpose, but gave no hint of the long life and powerful hidden potential that it would subsequently demonstrate.

discussions were going nowhere, so after a brief and formal meeting at the very top level, between the two chairmen, the whole deal was called off. Len Lord actually reported this to his directors at a meeting in July 1949, before authorising his publicists to release this statement to the press: 'The interchange of confidential information has ceased. No further steps will be taken with regard to the pooling of production, and no merger is contemplated.'

The timing of this 'divorce' is important – if only because it coincided with the point at which work on the new A-Series/A30 project moved forward from a 'why don't we . . .?' proposal to a definite project. In other words, the collapse of the merger proposals was one of several factors which led to Len Lord deciding to get his own back on Lord Nuffield, by authorising the birth of a new car to compete, head-on, with the Morris Minor. One understands that Lord told Lord Nuffield what he was going to do, though no technical details were revealed at that point.

CAB1

At Longbridge, therefore, two very important announcements would be made in 1951. One was the introduction of the new A30 model, complete with its A-Series engine, and the other was the completion of the vast new car assembly building (CAB1), which came on-stream in the middle of the year before the A30 was quite ready to fill it. Simply and basically, however, if CAB1 had not been finished and made ready there would have been no other place at Longbridge where the A30 could have been assembled. It was, after all, Austin's first ever chassisless product, and new assembly methods would be needed to mate engines, gearboxes and suspensions to the bodyshell.

Before then, cars and trucks had been assembled in increasingly cramped conditions, not to say in squalor, in South Works and West Works, in the former tucked into an increasingly over-burdened factory complex which could be expanded no further. This roughly triangular

If the Luftwaffe had got its way, German bombers would have flattened the Longbridge complex early in the Second World War. This reconnaissance shot, captured in 1945, shows the 'flying ground' which Austin would eventually cover with the two massive CABs (Car Assembly Buildings), and the other already established blocks. (*BMIHT*)

site, the core of which included the original Austin works of 1905, was bounded by two stretches of railway (one the LMS main line from Birmingham to Bristol and the south-west of England), and also by the higher plateau of Austin's 'flying ground', the airfield which (as already described) had also been extended to its absolute limits to cater for Austin's Second World War activities. The flying ground, in fact, was not used for anything other than open-air storage at this time.

Len Lord's solution, to satisfy his self-imposed plan to double or even treble the size of Austin's operations, was therefore to use the large area of the 'flying ground' to build a vast new assembly building which would be the largest, the most modern and the most mechanised of any car factory in the UK. Although this was an era when robots had yet to be invented, it was still intended to be as mechanically efficient as possible. This building would be linked to West, North and the existing South Works by a brand-new series of conveyors, tunnels and mechanised link ways. Trucks would still be needed to ferry in components; surprisingly, this would include complete bodyshells from one side of the main A38 road (West Works) to the other.

Since the building of military aircraft had ended in East Works in 1945, and since the largest of those aircraft (the mighty four-engined Lancasters) would have needed to take off from a longer runway than existed at Longbridge, the area had already been redundant for some time. Although it was roughly circular in plan the flying ground could only accept a building up to about 400 yards long, but this was ample for what Lord, and Austin, had in mind. Later it was extended, but it was never more than a third of a mile long.

The plan, simple but carefully thought out in the grand style, was that an integrated new CAB should be erected, aligned roughly north-east to south-west, in which the assembly of all the contemporary and planned mass-production Austin cars would be concentrated. For the time being, limited-production models such as the Austin A40 Sports, the Champ 4x4 and (soon) the Austin-Healey 100 sports car, would take shape in other, older, more 'traditional' areas of the factory – but that was to be a temporary, rather short-term arrangement. As far as the new A30 was concerned, one final assembly line would be totally dedicated to it, while the new A-Series engines, their related gearboxes and major components such as axles, would be delivered to that line by tunnel and overhead conveyor.

When it was finally shown off to the industrial media, CAB1 was boastfully advertised as being by far the most modern and sophisticated assembly plant in the world – which was undoubtedly true, though European giants such as Fiat and Renault would make haste to close that gap during the 1950s. That doyen of the British 'establishment' motoring magazines, *The Autocar*, was so impressed with the new factory that it devoted no fewer than four pages of highly illustrated material to a description of it:

'Few of those who have seen it would deny the proud boast. But it is not only the fine and imposing building, some 900 feet in length, fronted by lawns and flower beds, which impels one to accept the claim, for the complex machinery and equipment it houses reduce the task of assembling a car to virtually a series of automatic operations . . .'

The importance of CAB1 was not that it came into existence at all, but rather because of the way that it took advantage of the natural terrain. Not only this, but Len Lord had looked ahead with real vision, making sure that there was space to install several different, parallel and totally distinct assembly lines for the various models – A30s would have the use of two lines (though this detail was still secret when CAB1 was first shown to the press), A40s another, while A70s and A90s had a third. According to the drawings released at the time there was provision for four lines. Not only that, but an aerial view made it clear that there was still space on the flying ground for more big buildings to be erected alongside CAB1, if and when the demand arose: it would, for the second of Alec Issigonis' A-Series-engined front-wheel-drive cars (the Austin/Morris 1100 range) occupy what became CAB2 in the early 1960s.

The real advance of CAB1's layout was that major components were not fed into the building from doors at ground level, and from the outside world, but from under the floor or from overhead conveyors. Everything from bodyshells to engines, gearboxes to axles and suspension assemblies, would be assembled on other parts of the vast Longbridge site, then arrive ('oven-ready' as it were) exactly where they were needed.

In order to ensure that this process worked, an enormous 1,000ft-long tunnel and covered way was driven into the hillside, and under the assembly floor, from the northern side of the site (*ie* from the South Works area). For all the obvious reasons (such as being closest to North, South and West Works), the chassis frame delivery area and suspension installation zones were towards the northern end of the site, and at the south end the newly-completed cars could be, and often were, driven straight out through the doors, and sent on their way to holding compounds, or to their customers at home and overseas.

Because this was a highly mechanised progress, observers in the tunnel would see parts on slings, advancing inexorably, seemingly without purpose, but being delivered to one of several stations where they would pop up to meet the part-completed car for which they were intended. The cluttered old days of assembly lines holding piles of major components alongside the moving tracks themselves had gone for ever.

Amazingly, and in spite of the huge expense of effectively doubling the size and scope of the Longbridge factory, the construction of CAB1 seemed to have little negative effect on the company's activities, or finances, for there was no large-scale demolition or disruption of the existing Longbridge plant. In fact, between 1949 and 1951 vehicle production had moved up yet again, from 136,000 to 142,000, while the business' net profits had soared from £680,000 to no less than £2,841,000. Was it any wonder that in 1951 Len Lord took the opportunity of gaining board approval to raise his own salary from £12,500 per year plus 2½% commission on net profits, to £23,750 plus 1½% commission? That, in fairness, meant that his personal rewards would come down in the short term, but would soar in the late 1950s.

Engine and car – ready for launch

In the meantime, work on getting the new car, and most particularly its new engine, ready for sale went steadily ahead. Even so, Len Lord – thrusting, sharp, ambitious and as brutal as ever – was apparently never satisfied with progress. As someone at BMC who knew him and worked under him for years once said: 'He was usually as friendly as a bear with a sore head, but there were days when the head was even more sore than usual.'

Not even regular explosions of temper from the chairman could get the new engine ready any faster – and there were people at Longbridge who wondered what all that fuss was about, as it was becoming clear that the all-

important supply of bodyshells was likely to be delayed by several months.

Usually, and for many years past, Austin had manufactured its own bodyshells, and had bought in separate steel chassis on which to mount them, but in the case of the A30 new technology was involved. Austin's problem was that the new A30 would feature the company's very first true chassisless bodyshell, and since they had never tackled such a job before they were worried about their ability to do the job properly.

Even though it would have meant a certain amount of 'loss of face' within the motor industry, consideration was certainly given at the planning stages to putting out the manufacture of monocoques to an independent concern. There was, of course, only one Austin precedent to be considered, for when Len Lord rushed through the design of the new Eight and Ten models of 1939 the platform chassis (not complete shells, of course) had been provided by Pressed Steel of Cowley.

This time around, only three companies could possibly have dealt with the high volume of A30 four-door saloon shells to be produced – Pressed Steel, Birmingham-based Fisher & Ludlow, and Briggs Motor Bodies of Dagenham in Essex. In the end none was asked to do the job – at least, not the job of producing the saloon shell, though Briggs would later make several thousand van and Countryman (estate) types at their Doncaster factory. Instead, Longbridge's body engineers took the 'Brave Pill' and elected to tackle the job in West Works.

Finally, in October 1951, the 'new Austin Seven' was unveiled to the public on the very eve of the Earls Court Motor Show, though Austin made sure that no one realised it was still some months before cars could actually be put on sale.

Even though the new car was technically conventional, with 'traditional engineering', both of Britain's 'establishment' magazines – *The Autocar* and *The Motor* – greeted it with something approaching reverence. Both had known of the existence of the new model for many months, but always observed the embargo deadlines which applied (and which were observed) in those days.

The Autocar headlined its five-page description 'Once more an Austin Seven', noting straight away that: 'There has been no secrecy about the fact that the popular Austin Seven of the 1922–1937 era was one day to have a successor. Mr L.P. Lord announced that two years ago . . .'

'It is not too much to say that it is one of the

The A30 and the A35 (this is an A35) that followed were modest little family cars, small in every way, the A-Series engine being specifically designed as their power unit.

outstanding attractions of the [Earls Court] exhibition . . . an innovation for Austins is the adoption of unit or integral construction, the all-steel body having a fully stressed skin and there being no chassis frame . . . Altogether the Austin Seven is a remarkable car, both for its modern lines, and well-proportioned appearance, and for its technical specification.'

The new small engine ('A-Series' was not a phrase used at the time, nor even coined yet) looked so like the A40 unit, which was celebrating its fourth birthday, that it was received without superlatives: 'The new Seven engine, clutch and gearbox naturally follow the lines of design that have already been well proved on other Longbridge productions.'

Amazingly, *The Motor*'s headline was almost the same as that of its rival – 'Once again: An Austin Seven' – and the opening words in its analysis were: 'Probably the greatest guarantee of the future success of the new Austin Seven is the consciousness which is noticeable at Longbridge amongst all who have played a part in its evolution, that they are competing not so much against their normal competitors, as against their own reputation.'

This was their comment on the new engine:

'In the design of the engine, no concessions have been made to cheapness and, except for one or two

details where pure size has made simplification possible, the unit is virtually an 800cc edition of the familiar A40 power unit.'

For the time being, however, no new A30s (the 'Seven' title was soon abandoned) reached showrooms, or even made their way to the docks ready for export, as the bodyshell and engine production facilities at Longbridge were not yet in operation. This did not stop Austin from setting UK retail prices for the new car, and it is interesting to compare these with those of their immediate rivals:

Model	Engine size/ valve gear/power	Total retail price
Austin A30 four-door	803cc/ohv/30bhp	£507
Morris Minor MM		
(two-door)	918cc/sv/27.5bhp	£519
(four-door)	918cc/sv/27.5bhp	£569
Ford Anglia (two-door)	933cc/sv/23bhp	£479
Ford Prefect (four-door)	1,172cc/sv/30bhp	£572
Renault 4CV	748cc/ohv/21bhp	£689

Although its carrying capacity was limited, Austin found a ready market for the little A30 (later A35) Countryman.

Len Lord often asked his sales team what they wanted to charge for their new models, but next asked what was the price of the nearest rival, and then undercut it by a few pounds. Nowadays we have no written evidence to tell us what the original A30 *should* have cost, but the legend is that Len Lord was quite determined to sell his new car for less than the Morris Minor, and reduced it from an originally suggested £525. (Why not fight the Ford Anglia price too? Probably because this was a thoroughly obsolete model, with a 1930s-type chassis frame and beam axle suspensions, a side-valve engine, and pre-war styling. Len Lord preferred to wait for a new-generation car to arrive – which it would not until 1953.)

In the meantime, final testing and development of the all-new A-Series/A30 combination continued. Two cars (along with other new Austin models) made a high-speed dash around the warmer parts of Belgium, France and Spain at the end of 1951 into early 1952. As far as the Zenith-carburettor-equipped engines were concerned, there was one significant failure when a connecting

The fascia/instrument panel of the A30 was a modest affair, with no way of knowing how fast or hard the little A-Series engine was being used.

rod big end bearing failed, and as a result the priceless prototype had to be towed all the way back across France to Brussels, where a replacement power unit was fitted. A further long-distance test, with an upgraded experimental unit, was much more successful.

It was already becoming clear that, as originally designed, the A-Series was not a very robust unit, and Longbridge development engineers, led by characters like Gil Jones, would spend many months rectifying the problems. The miracle was that in due course it would become one of the most reliable and trouble-free power units that BMC/British Leyland ever manufactured.

Even so, in the initial stages there was no avoiding the fact that it was being built ruthlessly down to a price, was only to be rated at 30bhp, and was initially going to power a car which would reach a mere 60mph flat out. In the words of one latter-day tuning authority, David Vizard, the

crankshaft was 'just a shade on the spindly side . . . even in the early days of performance tuning . . . the crankshaft of the 803cc unit was often described as "a bent piece of wire with some journals ground on".'

Finally, after a traumatic three-year period in which the new little engine progressed from 'good idea' to 'in production' status, the A30 was ready for sale, and the first true off-the-line cars left CAB1 in May 1952. Although the build-up of series production would be agonisingly slow (only about 4,000 cars had been completed by the end of 1952), almost everyone had an excuse for this – that the merger with the Nuffield Organisation had just taken place!

BMC thought there was a ready market for this tiny 'Ute' (or pickup) version of the A35, but even the willing little A-Series engine couldn't deliver enough power to deal with an economic amount of payload, so the model did not last long.

CHAPTER 4

Founding and building BMC

When Austin suddenly announced a merger with the Nuffield Organisation in November 1951, almost everyone except the two boards of directors was surprised. Nuffield, after all, was still financially controlled by Lord Nuffield himself, attempts at a merger in 1948–49 had been a failure, and the two dominant individuals in this transaction – Len Lord and Lord Nuffield – had parted in acrimony more than once in earlier years.

Business, however, is business. Although it was never going to be easy, the far-sighted Lord could see that Austin would have to expand by acquisition if it was to survive long-term, whereas the stubborn and inward-looking Lord Nuffield could not (or, more likely, would not). In age, and in experience of course, there was almost a full generation between the two men, and this would have to be resolved. It was, one can surmise, the biggest obstacle of all.

At the time of the proposed merger, which was

Lord Nuffield (born William Morris)

Although Lord Nuffield had no part in the design of the original A-Series engine, it was his old-style stubbornness that indirectly led to its birth in 1951. As William Morris, he had set up Morris Motors in 1913, to build cars at Cowley, near Oxford. By the 1920s Morris was a direct and formidable rival to Austin, by the mid-1930s William Morris was Lord Nuffield, and by the late 1940s his company had become the Nuffield Organisation, embracing Morris, Wolseley, Riley and MG, plus Morris Commercial.

Len Lord, who went on to become Austin's supremo, worked for Morris during the 1920s and 1930s, then resigned abruptly in 1936 after a disagreement over pay. MD of Austin from 1945, by the late 1940s he had resolved to take over Nuffield, no matter what it took.

Although Len Lord had not completely signed off the new A-Series/Austin A30 project at that moment, it was Lord Nuffield's reluctance to talk logical business sense over a merger which tipped the balance. Lord then informed Nuffield that if he would not agree to an amicable merger, then the A-Series/A30 projects would go ahead, and that this was bound to harm Nuffield.

It was only after the new Austin venture had been announced that Nuffield agreed to a merger, which duly took place in the winter of 1951/2, the announcement coming in November 1951. The result was the formation of the British Motor Corporation (BMC), in which Lord Nuffield was the chairman for the first few months. In that time, however, Lord Nuffield had little influence on the evolution of the A-Series, but deserves to be remembered as one of the founding fathers of the new business.

He died in 1963.

George Harriman

Although it was Len Lord who authorised the new A-Series engine, it was his deputy (later BMC's managing director) Sir George Harriman who ran the factories that made it so. Not that there was much new in this arrangement, for Harriman had been Lord's faithful bag-carrier for many years. At a personal level the two were poles apart, but they seemed to get on well together for decades. Lord was abrasive where Harriman was emollient, Lord was the dictator while Harriman was always the consulting boss, and Lord was always decisive while Harriman often seemed to be diffident.

Coventry-born Harriman joined the Hotchkiss (soon to become Morris Motors) engine plant in Coventry as an apprentice in 1923, and finally stepped down as British Leyland's chairman at the end of 1968, having joined Austin (and Len Lord) in 1940. Because his father, also George Harriman, was employed at Morris before him, the son was always known as 'Young George', an affectionate title that stayed with him for decades.

First as an apprentice at Morris Engines, then a production superintendent, he briefly worked for Len Lord before their career paths split. Then, in 1940, he jumped ship from Morris (at Cowley by that time), joined Lord at Longbridge, and started his steady rise to CEO. Production manager in 1944, then general works manager in September 1945 (when he joined the board), he became Len Lord's official deputy in 1952.

As Austin founded BMC, eventually absorbed Pressed Steel, then took over Jaguar, Harriman became more and more powerful. After Len Lord went into 'semi-retirement' in 1956 (as I have made clear, no one really believed *that*), Harriman became joint managing director/deputy chairman, rose to become BMC's sole managing director in 1958 and finally added the chairmanship in November 1961 when Sir Leonard finally retired.

Through and around all these corporate promotions, 'Young George' was always respected, invariably gentlemanly and courteous, and interested – but not fanatically so – in cars like the Mini and the 1100 which Alec Issigonis brought to market. To Harriman, making profits, keeping the customer happy and projecting the right corporate image always seemed to be more important than cutting-edge technology and everything which Issigonis and acolytes such as Alex Moulton found fascinating.

It was, for instance, significant that Alec Issigonis was not originally interested in Mini-Coopers, or in the Riley Elf/Wolseley Hornet types, whereas Harriman saw all such types as valuable to the car's (and BMC's) image. Above all, he realised that he had to keep his multifarious dealer chain, at home and overseas, happy, and liked to give them all manner of derivatives to promote.

Accordingly, the Mini and all its derivatives, made on two sites (Longbridge and Cowley) prospered and became famous during his spell in the chair, so that no one, especially his shareholders, was seen to complain. Harriman became Sir George in 1965, saw BMC absorb Pressed Steel in the same year, and also took over Jaguar (which included Daimler) in 1966. It was during this period that so many different Minis were launched, flowered and prospered, and Issigonis began to evolve his engines/models/structures master plan and even began to dabble with a replacement Mini, the 9X.

Then came the biggest corporate merger of all, when the BMC/BMH conglomerate got together with Leyland to form the ill-starred British Leyland combine. At first it was agreed that Sir George would continue as chairman of the board, but that Leyland's Sir Donald Stokes would be his CEO. With Leyland more and more prominent in the new business this cosy arrangement did not last for long, and a physically ailing Sir George announced his retirement from business in September 1968.

Thereafter he took no further part in the motor industry, and died in 1973. He was only 65 years old.

announced on 23 November 1951, Len Lord was not yet at the height of his powers, or his ambitions (he was only 55 years old, and could be described as being in rude – often very rude – health), whereas Lord Nuffield, whose personally-owned companies had been building cars for 38 years, was already 74. Nuffield, a family man but without children, had no obvious successor lined up to take over from him, and seemed to be making no serious attempt to find one, whereas Len Lord already seemed to be grooming George Harriman to do his bidding in future years.

The announcement of a merger came, with typical financial obfuscation, on a Friday evening after the London Stock Exchange had closed, and opened with these weasel words:

'For some time past the boards of Morris Motors Ltd, and the Austin Motor Co Ltd have had under consideration the desirability of amalgamating the two companies. In the result they have arrived at the conclusion that unified control would not only lead to more efficient and more economic production, but would also further the export drive . . .'

The name 'British Motor Corporation' was obviously not finalised at that time, for it was not mentioned in a long and complex press release, but the statement went on to list the four directors who would be on the parent board, and who would run the company. They were: Lord Nuffield (chairman); Leonard Lord (deputy chairman and managing director); Reg Hanks (who was currently vice chairman of Morris Motors Ltd); and George Harriman (who was currently deputy managing director of Austin).

Much of the rest of the statement covered financial matters, and it was clear that this major manoeuvre would take time and could not be formalised until early 1952. It was also clear to all Austin-watchers that one of the new products to be intimately affected by the changes would be the brand-new A-Series engine.

At this point I really need to delve back into the recent genealogy of the two companies, for the birth of the A-Series engine was closely involved in what had already happened, and what was likely to happen after the merger was formalised.

Austin and Nuffield (for which, really, read Morris) had been bitter rivals for many years. In 1935, for instance, Austin sold 73,562 cars while Morris sold 96,512, but Morris made no further progress before the war, whereas Austin made no fewer than 89,175 cars in 1937.

Austin, BMC or . . . what's in a name?

In local patois, almost every worker employed at Longbridge over the years has called it 'The Austin . . .', but legally the name of the companies owning and running the operation has changed persistently:

From 1905, Austin was the original owner.

The British Motor Corporation (which controlled Austin and the Nuffield Organisation), as a holding company, took over in 1952.

When BMC took over the Jaguar Group in 1966 the parent company officially became British Motor Holdings (BMH).

The British Leyland Motor Corporation, which merged BMH with the Leyland group, was born in 1968. From this point, Longbridge officially became part of the Austin-Morris division.

British Leyland was nationalised/rescued in 1975, and in 1978 that title was truncated to BL.

The Austin-Morris Division of BL was then renamed Austin-Rover in 1983.

Austin-Rover was then renamed Rover Group in 1986.

British Aerospace took over in 1988, buying the rump of British Leyland (which included the Rover Group and Land Rover) from the British government.

British Aerospace then sold the entire Rover/Land Rover Group to BMW in 1994.

BMW tired of Rover's continuing financial troubles in 2000, and sold the company to the Phoenix consortium, who reconstituted and renamed Rover to become MG-Rover. At the same time Land Rover, which had also been owned by BMW, was sold off to Ford.

After five years of dodgy financial dealings, property sales and other panic measures, MG-Rover called in the Receiver in 2005.

George Harriman (later Sir George) was Len Lord's closest associate for many years, and was his deputy during the establishment and development of BMC. After becoming BMC's chairman in 1961 he held the post until he retired at the end of 1968. (*BMIHT*)

Immediately after the war both companies restarted civilian car production as briskly as possible, Austin, as an example, building 132,573 cars in 1950/1, along with 29,522 commercial vehicles, while at the same time Nuffield was already making 99,586 private cars, and light commercial vehicles at Cowley, 11,068 cars at the MG factory at Abingdon, and 16,110 vans and trucks at Adderley Park, Birmingham, a grand total of 126,764 vehicles. Austin, in other words, was already the most productive of the two interested parties, and likely to be dominant in the future.

In calendar year 1951, incidentally, the British motor industry produced 475,919 cars, which meant that Austin and Nuffield between them currently held no less than 51% of the market. Although by British standards this was a dominant situation, Len Lord was looking further afield, into Europe, at the way that VW, Fiat and Renault sales were progressing, and was convinced that further progress would be needed.

In those first five post-war years both companies had rejuvenated their ranges of private car models, but with one very important difference: Morris had already produced a new small car (the Issigonis-designed Morris Minor Series MM of 1948), whereas Austin had revealed nothing smaller than the A40 Devon, which was a full size, engine size and price class above that of the Minor. For Austin, though (and to Alec Issigonis' continuing

chagrin) there was the consolation that the Morris Minor was available only with an ancient (mid-1930s) design of side-valve engine, which appeared to have run out of development potential and which certainly had very limited market appeal.

What is also known is that although Len Lord had spent years at Austin in rivalry with Nuffield, his previous employers, he had still not forgiven Lord Nuffield for his treatment in the mid-1930s, and was still determined to get his corporate revenge.

To quote Graham Turner, from a magisterial study of the foundation of British Leyland (*The Leyland Papers*): 'Lord once remarked that they [Austin and Morris] were like two Second Division teams trying to play in the First Division. Altogether, there seemed a good deal of logic in a merger: the only trouble was that Nuffield and Lord had not been on speaking terms for a long time.'

As I have already explained, well before the design of the new A-Series engine – and the Austin A30 which it was to power – got started, the two companies tentatively tried to get closer together, even though it was distinctly at arm's length. However, even in October 1948 there had been no mention of a joint approach to marketing, or to a coordinated approach to new model development. The initial accord was considered too loose, and too tentative, for that.

Specifically, there was no mention of any

commonisation of work on new engines. On reflection this seems to be quite extraordinary, as both Austin and Morris were desperately in need of a new, modern, efficient, small engine design – but in 1948/9 Austin had nothing like that on the stocks, while Nuffield was still considering an overhead-valve version of the ancient Morris Minor engine, which had featured in the Wolseley Eight as early as 1939.

This accord was dissolved only nine months after it had been set up, with virtually nothing ever achieved. Little was said or written down about the end of the affair, which came in July 1949, and it left Len Lord's master plan, however patiently devised, no further ahead than before. Lord subsequently bided his time, then tried again in October 1950, when he approached Lord Nuffield again, ostensibly to wish him a happy 73rd birthday. This rapidly developed into a more businesslike discussion about a potential merger.

And still there were problems. Although Austin's board members were in agreement with a proposed deal (and so they should be, for this was shaping up to be no more and no less than a takeover by Austin of the Nuffield Organisation), Lord Nuffield's subservient colleagues (led by Reg Hanks, his long-serving vice chairman) were not. They resisted the idea of a merger quite vehemently, the result being that the deal (which

was still being pursued behind closed doors) was once again abandoned.

Lord's reaction can be imagined. Maybe the word 'treachery' was not mentioned, but he certainly seems to have been quite incandescent about yet another rebuff, and determined to get his own way at once. Apparently he called Carl Kingerlee (Lord Nuffield's personal secretary) in a state of high dudgeon, telling him that he was disappointed (knowing Lord's reputation, I suspect the words used were not as diplomatic as that). Austin, he made it clear, would now complete its plans to produce a direct competitor to the Morris Minor – the Austin A30, which would be powered by the new A-Series engine, and that this, effectively, was war.

Nuffield was stubborn ('petty-minded' is how some colleagues later described him), and his board colleagues backed him (they had careers to protect, after all), so it was a further year before Lord had simmered down a little, made yet another personal approach to Lord Nuffield, and finally got his backing for a merger. This time the proposals were pushed through, for on this occasion Lord Nuffield (who was still the Nuffield Organisation's major and controlling shareholder) told his fellow directors that the time for discussion was past – and the proposed merger went public within days.

Because of all the legal hurdles which had to be

When Morris introduced the Issigonis-designed Minor of 1948 it was fitted with this old-style 918cc side-valve engine. Soon after the BMC merger was finalised, Len Lord instructed that the A-Series was to take its place. (*BMIHT*)

The original 918cc side-valve engine fitted easily into the Morris Minor's engine bay from 1948 to 1952 – but the A-Series was even more compact, and would soon take its place. (*BMIHT*)

jumped, it took time to finalise the merger proposal – individual boards of directors had to be consulted, and shareholders informed, for instance – and the British Motor Corporation did not come into existence until 25 February 1952, and did not officially absorb Austin and Morris until 31 March.

To bring this story neatly, and briefly, to an end, when the new British Motor Corporation came into existence Len Lord became its managing director and (in American parlance) its 'chief executive officer', with what he saw as complete power. Lord had been at the centre of power for years at Longbridge, and he firmly intended that BMC's centre of gravity should be in the same location.

Unhappily for him, Lord Nuffield as chairman – titular and non-executive though he might be – continued to interfere in his habitual and well-practised way. Lord, whose fuse was notoriously short, and whose temper was volcanic, was furious. It was only after he threatened to walk away from Cowley (and Lord Nuffield) for the second time in less than 20 years that Nuffield saw his time was up. At BMC's first annual general meeting, held before the end of 1952, he announced his retirement, became president of the corporation (though with no executive power at all), and was never again involved in management: his motor industry career had lasted for 40 very fruitful years.

New horizons for the A-Series

In the meantime, as we saw in the previous chapter, countless millions had been spent on re-equipping North Works at Longbridge to put the little A-Series engine into production, the A30 'Seven' had met its public at the Earls Court Motor Show, and (because it was still not ready to go on sale), order books and waiting lists built up rapidly. Almost immediately, by the way, the engine took on its title of 'A-Series', as Bill Appleby confirmed when he read his paper to the IMechE more than a decade later.

When BMC officially began operations in the spring of 1952 Len Lord set about a dynamic programme of rationalisation, of which the new A-Series engine was a major beneficiary. After a whirlwind study of the new corporation's future, he and his colleagues decided that there was a pressing need to cut down the number of different engines – 'building blocks', if you will – being produced or planned for launch in BMC private cars.

In retrospect, it is quite astonishing to realise that in the spring of 1952 no fewer than 11 different types were being produced or were immediately available for a corporation which was building no more than 300,000 units a year – not merely of different sizes, but of different types. By any sane industrial and financial analysis, the annual average take-up of 27,000 units per engine type made little sense.

For interest, this is the line-up of engines – Austin *and* Nuffield – which were in existence at that time:

Make	Engine	Rated power/ rpm (typical)	Originally launched	Comment
Austin	803cc	30/4,800	1951	The new A-Series
Nuffield	918cc	27/4,400	1934	Morris Minor
Nuffield	918cc	33/4,400	1946	Wolseley 8*
Austin	1,200cc	42/4,300	1947	A40
Nuffield	1,250cc	54/5,200	1939	MG TD
Nuffield	1,476cc	41/4,200	1948	Morris Oxford
Nuffield	1,476cc	51,4,400	1948	Wolseley 4/50
Austin	2,199cc	68/3,800	1944	Austin A70
Nuffield	2,215cc	70/4,800	1948	Morris Six
Nuffield	2,215cc	72/4,600	1948	Wolseley 6/80
Austin	2,660cc	88/4,000	1948	Austin A90**
Austin	3993cc	125/3,700	1939	Sheerline/Princess

* This engine was in abeyance but ready to manufacture, as described below.

** This engine was an enlarged version of the 2,199cc unit.

It is also worth noting that the Nuffield engines which BMC had inherited were an eclectic, not to say illogical, collection, for there were side-valve, overhead-valve and overhead-camshaft units among them, some with only a single, restricted-volume application.

Lord's master plan, which was no less sweeping than the one with which he had signalled his arrival at Austin in 1938, was that there should be a major investment programme which would result in just four engines being on the stocks for any current and new BMC model: a small engine (A-Series), a medium-sized engine (B-Series, to evolve from the existing A40 power unit), a C-Series (a brand-new six-cylinder engine) and a D-Series (the existing 3,993cc power unit). Similar rationalisation was also proposed for gearboxes and axles, but the commonisation of Austin and Nuffield body styles would have to wait for a time.

Killing off Morris' new rival to the A-Series

This meant that one decision which affected the future of the A-Series, and of the Morris Minor, had to be made urgently.

Not many people realise that before the A-Series engine was standardised at the end of 1952, Nuffield already had its own small-capacity overhead-valve engine, which might just have done a great job instead (though not necessarily for a lengthy period). The story of this project had really begun in 1938/9, when Nuffield was preparing a new Wolseley Eight model as an upmarket version of the Morris Eight Series E.

Mechanically, for Wolseley the major change was that whereas the Series E had an archaic-type side-valve engine of 918cc (the USHM), the Wolseley Eight was to have an overhead-valve evolution of it, which was internally coded UPHW (the 'W' indicating Wolseley usage). Like the A-Series, though of course designed and developed by a different company, it was a simply-engineered, cast-iron unit with a small bore and long stroke (57mm x 90mm), this being usual for the days when British taxation legislation affected the general layout of power units.

The onset of war meant that the Wolseley Eight was not revealed in 1939 as originally planned, but eventually went on sale in 1946. In the next two years just 5,344 such cars were produced. Built at Wolseley's Ward End factory in Birmingham, with engines supplied from the Morris Engines Branch at Courthouse Green, Coventry, the ohv 918cc power unit of the Wolseley Eight used a single SU carburettor and produced 33bhp at 4,400rpm. As it had been designed by the same Nuffield team which also produced the larger and very versatile XPAG engines fitted to the MG TB–TF sports car range it was thought to have a great deal of potential.

In the meantime, at Cowley, Alec Issigonis had conceived his original masterpiece, the Morris Minor (or Mosquito, as it was known in the early days). He originally wanted it to have a new flat-4 engine, which was built in prototype form but was never committed to production, so that in the end he had to settle for the old (Morris Eight) side-valve 918cc unit instead.

By the end of 1950, however, and while Nuffield was still an independent concern, it had been decided to re-engine the Morris Minor with a developed version of the Wolseley Eight power unit. Morris Minor historians confirm that the engine transplant was easily carried out.

Before the BMC merger took place, Morris planned to fit this overhead-valve 918cc engine to the Morris Minor in 1952–53. It had originally been fitted to the post-war Wolseley Eight model, and was built at Courthouse Green in Coventry. The arrival of the A-Series immediately killed it off. (*BMIHT*)

Alec Issigonis was already noted for having designed the original late-1940s Morris Minor, before the A-Series was applied to the 1952/53 derivative of that car. Later, of course, he would take up the A-Series engine for use in his revolutionary Mini.

Alec Issigonis

Although Alec Issigonis had nothing to do with the design and continuing development of the A-Series, the front-wheel-drive BMC cars that he inspired could not possibly have prospered without his input. Although Sir Leonard Lord told Issigonis that he *had* to use a derivative of the A-Series in his Minis, and in the 1100/1300 range which followed, it was Issigonis' decision to turn them sideways in the engine bay which made all the difference. That, and the notion of putting the transmission in the engine sump and sharing the lubricant, were acts of faith – and of genius.

Born in Turkey in 1906, Issigonis moved, with his family, to London in 1923. After spending time with Humber Ltd (a subsidiary of the Rootes Group) in the 1930s, he joined the Nuffield Organisation in 1936, going on to make his name by designing the new-generation Morris Minor, which appeared in 1948. Later, finding himself in a technical and managerial backwater at Cowley, he moved to Alvis to design a new big car, but this project was cancelled and he was attracted to return to BMC at Longbridge, to open up a new long-term research department.

When his department designed ADO15 – the car which later became legendary as the Mini – he was obliged to use the A-Series engine, which would power nearly 5.5million such cars in the next four decades. He also inspired the birth of the ADO16, which is now more familiarly known as the 1100/1300 range.

After becoming BMC's technical director in 1961, he made sure that other new models also had front-wheel drive, and also used A-Series engine types, though if he had got his own way in the 1970s he would have seen that power unit replaced by a new-generation 9X engine.

After British Leyland was formed in 1968 Issigonis was rather brutally moved sideways to a pure research role. Then, having been knighted in 1969, he officially 'retired' from BMC in 1971, though he remained an arms-length consultant for some years thereafter.

He died in 1988.

The first such prototype car was built in June 1951, and a total of eight machines were put on the road before the BMC merger of November 1951 was even announced. Morris Engines, apparently, was immediately capable of providing 500 engines a week, but new tooling had already been ordered to make it possible for that to be doubled to more than 1,000 engines a week.

According to Issigonis' faithful collaborator Jack Daniels, who had a great deal of experience with every possible derivative of these machines, 'It was the best Morris Minor, in my view. I drove it for testing, and it was a gorgeous car. The Austin engine was a bit lighter, but it wasn't a good engine: and there we were, sitting with a 918cc overhead-valve engine.'

Alec Issigonis, however, recalled that 'the A-Series was already in full production, so Harriman very rightly said, look, there's no point in tooling-up for your engine, use the A-Series. So we did. And it gave the car a new lease of life.'

That, then, was the end for the Morris/Nuffield overhead-valve 918cc engine, which never went back into production and was never seen again. Nowadays only photographs remain.

An A-Series for everyone

As already noted in the previous chapter, the A-Series was only just crawling into series production when BMC was founded, with only about 4,000 of the new Austin A30 saloons being built before the end of 1952. Even then the logistics were quite simple, in that there was initially only a single specification – a Zenith-carburetted 803cc unit developing 30bhp – which was manufactured at Longbridge's North Works, and transported about half a mile (partly by conveyor, through the newly-built tunnels) to the CAB1 building where A30 assembly took place.

If the first of many Nuffield-versus-Austin disputes had not then taken place, a decision to fit the A-Series to the Morris Minor instead of the old side-valve Nuffield engine could have been implemented even faster than it actually was. The problem – not a technical problem, but one of the 'we have always done it this way' variety – was that

Nuffield's engineering team, led by technical director Vic Oak, with Charles Griffin in charge of all development (Alec Issigonis and Jack Daniels were concentrating on the Morris Minor), were completely wedded to the use of SU carburettors on their engines. They insisted that if the A-Series was to be fitted to the Morris Minor then it should feature an SU carburettor.

Because SU was a company owned by the Nuffield Organisation this was reasonable, but it infuriated the Austin design team, especially as a whole series of technical tests would be needed to clear it for use. Space for the installation was never going to be a problem, as the Minor was being produced with a very roomy engine bay, though the use of a large air cleaner above the SU carburettor quite dwarfed the carburettor itself. Even so, the very first of the A-Series-equipped Minors, to be known as Series II (SII) was built in July 1952, and by the end of the year the old Nuffield-engined (MM) type had come to the end of its career.

The proposed change was not popular with long-established Cowley staff, particularly the engineers who had developed a bond with 'their' Morris Minor, but

By the standards of the day the original late-1940s Morris Minor was a smart car, but badly let down by its old-type side-valve engine. The change would come in 1952, when the first A-Series derivative was put on sale.

opinions were split. One Cowley tester, Joe Gomm, is quoted as saying 'That 803cc engine was the biggest load of rubbish we ever had. What really upset us was that we had the Wolseley Eight overhead-valve engine scheduled for the Minor, and weren't far off putting that into production. That was a beautiful engine.' On the other hand, a colleague, Cyril Hodgkins, had this to say:

'The 918cc Morris engine was good in its day but . . . the Austin engine was a big improvement. Even as a Morris man, I give unqualified praise to the Austin engine. Not many Morris men would say that.'

Technically, Longbridge and Cowley moved fast to adapt the A-Series to the Morris Minor, and, as Bill Appleby pointed out in his seminal paper: 'The opinion of the

SU – the carburettor company

Way back in 1904, two brothers of the Skinner family – Carl and George (who were members of the Lilley and Skinner shoemaking hierarchy) – built their first prototype carburettor, and in 1910 founded a company called 'Skinners Union' to build them in quantity. It was logical, therefore, that the products of Skinners Union should be titled 'SU'.

Originally based in Kentish Town, North London, their carburettors (which were of the constant vacuum type) took time to become established in the British motor industry, and first appeared on the 'bullnose' Morris in 1922, but for a time Morris also employed Smith carburettors as an alternative fitment. SUs were not fitted to Austin cars at this time, nor would they feature until the 1950s.

Although they functioned well, early SU carburettors were expensive to manufacture and struggled to gain a market share, and at one time it looked as if the business might collapse. However, during the 1920s William Morris set out on a strategy of buying up his most important suppliers and incorporating them into the Morris Motors company. His gaze settled on SU in 1926, when Carl Skinner visited him and, confessing that his company was losing money, offered it for sale. After a short but brisk period of activity, during which Morris tested alternative carburettors, he bought SU for £100,000, and eventually installed Skinner on the Morris board of directors.

Within months the SU manufacturing operation was moved from London to Adderley Park, Birmingham (next to the Morris Commercial factory), and the company name changed to Morris Industries Ltd. Thereafter SU's fortunes changed,

all subsequent Morris cars were equipped with SU carburettors and, amazingly, supplies to rival concerns also increased.

However, Morris' holding company, the Nuffield Organisation, was always cautious about doing business with its rivals, and charged them handsomely for the privilege of using SU carburettors – indeed, much more than was charged in inter-company costs to the Morris, Wolseley and MG car-making concerns.

This no doubt explains why SU carburettors rarely figured on 1930s or 1940s Austins, for the designers at Longbridge knew well that although they might admire the SU, the political and financial realities meant that they could not economically be specified on their new cars. Although there is evidence that the SU might otherwise have found an immediate home on the new A-Series engine, the fact is that the Austin A30's 803cc engine was launched with the simpler and cheaper downdraught Zenith.

Even so, this was one area where the benefit of the merger of Austin with Nuffield in 1951–52 bore immediate fruit. When the Morris Minor became Series II during the winter of 1952–53, the newly-installed A-Series engine was rated at 30bhp (instead of the 27bhp of the original side-valve 918cc-engined Series MM) and was equipped with an SU carburettor.

Rationalisation within BMC, however, was neither rapid nor wide-ranging, for the Austin A30 *and* A35 which followed were still fitted with Zenith carburettors throughout the 1950s. Thereafter, of course, the Mini had an SU carburettor, as did the larger cars in the Austin range, and it was the 'Skinners Union' device that became the BMC carburettor of choice throughout the 1960s and 1970s.

road test drivers was that the use of the constant-vacuum [SU] as opposed to the fixed-jet [Zenith] carburettor smoothed out many of the induction troubles.'

Even so, there was a problem in slotting the A-Series engine into the Minor, for the Morris weighed about 250lb more than the A30. Accordingly, at the same time as the A-Series appeared in the Minor to make it the SII, the rear axle ratio was dropped from 4.55:1 to 5.286:1. Although the SII could just about keep up with the original MM on the road, it rapidly gained the reputation of a buzz-box, as it could reach only 62mph when absolutely flat out, and struggled to reach even 45mph in third gear.

Deliveries for export began in the autumn of 1952, but as far as British customers were concerned the SII broke cover in the winter of 1952/3, at a time when waiting lists for all new cars persisted, and customers would happily accept whatever they were offered. For the next four years BMC's 'tiny twins' – the A30 and Morris Minor SII – sold just as rapidly as they could be built, and the shareholders did not complain.

Not only did production of all BMC cars surge ahead in this period, but profits also boomed – from £1,766,450 in 1953 to £3,055,000 in 1956 – even though Longbridge suffered from at least one long and very damaging strike, and dipped into the corporate pocket to take control of Fisher & Ludlow, the bodyshell manufacturers whose headquarters were in the Second World War 'Spitfire factory' at Castle Bromwich.

Production of the A-Series engine, still concentrated entirely in North Works at Longbridge, rose inexorably, and by mid-1956, when the time came to refresh the two models which used it, more than 500,000 units had already been manufactured – as an example, there were 269,838 Minor SIIs. By then, however, it was clear that BMC would have to raise its sights, as there was now increasingly credible market competition from Ford (with the new-style but still side-valve-engined Anglia and Prefect 100E models) and particularly from Standard, whose modern Eight/Ten range not only matched their prices but included a new overhead-valve engine which was being built in 803cc *and* 948cc form.

It was not that the development and improvement of the A-Series had been ignored for five years, but rather that the introduction of new derivatives had never seemed to be urgent. John Barnett showed me a highly secret old development paper, dating from 1953, which listed a number of different possible engine sizes between 800cc

and 1,000cc which were all suggested (and occasionally even tried out), but never approved. Even at that time it was thought possible eventually to expand the engine to 998cc, but this was not done – except on paper.

In addition 'There was an aluminium A30 prototype at one time, and one idea was that it might have a twin-cylinder version of the A-Series engine. However, I don't think that ever got into a car, for its performance on the test bed was disappointing. I admit we only tested with SU carburettors, but it really lacked torque. It only produced 18bhp, in a project coded ADO11 . . .

'We got heavily involved with Joe Ehrlich, who wasn't only known for working on motorcycles, but on two-stroke engines. We were doing two-stroke engines for him . . . on new dynamometers which were capable of running up to 10,000rpm. At the time, believe me, the Austin Motor Co had two entries in the Isle of Man TT in the 125cc, or maybe it was the 250cc, class.'

By the mid-1950s the A-Series' shortcomings had already become clear: 'I was involved in the first German autobahn test of various BMC cars. The A30s didn't come out of that very well, particularly in terms of bearing condition. So there was an upgrade when we went to full-flow oil filters (originally they were bypass filters), and a change of crankshaft bearing material to lead-indium – and a repeat test was done, which was satisfactory. Oh, and the axle ratio was changed, because they were under-geared.'

These tests were not confined to A-Series cars, but also included B-Series cars – the Austin A40 Cambridge and Morris Oxford SII in particular. Based in Stuttgart, they involved a build-up of 25,000 miles per car in only a few weeks. Unheard-of by Austin or Morris test departments before this time, these rapidly became a sign-off test for all new models.

The first enlargement – to 948cc

The first major redesign followed in the autumn of 1956, when the Austin A30 became the A35, and the Morris Minor SII became the Minor 1000. There were small but significant style changes to each car, and in both cases the gearbox was given more carefully chosen intermediate ratios, and provided with a neat and very sporty remote-control floor change to replace the original willowy wand; but the most important update was that the engine was enlarged to 948cc, becoming more powerful and more torquey in the process.

After much deliberation, BMC decided to enlarge the engine by increasing the cylinder bore, but left the stroke alone, and a change from 58mm to 62.99mm resulted in a capacity of 948cc instead of 803cc. Although this sounds simple enough to achieve, it could only be done by making changes to the cylinder block casting itself, for although the cylinder bore centres were left unchanged (to simplify manufacturing operations), the casting had to be re-cored, and the cylinder barrels (1–2 and 3–4) had to be siamesed in pairs.

As feared, early tests showed a tendency for bore distortion to take place, but this problem was eventually traced to the use of an unsatisfactory type of cylinder head gasket. Once this was changed the problem disappeared, and development went ahead in a routine manner. At the same time the block and crankshaft were both beefed up, while the diameter of the big end bearings (now to be lead-indium, as already noted) was increased from $1^{7}/_{16}$in to $1^{5}/_{8}$in.

Amazingly (and this, don't forget, was five years after the BMC merger had taken place), although both cars had engines with an 8.3:1 compression ratio the A35 and Minor 1000 engines still had different carburetion. The result was that the Zenith-equipped A35 produced 34bhp and the SU-equipped Minor 1000 produced 37bhp. However, helped along by the use of higher ('longer') back axle ratios on both cars the performance was considerably enhanced.

The author particularly recalls buying a year-old A35 in 1958, and finding it suitable for use in club rallies because it now had a top speed of 70mph, and would thrum up to 56mph in third. When new my two-door would have cost £554, and a heater would have cost an extra £20 – but unhappily my car did not have such a desirable extra. With 3bhp more the contemporary Minor 1000 could reach 73mph, but could accelerate no faster, and drank more petrol.

No matter. This was the boost that the marketplace had been waiting for, and battle with Ford and Standard was once again in progress. BMC now produced A35 saloons, Countryman types, vans and – for a short time – pickups (with bodyshells coming from three sources: West Works, Fisher and Ludlow and, for a time, Briggs of Doncaster), while Minor 1000s were built as saloons, convertibles, Travellers, vans and pickups, their bodies coming from Nuffield Metal Products in Birmingham and Morris Bodies in Coventry.

Egged on by their voracious dealer chain in the UK and overseas, BMC kept on turning out more, and more, and yet more of the cars which were powered by the A-Series. The demand was certainly there, for in the UK there seemed to have been no attempt to bring Austin and Nuffield dealerships together. Every High Street in every British market town seemed to have Austin and Morris dealerships, many of them within sight of one another, so competition for sales was intense.

Taking 1957/8 as an example, that was a year in which 81,930 A35s were built, along with 130,969 Minor 1000s. In the meantime, two very important new models, the Austin-Healey Sprite and the Austin A40 Farina, were also about to join in. No wonder the production facilities in North Works were beginning to creak under the strain.

Sprite and Midget – the A-Series proves its worth

Amazingly, it was not until 1958 that BMC slotted the A-Series engine into a sports car of their own, even though studies had been made in the early 1950s and the engine had already found a home in a variety of independent specialist limited-production vehicles. In fairness to BMC, though, the original 803cc engine had been such a milk-and-water affair that there never seemed to be any point in trying it out in a two-seater.

Soon, though, the arrival of the more robust, more tuneable 948cc engine made a big difference. Although the increase in power of standard engines was modest – 30bhp at 4,800rpm (A30) compared with 34bhp at 4,750rpm (A35) – the potential for improvement now seemed to be there. It was not long before tiny racing cars and rally cars began to prove this point.

Except for MG's increasingly successful activities (for the Nuffield Organisation), early in the 1950s neither Austin nor Nuffield needed to know much about the sports car business. Neither company had tried to sell sports cars with their own badging, so Austin encouraged the growth of Austin-Healey while Nuffield persevered with MG. As already related in Chapter 4, Austin had dabbled with the development of an A30 convertible, while chief stylist Dick Burzi had schemed up a smart little 'sports car', but these never came to fruition.

The BMC/Burzi project of 1953 featured an unmodified (30bhp!) A-Series engine, had a tubular chassis frame (in other words it was not based on the A30's own platform)

Donald Healey

Born in Cornwall in 1898, Donald Healey had already made several reputations while making and losing substantial sums of money, before he joined forces with Len Lord at BMC to establish the Austin-Healey brand in 1952. When the time came to turn the A-Series into a sporty engine, Donald Healey's team provided the engineering know-how which led to the birth of the Austin-Healey Sprite in 1958, and kept that engine to the forefront of racing, rallying and record-breaking for the next two decades.

After flying aircraft in the First World War he opened a garage business in Perranporth, Cornwall, started out in trials and rallies, then won the 1931 Monte Carlo Rally in an Invicta. Attracted to industry in the 1930s, he became Triumph's technical director in 1934, worked with the Rootes Group during the Second World War, then set up the Healey Motor Co in 1945.

Healey sold hundreds of Riley and Nash-engined sports cars, then built an attractive Austin-engined prototype in 1952. BMC's Len Lord bought it, turned it into the Austin-Healey 100 sports car, and a new brand was born. Donald Healey, his son Geoff and a compact workforce then became successful sporting (and racing) consultants to BMC, and were asked to design the original Austin-Healey Sprite. With help from MG, and from various engine-tuning consultants, they produced many A-Series-engined record cars, racing cars and rally cars, while the Sprite inspired the birth of the MG Midget sports car.

When Lord Stokes of British Leyland cut off a raft of consultancy and royalty-paying agreements in 1970, including that with the Healey company, Donald Healey drew back, joined forces with Kjell Qvale (of San Francisco), took over Jensen, and launched the Jensen-Healey. That business, unhappily, folded in 1976, after which Donald retired reluctantly to his native and much-loved Cornwall, where he died in 1988.

with cutaway body sides, and had no need of opening doors. The running gear featured the 803cc engine and the A30 four-speed gearbox, along with the coil spring independent front suspension of that car. Even so (and, once again, to quote Geoff Healey) 'This car was neither sporting, nor much of a tourer . . .'

Then came the birth of Austin-Healey, and the whole approach of BMC to sports car motoring seemed to change. First there was the Austin-Healey 100 of 1953, then the even bigger 100-Six and finally, in 1958, the launch of the sensational little A-Series-engined Sprite.

Donald Healey was already famous before he began making cars under his own name in 1946. Way back in 1931 he had won the Monte Carlo rally in a 4½-litre Invicta, and later he had directed Triumph's design and engineering teams from 1934 to 1939. Starting from scratch in 1946, he then began building a variety of Riley, Alvis and even American Nash-engined sports cars, but it was his idea of producing a cheaper two-seater based around Austin A90 Atlantic running gear that brought him to Len Lord's attention in 1952.

Almost overnight, it seemed, the original Healey 100 project became the Austin-Healey 100, and went into production at Longbridge in mid-1953, after which the Warwick-based Healey Motor Co Ltd became a favourite of Len Lord, and soon equalled MG as a BMC provider of fast cars, race and record car projects, and sports car design work. Less than four years after Lord and Healey had forged their first agreement, the dapper little Cornishman was invited to think big – and fast. Writing in his gloriously detailed book *More Healeys*, Geoff Healey (Donald's son, who carried out much of the engineering work on all Healeys and Austin-Healeys), perfectly sums up what happened next:

'The Sprite was first conceived in the winter of 1956, the result of a meeting between DMH [these were Donald's initials, by which he was always affectionately known] and Leonard Lord. During a discussion on the sports car market, both men agreed that sports cars were becoming expensive, and that the market was contracting as the price went up. In his blunt, down-to-earth manner, Len Lord then commented that what we needed was a small, low-cost sports car to fill the gap left by the disappearance of the Austin Seven Nippy and Ulster models of pre-war fame. What he would really like to see, he said, was a bug. It is impossible to tell whether he was simply thinking aloud, or deliberately giving DMH a broad hint of what we should do, but this conversation certainly set DMH thinking as he drove back from Longbridge.'

Those were the days when neither BMC nor Healey had 'product planning departments'; but what they *did* have was decisive and powerful characters at their head. What Lord had done, in effect, was to set Donald Healey on a path, and Healey was quick to react. Once unleashed, it was the Healey company which did much of the design and engineering work of a car which ran on an 80in wheelbase, while BMC's planners not only arranged for the new sports car to be assembled at the MG factory at Abingdon (this was rapidly being recognised as BMC's dedicated sports car plant), but made sure that the new monocoque hull would be made by John Thompson Motor Pressings (platform) and Pressed Steel (bodyshell, and assembly to the platform).

Healey also tackled the styling, but originally wanted to include lay-flat headlamps with a flip-up mechanism. This arrangement was finally abandoned when costs and complications were realised, in favour of an arrangement that featured fixed headlamps. Not unnaturally the new car was instantly nicknamed the 'frog-eye' (in Britain) or 'bug-eye' (in the USA)!

In less than a year – effectively, throughout 1956 – Healey engineered the new car, which used an elegantly blended combination of Austin A30/A35 and Morris Minor/1000 pieces, the A-Series engine being absolutely central to the project. It was indeed fortunate for all concerned that the lustier 948cc version of the engine had just been finalised for use in the up-gunned family cars, and that the slick, sporty, remote-control gearchange with the more suitable intermediate ratios had also been designed for use in those two cars. It was, in other words, an ideal basis on which to build a new model. Tooling up for series production went ahead at great speed, so following approval by George Harriman in January 1957 (this was, incidentally, in the depths of motor industry gloom during the fuel-rationed Suez Crisis), the production car was launched in May 1958.

BMC's saloon-orientated engineers were happy to see the car take shape like this, and the very first engine installation was worked up by Healey, as BMC had not, so far, produced anything like that for its own use. The first 948cc-engined Sprite featured a twin-SU carburettor installation which Healey development genius Roger Menadue had modified from an MG TF installation, and

This was the original Austin-Healey 'frog-eye' Sprite of 1958, which was powered by a 43bhp version of the 948cc A-Series engine. Much more development would follow.

On the 'frog-eye' Sprite, the A-Series engine was very accessible once one lifted the entire front end of the car – grille, headlamps, front wings and all . . .

Geoff Healey's biggest niggle concerned the placing of the mechanical rev-counter drive, which eventually found a home at the rear end of the dynamo.

Much of the proper development work on this version of the A-Series engine took place at the Morris Engines plant at Courthouse Green, in Coventry, where Eddie Maher soon got heavily involved in extracting more, and yet more, power from sporty versions of the little power

unit: Eddie would later become feted for his work on race and rally engines, squeezing out more power and torque than their original designers can ever have envisaged.

By this time Len Lord had decided that Courthouse Green (which was, for instance, already building all the 2.6-litre six-cylinder C-Series power units) should become a second supplier of A-Series engines, especially to non-Longbridge sources. With major castings coming from an ex-Nuffield supplier in Wellingborough, this second line soon built up momentum, and soon began delivering them by the truckload to Abingdon as sales of Sprites, and later MG Midgets too, increased.

Maher's team soon found ways of increasing the 948cc

engine's output from 34bhp at 4,750rpm (with a single Zenith carburettor) to 42.5bhp at 5,000rpm with twin SUs), which sounds like a modest increment but was, of course, no less than a sturdy 25% improvement – and we now know that there was still a lot more to come. Even so, only a modest amount of more exotic detail had gone into the upgrade, for the compression ratio was still only 8.3:1, which was the same as that employed in the Austin A35/Morris Minor 1000 power units. The camshaft profile, of course, was different, special valve springs were

. . . which explains why many owners invested in aftermarket bonnets that looked better and gave even better A-Series engine access. This was a popular conversion of the period.

fitted, exhaust valves were Stellited, and twin H1 SU carburettors were standardised.

The new sports car got off to a great start, with nearly 50,000 built in three years, which was really no surprise, as its sporty performance (as road-tested, the original car had an 80mph top speed) was linked to eager and responsive handling, all at a very attractive price. For interest, these were the original UK retail prices of the three 948cc A-Series-engined cars:

Austin Healey Sprite	*£679*
Austin A35 saloon (two-door)	*£570*
Morris Minor 1000 saloon (two-door)	*£625*

– there being no other similar British sports car which could compete.

This was how BMC advertised the Austin-Healey Sprite, complete with its A-Series engine, when it was launched in 1958.

By the time Eddie Maher's team at Courthouse Green had finished developing the Austin-Healey Sprite engine, they had produced a neat-looking and potentially very powerful twin-SU version of the 948cc A-Series unit.

Farina style for BMC

Before I turn my attention to the front-wheel-drive revolution which swept through BMC in the 1960s, I must record the arrival of the first Farina-styled Austin, which was the A40 of 1958. By the 1950s George Harriman, more readily than Len Lord, had concluded that BMC was in danger of falling behind in the styling stakes, for Austin's Dick Burzi, though well-liked and capable, was no artistic genius.

Soon Lord, encouraged, of all things, by a visit to Longbridge by HRH the Duke of Edinburgh, approached Pininfarina of Turin, contracting them to produce shapes for the next generation of BMC family cars. The result was a flood of new shapes – A40 in 1958, B-Series 'Farinas' in 1959, and Austin A99/Wolseley 6/99, also in 1959. The same cars were retouched throughout the 1960s, and it was only the unique Mini (see Chapter 5) which was shaped completely in the UK.

The first commission became the A40, a square-back/hatchback car which was effectively a replacement for the A35, even though it was significantly larger and had its own unique platform. Styled in 1956 (just as the 948cc A-Series engine was coming on-stream), finalised in 1957/8 and launched in the autumn of 1958, it was a refreshingly attractive little four-seater. The first series had a fixed rear window and a drop-down boot lid, but in due course a two-piece (upper and lower) back, estate-car style also came along.

Much of the 'chassis' of this new machine came from the A35, including the 948cc A-Series engine, while for the moment Austin stuck stubbornly to its use of the downdraught Zenith carburettor. A change to SU carburetion would not take place until 1961. Even so, the new car was well received, the semi-hatchback arrangement was popular, and sales were buoyant right from the start. With full production established in 1959/60, 76,562 A40 Farinas were built at Longbridge during the year, compared with just 27,622 A35s and 105,985 Morris Minor 1000s.

So, was A-Series demand already at its peak? Not by any means, for in August 1959 the first of Alec Issigonis' legendary Minis had hit the headlines.

The A-Series was so compact that it could be fitted almost anywhere. This was the snug but nonetheless easy installation in the early 1960s Sprite/Midget engine bay.

By the early 1960s Innocenti of Italy had begun to build A-Series-engined BMC cars under licence, after which they evolved this very smart own-brand derivative of the Austin-Healey Sprite. Unhappily this car was never officially marketed in the UK.

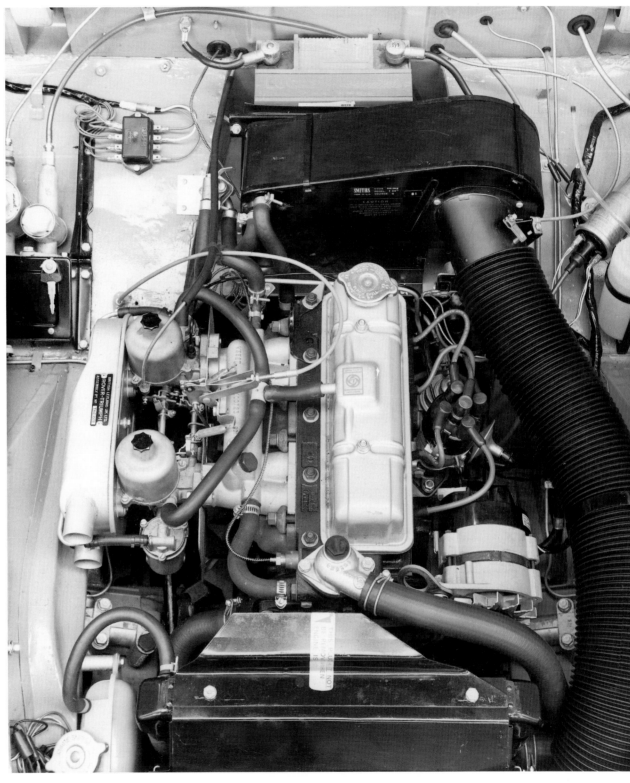

When US exhaust emission regulations became so stringent in the early 1970s, the A-Series engine was finally unable to meet them. This meant that the Triumph Spitfire 1.5-litre engine (seen here in the Midget) had to do the job instead.

From 1964 the Sprite/Midget sports cars had wind-up door windows and more sophisticated rear suspension to go with their 59bhp 1.1-litre A-Series engines. It was an extremely successful combination.

The Sprite Mk IV/Midget Mk III of the late 1960s was one of the most popular of all A-Series-engined sports cars, particularly as it had a sturdy 65bhp/1,275cc version of the power unit – effectively a detuned derivative of the S-Type engine.

The Sprite/Midget family was always very popular and very successful in the 1950s, 1960s and 1970s. This was the scene at Abingdon in December 1959, when the placard notes that all previous output records had been broken.

By the end of the 1950s the A-Series engine was probably the most important 'building block' in the entire BMC range. This is the 'chassis' that made up the running gear of the Austin A40 Farina, as introduced in 1958. (*Barney Sharratt*)

The A40 of 1958 was the first new Austin model to
be styled by Pininfarina. In its first full production
year – 1959–60 – no fewer than 76,562 of
these smart little A-Series-powered cars were
manufactured at Longbridge. (*BMIHT*)

the latest expression of the Austin line

This artist's rendering does justice to the smart lines of the Farina-styled Austin A40, which used a 948cc A-Series engine when launched in 1958.

During the 1960s MG dabbled with producing this car – coded EX234 – as a possible replacement for the Midget, or even for the MGB. There would have been a range of engines, but the A-Series was always to be the 'entry-level' choice.

CHAPTER 5

Mini and 1100

In August 1959 the A-Series took on a completely new lease of life, for it was central to the new Mini project, to the 1100/1300 which followed, and to cars like the Allegro, Maestro and Montego which all ensued in the next generation. From the day that the Mini was put on sale, A-Series production was pushed up just as hard as possible, so that major changes and expansion had to take place at Longbridge and, of course, at Courthouse Green in Coventry.

It all started with the Suez war of 1956, the petrol shortage that followed, and the boom in 'bubble car' sales which upset the marketplace. BMC's chairman, Sir Leonard Lord, knew he must move swiftly. BMC had most to lose if its A35/Minor 1000 models stopped selling, and needed smart new economy cars.

Cometh the hour, cometh the man. Alec Issigonis, who had designed the Morris Minor in the mid-1940s and then left Morris to work at Alvis, had recently returned to Longbridge. His small special projects team was working with a very broad, unfocused brief on long-term ideas.

In March 1957 Len Lord, so the legend says, swept into the Issigonis conclave, cornered the brilliant engineer, and succinctly told him to 'Drop everything, start again, and build me something tiny to beat the bloody bubble cars. We must drive them off the streets by designing a proper miniature car.'

Within weeks of Len Lord asking Alec Issigonis to produce a new tiny BMC car, with an A-Series engine, this mock-up had been produced. Except that the front grille style was simplified, it went ahead virtually unchanged.

This cutaway drawing of the original Mini of 1959 shows just how small Alec Issigonis' team had managed to make the engine bay, complete with its transversely-positioned 848cc A-Series engine. More than five million Minis would be produced in the next 41 years.

It was quite startling to discovery that so little space in the original Mini was taken up by the A-Series engine, but here is photographic proof.

When the miraculously packaged Mini was designed, its transmission was arranged to live 'in the sump' of the much-modified A-Series engine. It was all a very tight squeeze.

Alec Issigonis, the compulsive sketcher, is credited with refining the concept of a transversely-mounted four-cylinder-engined car.

Thus the XC9003 project was born, which soon got a mainstream project code – ADO15. Was this Mission Impossible? Issigonis had not only to build the smallest possible car, but provide space for four adult passengers too. He also knew that this car would have to replace the A35 and, as Lord had already told him, 'You can use any sort of engine you like, just so long as we have it on our present production lines.' Which, in reality, meant that it would have to be a derivative of the A-Series. Lord did not consult his production experts in advance – if increased A-Series production was needed, so be it; they would just have to cope.

For ADO15, Issigonis chose front-wheel drive. But if he needed a length of more than eight feet to package the cabin and the luggage boot, how small could he then make the engine bay? Way back in 1952, when a front-wheel-drive Morris Minor-based car was built, it used a transversely mounted engine. That, no question, was the inspiration for a new car, but this one would also have its transmission under (not alongside) that engine.

Changes, though, were needed along the way. The first prototype cars used 948cc A-Series engines, which gave too much performance for what Len Lord and Issigonis required (92mph was talked of – real Mini-Cooper performance before that version had even been invented, though on only 37bhp I find that claim far-fetched); and

they were mounted with the SU carburettor and the manifolds facing forward. This gave so many problems (carburettor icing, and difficult access to electrical components such as the distributor, dynamo and starter motor, for instance), that the engine was turned through 180°, with the carburettor/manifolds now pointing backwards, the cooling radiator swapped sides, and an extra idler gear was added to the transmission to make sure that the car still drove forwards (think about it . . .).

At the same time, the engine was reduced in capacity. For a moment (a very brief moment, it seems) there was thought of reverting to the original 803cc, but in the end it was decided to retain the existing 948cc block (complete with siamesed bores in the casting), but with a stroke shortened to 68.26mm ($2^{11}/_{16}$in), which produced 848cc. All engines were to use a single SU carburettor, a new crankshaft was required to shorten the stroke and to accommodate the transmission drop gears, yet remarkably few other changes were needed. Remarkably too, when it was launched the 848cc engine produced 34bhp at 5,500rpm, which was enough to give the new baby car a top speed of 75mph – which was faster than either the Austin A35 or the Morris Minor 1000 of the day.

Reasonably, therefore, in 1957/8 no one at BMC even considered making faster versions (the invention of the Mini-Cooper was three years into the future), nor dressed

This was the finalised A-Series installation in the original Mini of 1959. Not many engines would have slotted so neatly into such a small area.

The A-Series engine fitted neatly, in transverse location, into the subframe of the legendary Mini for many years. This, in fact, is the Hydrolastic-suspended version of 1964–69.

up Rileys and Wolseleys. Vans and estate cars would follow, but that would all take time. For the moment, BMC planned only to make two near-identical saloons – Austin Se7ens (yes, they really did advertise it that way) at Longbridge, and Morris Mini-Minors at Cowley.

Company politics within BMC made it certain that the Mini would originally be assembled on two sites. BMC planned to use two badges and grilles – Austin Se7ens, it was decided, would be assembled at Longbridge, while Morris Mini-Minors would be built at the Nuffield factory at Cowley, near Oxford. Most A-Series engines would still be made at Longbridge, though an increased proportion would be manufactured at the 'Morris Engines' factory at Courthouse Green in Coventry. The complex front-wheel-drive transmission was made both at Longbridge and at Drews Lane, in Birmingham (which was another BMC subsidiary); engines and transmissions, therefore, would be delivered by the truckload – many trucks every day – down the road to Cowley.

By 1960/1, when the Mini was fully established, the A-Series production facilities must have been bursting at the seams, and the machinery was being worked all day, all night, all weekend, and taking minimum 'down time'

for maintenance. Just look at these official production figures for that 12-month period:

Austin Se7en	94,499
Austin A35	34,568
Austin A40	63,830
Morris Mini-Minor	45,329
Morris Minor 1000	63,573
Morris Minor van	21,893
Austin-Healey Sprite	8,480
MG Midget	1,647
Total	*333,819*

Then, of course, there were the engines being supplied to outside customers as varied as the Turner sports car company and the Ministry of Defence. All in all it was a remarkable period, and there was more expansion to come. Even as these figures were being achieved, BMC was preparing to launch its second type of front-wheel-drive car (the 1100 range), which is described below, in which the A-Series would be an essential component.

Alec Issigonis posing with 'Old Number One' – reputedly the oldest surviving Mini, complete with A-Series engine, which was built in 1959.

In 1959 the A-Series-powered Mini, with just 34bhp from 848cc, was as close to minimal motoring as BMC could possibly provide. It was the right car, with the right engine, at the right time . . .

Alec Issigonis and Sir George Harriman pose alongside the newly-launched Mini in the summer of 1959.

During the 1960s Marcos used the underpinnings of the Mini – engine, transmission, suspension and subframes – to develop the glass-fibre-bodied Mini Marcos. Hundreds were sold, even though the build quality was poor.

A-Series engines in Mini form went into all manner of oddities in the 1960s, this being the Mini-Moke. Built at Longbridge from 1964 to 1968, it later found new homes in Australia and Portugal.

UNIPOWER GT UPD

One of the most handsome of all A-Series-engined specials, no question, was the Unipower GT of the mid-1960s, which used a transversely-mounted 'Mini' pack behind the cabin . . .

. . . and it really was as small, and as sleek, as becomes obvious from this shot.

Mini-Cooper and Cooper S

It was at this time, of course, that the A-Series' most glamorous period opened up – and also the period in which so many detail changes were made to the design. In almost every case this was done to try to provide a larger-capacity A-Series without harming its long-term reliability, to make it possible to extract more torque and horsepower – or to achieve all these things at the same time.

Since this was a time when important A-Series changes were either proposed or actually carried out to the cylinder block casting, the head casting, the delineation of the cylinder bores, and the bore *and* the stroke, there was always a danger that it would become messy, expensive and downright undesirable to try to manufacture all the latest engine types which found favour. Fortunately for BMC's profits, however, some semblance of common sense always prevailed – and the fact that the truly special derivatives that were developed could be made at Courthouse Green in Coventry (well away from the epicentre of major A-Series production at Longbridge), was a great advantage.

It all began, really, when the A-Series' worth as a tuneable little competition power unit became clear, and the principal developments in the field of racing, record breaking and rallying are covered in detail in the next two chapters. By this time, not only had BMC's first sports-car applications (Sprite and, from 1961, MG Midget) been launched, but the noted racing car owner/engineer John Cooper had got his teeth into a new single-seater formula – Formula Junior – and was urging BMC to produce a high-performance version of the Mini itself.

As will be clear from the next chapter, the original impetus behind the development of new, high-output versions of the A-Series came from motorsport, and not from BMC's own rather unimaginative marketing staffs.

In fact, as soon as he got his hands on an original Mini, John Cooper started looking for ways to make it quicker, even though Alec Issigonis, on the other hand, did not really approve of high-performance versions. The very first prototype 'Mini-Cooper' was built in the Cooper Car Co Ltd's workshops in Surbiton, Cooper having co-operated with Eddie Maher of Courthouse Green to enlarge the engine and fit it with twin SU

BMC Engines Branch

Do not visit Coventry today and expect to find much evidence of that city's great motoring heritage. Almost all of it has been swept away. The bulldozers and so-called 'developers' who attacked Coventry in the 1970s, 1980s and 1990s got rid of every trace – including the vast Standard-Triumph, Rootes Group, Massey Ferguson, Daimler and Jaguar complexes, along with the old Riley and Morris Engines factories.

To flesh out this archaeological story, the once-famous Morris Engines plant, in Courthouse Green to the north of the city centre, has been obliterated and redeveloped. Way back – way, way back – after the First World War, there was a large engine factory at Gosford Green, near the city centre, owned by Hotchkiss, which supplied engines to Morris Motors. Morris bought the business in 1923 and soon discovered that one of the company's 'assets' was a young Len Lord, who went on

to rationalise production and begin his rise to chairmanship of BMC.

Renamed the Morris Engines Branch, the Gosford Green factory (itself originally a textile plant) was ideal at first, but eventually ran out of space as demand for Morris and Wolseley cars boomed. In 1938 Morris therefore built a new factory at Courthouse Green. Although it was badly damaged in the Blitz of November 1940 it was soon returned to full production, and in post-war years was always a very important unit in the Nuffield, later BMC, operation.

In the 1950s and 1960s much engine development, particularly of high-performance and motorsport power units, took place at Courthouse Green, and many thousands of specialised Mini-Cooper S engines and the short-lived A-Series diesel were also built there. In the 1970s, as British Leyland descended into terminal chaos and all engine assembly was concentrated at Longbridge, Courthouse Green became redundant, was finally closed and the site soon sold off.

When the Mini-Cooper was introduced in 1961, this shot of the new saloon alongside the contemporary Cooper Formula Junior single-seater emphasised how the same type of A-Series engine powered both cars.

carburettors, and even persuaded Lockheed to produce tiny front-wheel disc brakes.

BMC boss George Harriman eventually approved a minimum production run of 1,000 cars – originally planned for a mere 25 cars a week, though some BMC sales staff thought they couldn't possibly sell 1,000!

John Cooper persuaded BMC to develop a 1.0-litre version of the A-Series engine, that being a convenient competition capacity class limit. To do this speedily, yet not spend a fortune on tooling, BMC adopted a long stroke crankshaft dimension (which was already being considered for the 1100 models, though subsequently increased yet again for 1962/3), and matched it to a new and slightly narrower cylinder bore. This was the comparison:

850 Mini   *848cc, 62.9mm bore x 68.3mm stroke*
997 Mini-Cooper   *997cc, 62.43mm bore x 81.3mm stroke*

Along with a better-breathing cylinder head, a 9.0:1 compression ratio, twin SU HS2 carburettors, a three-branch tubular exhaust system, a torsional vibration damper on the end of the crank and a more enterprising camshaft grind, the engine produced an impressive 55bhp at 6,000rpm. Not only that, but these cars were fitted with a sturdy new remote-control gearchange. The engines were all built at Courthouse Green.

Once the public discovered that the first Mini-Coopers could beat 85mph (many could approach 90mph), they queued up to buy, and the 1,000 sales target was soon left far behind. Maybe the disc brakes promised more than they could deliver, and maybe the engine felt frantic when pushed hard, but nobody complained – much. Once the Mini-Cooper started winning in races and rallying, John Cooper's original vision was confirmed.

Although 997cc-engined cars were in production for little more than two years, they sold extremely briskly – 14,000 in 1962 alone. Baulk-ring synchromesh transmissions were standardised from mid-1962, but there were few other changes.

It was John Cooper's desire to have a race-winning Cooper Formula Junior car that led to the Mini-Cooper engine and S engine being developed. This is John himself, with a 1962 1.1-litre Cooper FJ car ahead of a 997cc-engined Mini-Cooper of the period.

998cc: tiny difference, or big difference?

From January 1964, and with very little fuss, Mini-Coopers started being built with a 998cc instead of a 997cc engine, the basic engine having already been put on sale in Mini-based Elf/Hornet models. Peak power was unchanged, there were only minor torque improvements, and there were no badging nuances to flag up the change. Internally, though, there were several important differences, which made this into an even more desirable little car. The Cooper's 997cc engine had always been unique (that engine size was never used in any other BMC production car), whereas the later 998cc engine would become a standard A-Series dimension, to be used in many other models, and it was produced in millions. Several BMC and independent tuning experts label this as the best and most all-round capable of any A-Series engine.

These were the dimensional differences:

997cc	*62.4mm bore x 81.3mm stroke*
998cc	*64.6mm bore x 76.2mm stroke*

Within the same block, the revised engine featured a wider bore and a shorter (the original, from 1951) stroke. It felt smoother when revved hard, and could theoretically breathe that important bit deeper.

Magazine road tests showed that 998cc cars were that important bit faster than 997cc types, which confirms that there was, indeed, more power and torque than before, though official figures did not back this up. Does this mean that the original claim of 55bhp for the 997cc engine was optimistic, or that the later claim of 55bhp for the 998cc engine was too modest? No one ever admitted to anything, but I suspect it was that the 997cc engine was not quite as lusty, in standard form, as was claimed.

By this time, in fact, the Mini-Cooper S had arrived on the scene and the launch of the very special little 970S was imminent, so BMC was about to lose all further interest in the original Mini-Cooper for competition purposes.

Originally for the Mini, and later for other A-Series/front-wheel-drive installations, the AP (Automotive Products) automatic transmission was another miracle of tight packaging.

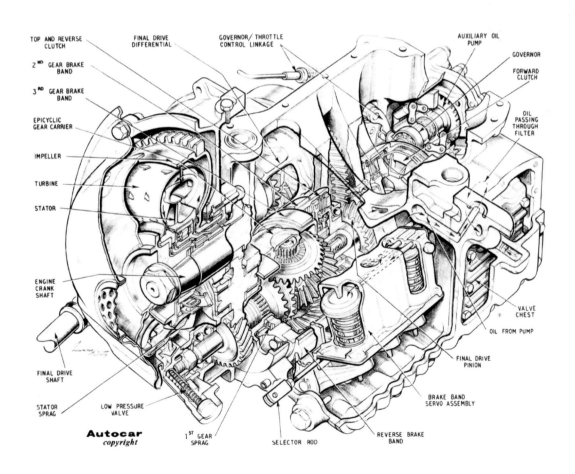

Although the Cooper S engine was much more powerful than the basic A-Series from which it had been developed, it was physically no larger than before. To prove the point, compare this 970S study with that of the 848cc engine pictured on page 76, for both units are in the same type of Mini engine bay.

Mini-Cooper S – the ultimate performance Minis

The cream, they say, always rises to the surface. Maybe this explains why more than five million Minis were made, yet the vast majority of surviving 'classic' Minis seem to be Cooper S models of one type or another.

That's reasonable, of course, for it was the A-Series-powered Cooper S which made most of the headlines in the 1960s, winning the Monte Carlo rally several times, becoming a crowd-pleasing saloon car racer, and being

one of *the* fastest ways of getting round our crowded towns and cities.

However, even though it had taken time to persuade BMC's management that the 997cc Mini-Cooper would sell, it took even longer to convince them that a trio of extra-special Cooper S engines should then be developed. This time it wasn't just bores and strokes that were to be altered, but the entire structure and basic layout of the A-Series engine itself. And it wasn't only racing-car constructor John Cooper, but his rival Ken Tyrrell (who would be running racing cars in Europe) along with the newly-appointed BMC competitions manager Stuart Turner, who were lobbying for BMC to produce yet more powerful engines.

With more power, this trio urged, not only could Mini-Coopers be better racing saloons, but Formula Junior (and, from 1964, Formula Three) cars using a 1.0-litre version of the new type of engine would also be quicker.

But before such cars could be used in motorsport, 1,000 would have to be produced for homologation purposes – the quicker, the better.

By this time, apparently, Alec Issigonis had come to approve of the use of Minis in motorsport: the favourable publicity it brought his product was appealing. With BMC's engine-tuning genius Eddie Maher and Downton's Daniel Richmond all lobbying as hard as possible, approval came during 1962. In little more than a year the very first Mini-Cooper S road car, the 1071S, went on sale.

As everyone surely knows, three types of Mini-Cooper S – 970S, 1071S and 1275S – were eventually put on sale, each for different reasons, and eventually a much down-tuned version of the 1275S became a mainstream engine too. In 1962 the medium-term strategy was to develop special 1.0-litre and 1.3-litre engines of the type known as A-Series 'S', but the 1.1-litre unit came first. All the S engines would be developed at Courthouse Green, then put into production at Courthouse Green too: in this way, not only would performance benefits be concentrated on the same site, but manufacturing would be kept close to the centre of that expertise too.

In later years the 1,275cc engine became a standard size used in all modern Minis: millions more would be made in the 1970s and 1980s for cars as diverse as the Marina and the Metro, yet in the early 1960s that engine size did not yet exist.

Compared with earlier A-Series engines, including the 997cc Mini-Cooper unit, two major changes in construction and layout had to be made (and this is why there was so much debate, and so much resistance from Longbridge, who could see the possible expense in changing things on the machine lines in North Works). One was that the cylinder bore centres in the block casting were juggled around so that a larger bore could be used; and the other was that the head casting was revised, not only to give better breathing, but to incorporate what is known as the 11-stud head pattern, with an extra holding-down stud (at the heater tap end) and a new holding down bolt (at the thermostat end) – this being done to provide better clamping of the cylinder head gasket. At the same time, the combustion chambers were somewhat re-profiled, and significantly larger inlet and exhaust valves were fitted. Larger diameter big-end bearings (2.0in diameter) were specified.

As Bill Appleby commented (of the initial 1,071cc engine) in his detailed IMechE paper of 1963: 'This engine is not mass-produced . . . but the specification is interesting in that the materials used are the best for the job they have to do. This engine is the direct result of work carried out by our Competitions Department in Formula Junior racing.

'The crankshaft, for example, is made of nitrided steel, which does not wear. The bearing clearance is therefore maintained at a minimum during the life of the engine, and the initial balance of the engine is maintained within close limits. This is very important in an engine with crankshaft speeds up to 7,000rpm, and up to about 7,800rpm when racing.

'We also use Nimonic 80 for both inlet and exhaust valves. The stems of these valves are tipped with Stellite. These materials, of course, are extremely expensive and could not be fitted in quantity-produced cars selling at a competitive price.

'For the first time in the history of the A-Series engine, the cylinder centres have been changed, but it is not, of course, manufactured on our quantity-production plant.'

That first derivative, which was produced in a real hurry, was the 1,071cc unit, which used the new 'S' bore of 70.6mm, but retained the 68.26mm stroke of the 850 Mini. In fact – as I shall explain in depth in the next chapter, when detailing the A-Series' career in Formula Junior racing – no version of this would appear in a single-seater Cooper until 1964.

The whys and wherefores were all connected with whether the production machinery at Courthouse Green could be altered with the least disruption to other A-Series assembly, and at the lowest investment cost. In fact, not only was it convenient to machine the new S-Type's EN40B steel crankshaft on existing tooling, but it helped produce a high-revving over-square power unit. Even so, it was only intended as an interim unit while the two definitive 'S' engines were finalised.

The 1,275cc version of the 'S' engine, which followed in 1964, used the same sturdy cylinder block but with a new long-stroke crankshaft and 81.3mm/3.20in stroke. This, in fact, was the same stroke as that used in the original 997cc Mini-Cooper engine, and on the Cooper S engine it also resulted in the cylinder block being a little deeper.

Finally (for deliveries of Minis with this particular engine did not begin until June 1964) came the 970cc 'S' engine, still using the same block and large bore, but with a unique 61.91mm stroke: this was never used in any other A-Series unit, but featured in the 1964 and 1965 Cooper F3 single-seater engines. By any standards, in fact, the 970cc power unit was an 'homologation special', solely produced to get sporting approval for the ultimate in 1.0-litre Mini-Coopers. No sooner had enough been built, than this model, and the 970cc engine which went into it, disappeared from the listings.

It was not, of course, the ultimate A-Series, even at that time in history. Years later, BMC competitions manager Stuart Turner commented that the Mini-Cooper S would have been a much better sports saloon 'if Sales hadn't insisted that it be usable by the District Nurse!' But how many District Nurses used Mini-Cooper Ss when they were on the market? Not many, I'm sure.

Even the 970S, which was a high-revving, limited-production model, was still a totally practical road car, with the same equipment, sound-deadening, instruments and seating as other Mini-Coopers – yet it was this car, more than any other Mini, which BMC-engined race and rally cars needed in order to dominate the 1.0-litre class, and nothing more. Since only 1,000 such cars had to be sold, they would put little marketing effort behind it.

Incidentally, it is not generally known that at this time (1963–64) there was a definite proposal to start building special 1071S-engined versions of the Sprite/Midget – the Midget, for instance, would have been called 'Midget S' – in order to face up to competition from newly-launched rivals like the Honda S800; but this was dropped when it was realised that costs would be too high, and that such a Midget would exceed 100mph, making it faster than the contemporary MGB –

which would have been highly embarrassing . . .

However, it certainly confirmed that Courthouse Green was now a very significant factor in the development *and* manufacture of A-Series engines. When the 1071S was launched in the spring of 1963, Bill Appleby reminded his listeners that although A-Series assembly had only begun at Courthouse Green in October 1957, more than 190,000 units had already been built there in less than six years.

1,098cc for the 1100 – a big stretch

Now we come to one of the most controversial and (as it happened) protracted development programmes to which the A-Series engine was ever subjected, and which eventually resulted in the launch of the long-stroke 1,098cc unit, initially for use in the front-wheel-drive 1100 range.

This story originated in the mid-1950s, even before the Mini programme finally took precedence over every other idea that Alec Issigonis' little research team had. Before Len Lord commanded him to produce the new Mini, one of the projects on which he was working was coded XC9002, and was effectively meant to be a replacement for the Morris Minor, fitted with a transversely-mounted engine and what the industry knows as an 'end-on' gearbox (the transmission being at the end, rather than under, the engine itself). Only a mock-up was produced at the time.

Not that it was forgotten – just sidelined. In 1959, and even before the Mini was introduced, Sir Leonard Lord

A-Series volumes – what a difference a decade makes

Although the idea of a merger with Nuffield (to form the British Motor Corporation) was only a pipe dream when Len Lord asked his team to design the A-Series engine, it soon became an absolutely vital cornerstone of the corporate line-up.

Purely as an example, this is how A-Series usage mushroomed in the first ten years. The dates quoted are for financial years:

1951–52	309	The A30 only went into production in May 1952
1952–53	18,436	The first full year of A30 production
1961–62	363,310	Of which no fewer than 182,864 were Mini types and 29,011 were Sprites and Midgets being built at Abingdon. By this time many engines were being built at Courthouse Green in Coventry.

There would be more to come, for in 1967–68 (the year in which British Leyland was formed), 602,660 units were produced, of which 267,678 were Minis and 249,500 were 1100/1300 types.

When A-Series engine manufacture was moved into East Works in the early 1960s there was really no shortage of space in which to do it. East Works was the original Austin 'shadow factory', set up in advance of the Second World War, first to build aircraft engines and later to build complete bomber aircraft, like this short Stirling. (*BMIHT*)

and George Harriman had decided to go ahead with the second important front-wheel-drive project. Like the B-Series 'Farina' range which was just hitting the showrooms (Austin A55 Cambridge, Morris Oxford, MG Magnette, Riley 4/68 and Wolseley15/50), the new car would have to take on several identities, all to be based on the same new structure.

And so it was that XC9002 (which immediately became ADO16 in the official BMC list of projects) was revived. However, although Alec Issigonis should have taken

control of the new model (his team, after all, had started it), it was his well-liked and extremely capable deputy, Charles Griffin, who steered this model almost all the way through. Griffin, one-time chief engineer at Nuffield in Cowley, and still facing weekly, often more frequent, trips to Longbridge, later recalled how this happened:

'Alec was blinkered. He only ever worked on one car at a time – at Cowley he had concentrated on the Minor, and at Longbridge it was only the Mini – and he had other models in his peripheral vision, but no concentration on them at all. So I had to take complete responsibility for the Pininfarina-styled 1100 [which is what ADO16 became], and later for the even larger front-wheel-drive 1800.'

Right from the start, however, there was the problem of an engine for ADO16 – for, as Bill Appleby commented: 'As engine designers we were confronted with a big problem, whether to design a completely new power unit to give a

By the early 1960s Longbridge had expanded virtually to its limits. CAB2 (closest to the camera in this aerial shot) had been built to accommodate the new A-Series-engined 1100 range. A-Series engines were still part-manufactured in North Works (to the extreme right of the frame), though a vast new facility was being built inside the underused East Works.

The Morris 1100 originally went into production at Cowley in 1962, and was joined by this sister-car, the Austin 1100, in 1963, which was always produced at Longbridge. Each and every UK-built 1100/1300 had an A-Series engine. (*BMIHT*)

Amid the blizzard of badge-engineering which emanated from BMC in the early 1960s, one result was the MG 1100 version of the Austin-Morris 1100, which featured a twin-SU/55bhp version of the 1.1-litre A-Series engine.

The Vanden Plas Princess 1100, effectively an MG 1100 in a party frock but still with an A-Series engine, was a real marketing success in the 1960s.

capacity of 1,100cc, or whether we should keep to A-Series overall dimensions. Actually, on the drawing board we did both, but in the end practical considerations gained the day and the latter course was chosen.'

First of all, Gerald Palmer, who had become BMC's 'chief engineer, body and chassis' in 1952, found time to sketch up his ideas for a 60° V4 engine, but as this was quite bulky it was only really suitable for in-line mounting. Palmer comments in his autobiography that later, after he had left BMC, 'I was told that the Austin side had also experimented with the narrow V engines based on Lancia designs.'

And indeed they had. For a time the engine design team, still led by Eric Bareham and with Eric Duncan at the head of this particular project, slaved away on a whole family of V4 and V6 power units, which might have been useful in transverse (front-wheel-drive) or even in-line (MGB, perhaps) configurations.

The vee-angle was reported to be no more than 18°,

a common cylinder head (to serve both banks) with a single overhead camshaft was proposed, and there would have been one SU carburettor at each side of that head, to serve the appropriate inlet ports. Although it promised to be quite heavy (compared with the A-Series), one of the models for which the V4 might have been potentially suited was the new ADO16. It was for this reason that there was truly generous space in the engine bay of ADO16 – generous, that is, when the A-Series was finally chosen, and enough for the V4 to have been slotted into the space therein. Bareham later confirmed that the front panel and grille of the new car was pushed forward by a full four inches to make this possible.

In the end BMC's top management concluded that

Not only was the 1100 a best-seller in Austin and Morris guise, but the more powerful twin-carb version of the A-Series engine helped turn the MG1100 derivative into a nippy little sports saloon. (*BMIHT*)

By the early 1970s demand for the A-Series engine was at its peak, for each and every Mini and every single car of the 1100/1300 range was powered by one version or another.

they were not convinced about the potential of a V4/V6 family, and that a massive investment in new transfer line and machine tooling would not be justified. Instead it was decided to look for a further stretch of the existing 848cc/948cc/998cc engine, and to move the entire existing production from North Works to East Works, which had been looking underused since the last of the Austin Champ 4x4s, and the Rolls-Royce engine which powered them, had been cleared away. East Works was also still assembling trucks, but these were about to be moved to the brand-new Bathgate plant – so there *was* a coherent BMC 'master plan' after all!

When totally finished in 1963, not only was it possible for the re-equipped East Works to build up to 12,000

engines and transmissions every week for the Mini and 1100 ranges, but the ability to carry on making in-line engines (for cars like the Midget, the Minor 1000 and A40 Farina) was retained. Not only that, but a further extension of assembly facilities – CAB2 (Car Assembly Building No 2) – was erected, to take shape alongside CAB1, with new assembly lines devoted to the assembly of ADO16 and the Mini. This was a new 207,600sq ft facility costing £3,000,000 when fully equipped at the end of 1962, and it brought Longbridge's ultimate build capability up to at least 600,000 cars a year – though the most it ever actually produced (in 1964/5) was 376,781: you can blame the almost constant turmoil of industrial unrest for the shortfall, as demand was certainly high in that period.

Thus it was that by the summer of 1962, when ADO16 (originally known only as the Morris 1100, though other derivatives were to follow) was launched, the A-Series had taken on a new lease of life – one which made it even more vital to the continued existence of this colossal business. Before this could be done, however, there was a problem. For obvious marketing reasons, the new ADO16/1100 model had to be quicker than the Mini – yet it was all set to be a lot heavier. Specifically, the Mini weighed about 1,400lb, and its 34bhp A-Series engine provided about 75mph. The ADO16/1100 weighed 1,820lb, and the sales staff wanted it to reach nearly 80mph: not only that, but there was to be an MG-badged version which ought to be even faster.

BMC's slide-rule merchants reckoned that they would need at least 48bhp – ideally more – from a single-carb engine, and 55bhp at least for use in the MG-badged version. Because the 997cc engine was not a mass-production version, and not over-endowed with low-speed torque, there was only one solution: to enlarge the existing 948cc engine by increasing the bore *and* the stroke.

But how? No allowances for a substantial 'stretch' had ever been built into the original 803cc version, and even pushing it out to 948cc had involved siamesing the cylinder bores; although this had largely been trouble-free in service, BMC's engineers were reluctant about trying to do any more. Because there appeared to be no other solution, however, it was decided to see if any more capacity could be squeezed out of the existing 948cc-type cast iron block without destroying the little engine's great reliability.

The measured tones used in Appleby's and Bareham's published IMechE papers make it all seem to have been easily achieved, but it was not. As Appleby reported in 1963: 'To obtain an 1100cc engine from a length of cylinder block originally designed for 803cc was a major design problem. After consideration, we decided on a bore and stroke of 64.58mm x 83.72mm [2.54in x 3.30in] respectively, still retaining the 948cc cylinder centres. By this the amount of metal between the bores was reduced to 6.5mm and it was doubtful whether or not we should be able to hold this in production, and return round bores without a great deal of scrap, bearing in mind that we have to use dry liners of about 0.070in thickness when we strike porosity . . .

'However, we bored out several cylinder blocks to suit the outside diameter of the liner and, somewhat to our surprise, they were entirely successful.'

Finally there was the decision to increase the stroke. When the 997cc Mini-Cooper was being developed, an 81.3mm/3.20in stroke was chosen for that power unit, because it was being considered for the ADO16/1100.

The capacity of that engine would have been 1,065cc – but in the end it was decided to add even more to the crank throw, leaving it at 83.72mm/3.30in. (Notice how the Imperial measures were invariably neat, whereas the metric equivalent had to fit in with Olde Worlde 'Black Country' custom and practice!)

Although this was not an ideal solution for a new-for-the-1960s range of cars (Ford-UK, for instance, was moving precisely the other way with a series of very *over* square engines for its new Anglia, Classic and Cortina types), it worked surprisingly well, and the upgraded A-Series went from strength to strength. Not only did the Morris 1100 (there would be no 'Austin' equivalent for another year) and the twin-SU/55bhp MG1100 become best-sellers as soon as they went on sale, but several existing models – the Morris Minor 1000, Austin A40 Farina and the Sprite/Midget sports cars – were all provided with their own versions of the 1,098cc engine too.

So, with A-Series activity, and models using it, all at a new high, this is how the figures stacked up for the 1963/4 financial year:

Austin A35 Van	*15,040*
Austin A40 Farina	*29,596*
Mini family	*174,682*
Austin 1100	*81,238*
Morris Mini	*71,169*
Morris Minor 1000	*38,817*
Morris 1100	*138,235*
Austin-Healey Sprite	*9,389*
MG Midget	*8,279*
Minor derivatives (including van)	*17,598*
Total	***584,043***

– and this, as far as BMC was concerned, was by no means the end of the expansion which they had in mind.

In the meantime, many other A-Series experiments were ongoing, though none of them came close to being adopted. In the early 1960s, and while BMC was making good money (published AGM accounts showed that no less than £15.6 million net profit was made in 1962), consideration was given to developing an aluminium-blocked version of the sturdy little engine, where such a block had to be suitable for high-pressure die casting.

ERA of Dunstable (who were technically and intellectually close to Sir George Harriman) got the contract to develop such a 1.0-litre power unit, which was called the BA1000 – incidentally, the expensive-to-manufacture cast iron/five-port cylinder head seems to have been retained – but in the end nothing became of it.

Attempts to update the cylinder head, whose limitations were, by this stage, well-known, would continue for some years.

The A-Series diesel

While all the high-profile engine enlargement, and high-performance work, was going ahead on the petrol-engined A-Series, yet another derivative was evolving. In the early 1960s, BMC sponsored the design of a diesel version of the A-Series engine, its original use to be in a small tractor.

The story goes back to 1960, when Nuffield (a subsidiary of BMC) approached Harry Ferguson Research, looking into the possibilities of adding a new small tractor model to its existing range. Although Ferguson's illustrious founder, Harry Ferguson, had recently died, his well-funded research organisation lived on, based at Baginton airport, close to Coventry.

Recently freed of its remaining links both with Massey Ferguson and with Standard (both of which had built its tractors in big numbers), HFR was steadily building up its own independent consultancy in many forward-looking engineering projects, and was happy to get involved. HFR, for instance, had already delved deeply into the art and detail of four-wheel-drive systems, but was still interested in tractors and the development of the breed.

It was fortunate for all concerned that when Harry Ferguson sold his tractor interests to Massey Harris in 1956, the severance deal allowed him to return to tractor production under his own name after five years had elapsed. Accordingly, by the time the Nuffield approach came in 1960 a new 'small Ferguson' tractor project (which Ferguson was convinced could sell for a mere £400) was well advanced.

To finalise this project, Nuffield asked HFR to use a BMC transmission instead of the complex Ferguson-Teramala transmission originally chosen, and at the same time it pushed ahead with plans to produce a small diesel engine that would be closely based on the current A-Series unit. In the end, the first BMC 'Mini tractor' started running in 1962, but was not put on sale until the close of 1965.

Because it was still building up diesel-engine expertise of its own, BMC had already turned to a highly-respected consultancy, Ricardo of Shoreham-by-Sea in West Sussex, for advice. Harry Ricardo himself had already been involved in new engine design for more than half a century, producing anything from

Ricardo

Well before any post-war Austin engines were designed, Sir Harry Ricardo and his company Ricardo Consulting Engineers (RCE) were justly famous. Born into a wealthy family in London in 1885, Harry Ricardo had been working on engines since the early 1900s. His first company, Engine Patents Ltd, developed the successful engine used in British Mark V military tanks during the First World War.

Ricardo started work on the improvement of diesel engines in 1919, and designed what became a famous diesel feature, the 'Comet' compression swirl chamber, which eventually led to the formation of Ricardo Consulting Engineers in 1927. Before and during the Second World War RCE made much of sleeve-valve engine design, then turned to the enhancement of the legendary Rolls-Royce Merlin V12 military aircraft engine. It was this sort of stellar activity that ensured the company was never short of work in the years that followed, a period in which the company once again got involved in new engine development for Austin/BMC, Saab, Standard-Triumph and other prestigious clients.

Although Sir Harry Ricardo (he was knighted in 1948) retired from active business in 1964, he kept in touch with the company that he had founded four decades earlier. He died in 1974, aged 89. In the fullness of time Ricardo, which had continued to expand, absorbed FF Developments (which was itself a descendant of Harry Ferguson Research), and by the 2000s had became a design/developer of all technological aspects of the automobile industry.

The BMC Mini tractor was introduced in 1964, the only BMC model ever to use a diesel-fuelled derivative of the A-Series engine. (*BMIHT*)

super-powerful military tank engines in the First World War to a pioneering diesel feature known as the 'Comet' compression swirl chamber, and was instrumental in improving both the Rolls-Royce Merlin aeroplane engine and the first successful turbo jets. Although Sir Harry would retire in 1964, his company continued to prosper.

The first joint BMC-Ricardo diesel project was the 2.2-litre four-cylinder unit which was used in Austin-badged, but Carbodies-inspired, London taxi-cabs (and later in other BMC commercial vehicles), after which the team turned to dieselising the 1.5-litre B-Series engine. It was this team, of which John Barnett was a member,

that was then asked to do the same transformation on the A-Series engine.

The original unit was of 948cc, and was developed at Longbridge but was always intended for manufacture at Courthouse Green, where most 'specialised' A-Series types seemed to settle. It was, of course, a considerable if not total redesign of the existing 948cc unit. Not only did it have a new, purpose-designed, cast iron cylinder head, complete with CAV fuel injection, but to meet Ferguson's demanding tractor standards it had to pass 1,000-hour durability tests, and be able to run at a variety of inclined angles as the tractor struggled with uneven terrain.

The block was reinforced, the front end of the block also being changed to allow the diesel injection pump to be driven off the front of the crankshaft (rather like the layout of the BMC 2.2-litre diesel), and of course a more rigid crankshaft was also specified. Complete with the

Ricardo-patented 'Comet V' combustion chambers, and the very high compression ratio of 23.6:1, the new little diesel produced a mere 15bhp at 2,500rpm, and never stood a chance of being adopted for pure private-car use.

To power its new 'mini-tractor' (which was, indeed, considerably smaller – physically and in its working capabilities – than any other tractor on the British market, and specifically from Massey Ferguson or Nuffield), Ferguson and BMC chose this diesel engine – their very first 'car-sized' diesel – based on the A-Series. This choice was not necessarily made because BMC thought it was the ideal solution, but rather because they saw it as the only viable choice that made commercial sense. An all-new small diesel would cost a fortune in new tooling, machining and assembly facilities, whereas a unit based on the A-Series might just work. It might also be viable for light-duty marine work.

The mini-Ferguson, which soon transmuted itself into a BMC Mini-Tractor, was always intended for sale primarily in the Far East, for use in market gardening and in paddy fields. This explains why much of the field trial work was carried out in an area between Knowle and Coventry, where BMC leased a stretch of swampy land with a lot of standing water, which apart from the lower ambient temperatures had all the same characteristics as a rice-growing paddy field!

BMC always intended that the mini-tractor should be produced, in quantity, at Bathgate, a newly-built factory halfway between Glasgow and Edinburgh (an area badly hit by unemployment as old-technology coal mines progressively closed down). Bathgate opened up in 1961,

This was the diesel version of the A-Series engine, which was only produced (at Courthouse Green) in the 1960s. (*BMIHT*)

originally assembling BMC trucks, but the first tractors followed in 1963. By December 1965, when the Mini-Tractor was finally launched as the 9/16 model, Bathgate was producing 18,000 tractors a year (alongside 27,000 trucks).

The new 948cc diesel-engined machine weighed in at about 2,100lb, had disc brakes as standard, and cost from £512.50 on the British market, where it created quite an initial stir, as this was the smallest-capacity volume-produced diesel engine in Britain. However, it was not a lasting success, either in the UK or in the Far East, especially as tractors seemed to be getting bigger and heavier all round the world. After only three years, in November 1968 the little 9/16 was replaced by an updated model, the 4/24 version, which was fitted with a 25bhp version of the 1.5-litre B-Series diesel instead.

No more was ever heard of an A-Series diesel, which died at the end of 1968 and was never revived.

Downton magic

Although his influence on the company's engine design work – and particularly on the evolution of the A-Series – took some years to mature, it was in 1961 that BMC first began to have dealings with a scholarly, other-worldly, character from deepest Wiltshire who was to become one of Alec Issigonis' most influential gurus. His name was Daniel Richmond, and his company was called Downton Engineering.

Except to the vintage fraternity, who knew all about him, Daniel Richmond seemed to have come from nowhere, and soon after he died in 1974 his little company began to shrivel away. When his much-loved and eccentric partner Bunty died two years later the business was wound up. Not that this was the end of Downton's magic, for a number of his staff who had learned so much from the master – not least legends like Richard Longman – subsequently carried on A-Series work under their own names.

By the mid-1960s, Minis and Downton were often mentioned in same breath; yet it was Alec Issigonis, rather than the BMC hierarchy, who had brought them together in the first place. Richmond, however, was a 'character'. My esteemed contemporary, Jon Pressnell, once noted that: 'Eccentricity, alcohol, and dogs – along with fishing – are key motifs in the story of Downton Engineering, an enterprise famous for its colourful way of doing business, often in the next-door pub.'

Way back in the late 1940s, after having spent some of his early working life with British European Airways, Richmond bought a tiny garage in the village of Downton, in Wiltshire, where he started working on cars as various as Rolls-Royces, Bugattis and Lagondas, mainly for his chums in the Vintage Sports Car Club.

Richmond was born to a life of privilege, his father being Sir Daniel Richmond (of the Indian Forest Service), his mother the daughter of Sir James Davy. Daniel himself eventually got together with the Hon Veronica ('Bunty') Romer, who was author Somerset Maugham's niece. They were, to put it mildly, eccentric in their lifestyle, for Richmond's 'working' afternoons were often devoted to drinking, fishing, or a combination of the two. Even so, Downton soon gained a reputation, with Richmond as its intuitive engineer, his inspiration being encouraged by the presence of a bottle of booze in a drawer of his desk, and by the presence of a salmon fishing river just behind the premises.

Richmond certainly got to know Alec Issigonis through the VSCC movement. His first encounter with the magnificent little A-Series engine followed in the 1950s, when a customer asked him to tune up a Morris Minor. Deciding that the kit offered to him to fit was not up to his standards, Richmond concluded that he could do better, and started a thriving development process which made Downton famous worldwide.

Colleagues such as Paul Ivy, Jan Odor (who would set up Janspeed), George Toth (who became an airflow wizard and later joined Richard Longman's company in nearby Christchurch) and Richard Longman himself were all prime movers. However, it was only when Downton produced a magnificent little 1.1-litre Mini-Cooper road car (which became affectionately known as 'Mini Ton Bomb' after *Autocar* magazine clocked a 103.5mph top speed) that the factory took interest.

Shortly after this Alec Issigonis contacted Richmond and invited him to visit Longbridge, where he was soon seen to have a magic touch regarding cylinder head profiling, combustion chamber shapes, and airflow work in particular. This was all very official, and very progressive: Richmond was allocated an office not far from that of Issigonis, and made regular weekly visits to Longbridge.

Richmond and Issigonis, it seems, got on famously, because both were languid, laconic, sometimes ethereal in their attitude to the economic realities of running a business, but could be totally dedicated to making a good engine better. Richmond was soon involved in new-product work, and had much to do with the detailing of the Mini-Cooper S engines, which started life with the 1,071cc unit in 1963.

In particular, he rapidly came to terms with the original 'kidney' shape of the combustion chamber, as laid down by Harry Weslake, but for truly high-performance applications he altered it considerably as time, and development, passed. To BMC's enormous advantage, incidentally, he also applied similar magic to the larger B-Series engines.

Because the A-Series was used in so many models (including, of course, the MG Midget and the 1100/1300 family), it was now possible for the little company to sell kits, and to 'Downtonise' a whole range of models. More and more staff were taken on to keep up with demand, especially after Downton was made an official BMC supplier of what were called 'Stage One' tuning kits, through the Abingdon-based Special Tuning Department.

By the end of the 1960s Downton had grown to a considerable size, with a total workforce of at least 80 people (machinists, engine builders and testers), and 100 kits were shipped out every week, many of them overseas. Daniel Richmond had bought himself a Ferrari (and was heard to say that he could make many improvements to the famous V12 engine when he could find the time), but

was losing interest in a business that was producing a lot of kit but was innovating very little.

At the height of Richmond's influence at BMC (and really quite independent of Downton itself), Issigonis invited him to help design the neat little overhead-camshaft engine fitted to the 9X prototype; but no sooner had this been done than British Leyland was formed and the engine was swiftly sidelined. The 'Stokes Axe' then cut a swathe through the various design and motor consultants, which meant that famous names such as John Cooper, Donald Healey and Downton Engineering were all cut adrift.

In due course, therefore, Richmond began to disappear to a country cottage in the West Country for weeks at a time, leaving Bunty to cope on her own. And then, suddenly, it all fell apart, for Richmond suffered two heart attacks, the second of which felled him at the age of only 47; Bunty died just two years later, in 1976.

That, in effect, was the death of Downton, though a company of that name survives to this day. Even so, today's owners would surely agree that Downton without Daniel or Bunty can only be a shadow of its original self.

More variations on an 1100 theme, this being the Riley Kestrel of 1965, which was mechanically almost identical to the MG 1100 and Wolseley 1100 types.

CHAPTER 6

Racing and record-breaking

Although the gallant A-Series went on to have a distinguished motorsport career (the 1.3-litre unit was capable of at least 200bhp in turbocharged form when used in the Metro Turbo in the British Touring Car Championship of the 1980s), I think it fair to suggest that this sort of use never entered the minds of engineers at Longbridge when the engine was first sketched up in 1949. If it *had* been in their minds they would surely have provided the original engine with a more efficient and more enterprisingly detailed cylinder head, and more favourable bore and stroke dimensions.

Is it not a miracle, therefore, that it went on to provide power for a whole generation of rallying and racing Mini-Coopers that performed with honour at prestigious race circuits like Le Mans, and gave a generation of young drivers a start in single-seater Coopers in Formula Junior and Formula Three? To this day, indeed, there are tuning shops all around the globe that still do most of their business working on an engine which was designed more than 60 years ago, and whose development secrets have long since been revealed.

After all, when the A-Series was young the only cars in which it was used were the Austin A30 and the Morris Minor SII. Neither could ever be described as sports cars, and neither had any obvious uses in motorsport, so why should anyone take an interest in what could be done with them? A look back at the first-generation saloon car races held at Silverstone in the early 1950s show that no A-Series-engined car – neither Austin A30 nor Morris Minor SII – was entered until 1955, when they were trounced by 896cc-engined two-stroke DKWs.

Nor did BMC's newly-formed 'works' competitions department, based at Abingdon and managed by Marcus Chambers, bother itself with such cars at first. Amazingly, it was a purely private entry – an Austin A30 driven by Ray Brookes and his son Ted – which recorded the first 'International' win for an A-Series-engined car, when the duo took advantage of an extremely favourable performance handicap on the 1956 Tulip rally to win the Dutch-based event outright. (To emphasise that the handicap favoured small cars, I should also point out that 803cc-engined Standard Eights finished second, third and fourth behind the nimble little A30!)

Shortly after this, of course, the much more promising 948cc-engined Austin A35 and Morris Minor 1000 cars were introduced, and, under some pressure from the BMC marketing department, Abingdon took both types – two of each – on to their strength, and began to use them, sparingly, where event regulations looked promising. Even so, success was still hard to achieve.

Amazingly it was a wonderfully amateurish records-breaking foray – by an Austin A35 to the banked circuit at Montlhéry, near Paris – which made the next headlines. At the end of 1956 Gyde Horrocks, the secretary of the Cambridge University Automobile Club, approached BMC, asking for the loan of a car for his members to attack a series of long-distance 'endurance' speed records in Class G (750cc to 1,100cc), up to seven days in duration. After a lot of discussion an A35 was prepared, five undergraduate drivers were chosen, and in July 1957 the record attempts were duly made. Except for the use of an extra-large fuel tank, and slight front-end aerodynamic changes, the car was virtually standard (and, most importantly for the publicity chiefs, it *looked* standard too), still running on a downdraught Zenith carburettor and cast manifolds.

With stops for refuelling and a change of driver planned at three-hour intervals, this could have become a very boring exercise for the drivers (Gyde Horrocks, Tom Threlfall, Peter Riviere, Ray Simpson and John Taylor) and, in high summer, indeed it was, so Marcus Chambers was also dragooned into a driving stint. With only one breakdown – a fractured rear spring shackle pin, which was soon replaced – the little car kept on, relentlessly lapping at about 75mph.

At the end of the week, new records had been set at times from four days (74.91mph) to seven days (74.90mph), and all the way up to 20,000km (74.89mph). All this was achieved at a running average of 28mpg fuel economy, and with only seven tyre replacements. When the near-standard engine was stripped and examined it was found to be virtually unworn, this impressing not only BMC's engineers but also Vandervell (who provided all the crank and big-end bearings) so much that they were confident about boosting the engine considerably in future events and applications.

BMC made much of the Cambridge University AC's gallant seven-day endurance record run on the Montlhéry banked circuit in France in 1957, using a lightly-tuned Austin A35 which had been loaned to them by the BMC Competitions Department at Abingdon.

EX219

BMC's first serious involvement with the A-Series in motorsport came in 1957, and appears to have been the only instance of a 'works'-backed programme using a supercharged A-Series engine. In 1957, and again in 1959, this came in an Abingdon-built record car.

The story, in fact, really begins in 1954, when MG built the first of their post-war record cars, development of which involved two phases. An earlier test car, EX135, had, of course, been famous since the 1930s, but it was now long in the tooth, and no longer belonged to the company (Lieutenant-Colonel 'Goldie' Gardner had bought it, rechristening it the 'Gardner-MG'). Accordingly a new machine, coded EX179, was designed to take its place.

EX179 used a prototype MGA chassis frame, had MG TD/TF-type independent front suspension, a conventional beam rear axle and half-elliptic leaf springs, and a sleek streamlined bodyshell, with a left-mounted steering column/driving position and a massive fuel tank on the right-hand side of the car to balance the driver's seat. Originally the engine was a much-modified MG TF1500 power unit producing 84bhp.

EX179 went on to have a varied and successful life. As originally built it broke eight international records at

Rev. Rupert Jones, at work.

the drivers drink two pints of liquid an
take salt pills before getting in the car.
The A35 came in for driver changes
every three hours and a rapid service.
We had a fantastic backup of Abingdon
mechanics, although this was very muc
a Cambridge University show . . . we
provided drivers and supporters, and
timekeepers to watch the official
timekeepers.

In all it was a matter of routine of
keeping the car constantly rounding the
banking at an even speed and it became
quite dull at times, as nothing would g
wrong. Days went by and the car
refused to miss a beat. The only
problem apart from flies blocking the
radiator was a spring shackle bolt,
which broke half-way through the week

Every 12 hours gearbox and back axl
oil were checked steering greased and
tyres changed, battery level checked an
radiator cleared of all the flies with a j
of compressed air. The sump was
drained every 24 hours and the filter
changed every third day.

There was a constant communication
between the driver and the pits, and
since the two-way radio used a lot of
batteries, conversations were conducted
on a blackboard or on hastily scribbled
notes thrown out of the car window. T
relieve the boredom, pit signals often
said "Tea up!" or "Post Arrived" and
"Letter From Your Girlfriend . . . We
Are Reading It!"

Then the records began to come in.
At the end of it all we took the four da
record for 11.572 kilometres at 74.91
and also the five day record, the 15,00
kilometres, the 10,000 miles, the six
days, the 20,000 kilometres, and the
seven days, all at 75mph.

The French test drivers, who were
using the track at the same time as us,
cheered the little car home showing fa
greater enthusiasm than some of the
team. But the job was done, the
experience gained, the team basis
formed. Other things were to spring
from this beginning . . . we were to
have a further attack at endurance
records, in a Healey and also a TR2,
both not up to the A35's reliability, b
that's another story.

Mexican hat with Rupert Jones and Royal Marine-issue shorts, out in the midday sun.

For seven days and seven nights this production model Austin A35 lapped the famous French track at Montlhéry at an average speed of 74.9 m.p.h. to capture seven international records. The drivers were Cambridge undergraduates:- Gyde Horrocks, J. R. Simpson, T. J. Threlfall, P. G. Riviere and J. A. B. Taylor. Like their fellow record breakers at Monza they relied on Castrol. When the engine was subsequently stripped, the British Motor Corporation reported " No measurable wear and all bearings perfect."

AND AT MONTLHERY

This is how Philip Young's excellent but short-lived magazine *Sporting Cars* recalled the 1957 Montlhéry escapade.

up to 153.69mph, and exceeded 120mph for 12 hours using a carefully surveyed ten-mile circular course on the hard-baked surface of the Utah Salt Flats. Two years later, in 1956, the same car returned to Utah, this time using a prototype MGA Twin-Cam engine (this was based on the B-Series power unit) and with steering transferred to the right side; on this occasion it captured no fewer than 16 endurance records at speeds up to 170.15mph, with 12 hours covered at 141.71mph.

In 1957 MG revisited the Salt Flats in search of new records and more publicity, and this time EX179 was re-engined with a tuned-up (but normally aspirated) 948cc A-Series unit. After attention by the special tuning department at Morris Engines in Coventry, the little engine produced 57bhp at 5,500rpm. To do this, twin 1¼in SU carburettors, a 10.2:1 compression ratio and a different camshaft profile were all needed.

The object – to establish new International Class G records (751cc to 1,100cc) – was achieved by British journalist Tommy Wisdom and American driver David Ash, with new marks at up to 12 hours and up to 118.13mph. Not only that, but at the same time no fewer than 25 American national standing start and 25 flying start records were also set.

That, however, was just a start, for in the Utah workshops the MG team changed the A-Series engine, the new unit being one with a small Shorrock supercharger, which provided a modest 4.5lb/sq in of boost yet resulted in a peak power output of 73bhp at 5,500rpm. This time it was David Ash and American racing driver Phil Hill who drove the car, setting new records for from three hours to 1,000km, at speeds between 131.38 and 132.62mph. Finally, to top off a very successful week in the USA, Tommy Wisdom took the supercharged car on a straight sprint course, his most outstanding achievement being to clock 142.08mph over a flying ten-kilometre run. Why a Shorrock supercharger, by the way? Really because Shorrock, which had originally

In 1959 the ex-MG record car, EX179, became EX219 when it was fitted with a Shorrock-supercharged A-Series engine. At the Utah Salt Flats in the USA it reached speeds of up to 138.75mph in a lengthy 12-hour endurance run.

been called 'Centric', had a great deal of previous successful history with MG, with records exploits stretching back to the 1930s. (Shorrock actually granted Donald Healey a sales concession for its supercharger kits, but few seem to have been fitted to road cars.)

With EX179 now coming to the end of its useful competition (and publicity) life, it was discreetly stored. Then in September 1959, as if by magic, a 'new' record-breaker, coded EX219, was unveiled at Abingdon, a car known as an 'Austin-Healey', which was sent out to attack a raft of endurance speed records, once again on the Bonneville Salt Flats.

New? No, not at all – though neither Austin-Healey, nor BMC, nor MG spelt it out at the time. Complete with an A-Series engine, and a lot more development work, EX219 was in fact a thoroughly redeveloped EX179, which, therefore, simultaneously disappeared from the scene.

Although I would never describe EX219 as having a shadowy history, the fact is that it appeared suddenly as if from nowhere, and is only very sparsely covered in Austin-Healey, MG and BMC histories – yet it achieved notable results in its short career with BMC. Except for noting it in its record results appendix, Wilson McComb's seminal MG history (*MG by McComb*) takes no notice of it; David Knowles' *MG, the Untold Story* takes no more notice, nor does Geoff Healey in any of his much-respected publications.

Peter Browning's book *Healeys and Austin Healeys* is more forthcoming, and with his blessing I quote from

In 1959 EX219, when fitted with a Shorrocks-supercharged A-Series engine, broke a whole series of sprint and endurance records at the Bonneville Salt Flats in the USA. One of the drivers, Fleet Street journalist Tommy Wisdom, is at the wheel, talking to MG development engineer Alec Hounslow.

his comments regarding the 1959 expedition to the Salt Flats. The fact that no fewer than 15 new Class G records were achieved with a Shorrock-supercharged A-Series engine is greatly to the car's credit, though these achievements were not entirely without incident. Tommy Wisdom, Ed Leavens and Gus Ehrmann were the three drivers, each of them covering about three hours per 'shift' around the circular track. Refuelling was needed at such intervals in any case.

As MG general manager John Thornley told Peter:

'Driving round and round this circle is a monotonous occupation, even at 140mph . . . As each record fell the news was conveyed on a blackboard and, as the end of each stint approached, illustrations of mugs of beer and rows of bottles arranged on the top of a crate also appeared by way of encouragement.'

Nine endurance records were achieved at speeds up to 138.75mph for 12 hours before the car was called in and sent back to its workshops in Utah, where what Thornley called the 'sprint' engine was then installed for attacks on the shorter-distance (up to one hour) records.

Then the dramas began. First of all a clutch failed, then Gus Ehrmann twice spun off the circular track trying to avoid a rough patch, which meant that the effort had to be started again. Fortunately, Gus then kept the repaired and re-tyred car going, and set up six more records, the shortest (50km) at 145.56mph, the longest (the hour) at 146.95mph. In spite of these indignities, by the way, the supercharged A-Series engine did not miss a beat.

This, though, was the end of EX219's career, for BMC were now keen to involve the A-Series engine in a new low-cost racing formula that could boast that its engines had been developed from those of production cars.

Cooper Formula Junior and Formula Three cars: A-Series single-seaters

This was where the very first link between John Cooper and BMC was forged. It was not connected with the Mini-Cooper road-car project, but with European Formula Junior motor racing. And, to quote that British film superstar Sir Michael Caine, 'Not a lot of people know that . . .'

Well, they do, actually – especially in Britain, where the Cooper story is now well known. Well before the Mini-Cooper was even conceived, John Cooper had produced a series of fast and nimble little single-seaters – 'Juniors' – for the latest racing category which was sweeping through Europe; with much help from BMC's ex-Riley tuning guru in Coventry, Eddie Maher, he eventually raced cars with 1.1-litre engines developing nearly 100bhp. In view of the A-Series' known limitations on cylinder head breathing, this was quite remarkable.

Formula Junior was born in Italy, and became an international formula in 1958. The idea was to encourage a 'beginners' formula, where the open-wheeler single-seater cars could weigh as little as 360kg (792lb) using 1.0-litre engines, or 400kg (880lb) with 1.1-litre engines. The basic engines – block, head casting, crankshaft layout – had to be those of current mass-production units, and had to stay 'as standard' (though re-machining was authorised), though almost everything else could be changed.

Fiat-engined Italian cars had it all their own way at first, but John Cooper saw an opportunity and moved very quickly to match them. His mid-engined chassis, with four longitudinal main tubes, cross-bracing, all-independent suspension by coil springs/wishbones at the front and transverse leaf spring/wishbones at the rear, was effectively a current F1 frame which had been put on a severe diet – but finding an engine was more difficult.

John Cooper wanted to use a British engine, and at the time the only real choice was between BMC's A-Series and Standard-Triumph's very similar Triumph Herald unit,

for in 1959 Ford's short-stroke Anglia 105E engine was still on the secret list. 948cc versions of both BMC and Triumph engines existed, but the Triumph unit had very little 'previous', whereas the A-Series had already been used in 'works' Austin-Healey Sprite racing and rally cars and looked promising.

Cooper made the phone call, visited Coventry, discovered Eddie Maher at 'Morris Engines' (Eddie had been diligently tuning race engines since joining Riley in the 1920s – Morris bought Riley in 1938, and Maher was 'one of the assets' – and had done some racing when young), and set out to see what could be achieved. Although the A-Series was small and light, not much was yet known about its ultimate tuning potential. Current Austin-Healey Sprite road cars used 43bhp/948cc engines with twin SU carburettors, while the Morris 1000 saloon used a single carb/37bhp version of the same unit.

Because existing Fiat race engines were producing up to 80bhp, that wasn't encouraging, but chief experimental engineer Maher used all his accumulated knowledge, set to, and transformed the engine. Within weeks, he – not Cooper – had developed a power unit with twin semi-downdraught SU carburettors, a racing camshaft profile, special pistons, and a cylinder head which had been reworked by Harry Weslake, all this being mated by Cooper to a Citroën-based transaxle.

Other British racing-car makers also approached BMC for engines, and some were either supplied or, in some cases, self-tuned and prepared, but the Cooper Car Co was always the preferred customer, and Eddie Maher's people spent most time keeping them happy.

The original Cooper T52 racing car was ready before the end of 1959, with a slightly-over-bored A-Series 994cc engine (the bore being 64.4mm), with twin SU carburettors and a claimed power output of 70bhp. The production run of cars went on to have a busy, partly successful year's racing in 1960. Walter Hansgen gave the car its USA debut at Sebring in March and won many races during the year. Ken Tyrrell's team began racing them in Britain at Easter time, and before long there was a running battle between his T52s and the 'works' Lotus 18s, which were using the new Ford 105E engine, an ultra-short-stroke motor which was being developed by Cosworth. The cars would have been even quicker, around a circuit, if only they could have used the newfangled disc brakes, but these were still banned by regulations which, after all, applied to everyone.

This was a season in which the Coopers were driven by famous personalities such as John Surtees, Henry Taylor, Jo Schlesser and Denny Hulme. Even so, the fact is that these first-generation cars didn't handle very well, and Cooper had to neglect their development while he and Jack Brabham got on with winning a second F1 World Championship.

Second thoughts, it must be admitted, often don't work, but in the case of the Cooper Formula Junior programme there's no doubt that the 1961 model, called T56, was much more successful. To quote that eminent Cooper historian Doug Nye, 'the new 1961 Mark II showed far greater investment in time, thought, and money'.

It wasn't just that the new car was lower, lighter, had coil spring suspension all round, used 13in wheels (instead of the 15in wheels of the original type) and was a better-handling machine, it also benefitted from a much lustier engine. Not only had Eddie Maher and Morris Engines spent many hours honing the specification, but in the meantime they had also 'borrowed' a rival Ford 105E engine for testing, to see where they could adopt some technology.

The 1961 BMC engine, still measured at 994cc, now used a single dual-choke Weber 45DCOE4 carburettor to replace the twin SUs, and an 11.5:1 compression ratio, meaning that at least 80bhp was available. It was linked either with the original Citroën-based gearbox or with a similarly modified component sourced from Renault.

The T56 was an altogether more successful car than the T52 had ever been, especially as its South African driver Tony Maggs won eight major races for Ken Tyrrell's organisation, his team-mate John Love often being close behind him, and beating him on occasion too. Once again, Hansgen was successful in North America. These, by the way, were small, sleek and very fast little cars (the T56 was once timed at 142mph in a straight line), although they were still slightly behind the Ford-engined-cars in peak power.

1.1-litres for 1962 and 1963

For 1962, therefore, it was deep-breath time for Cooper, who made good money by selling new FJ cars 'off the shelf' to customers all over the world and wanted to increase such sales in the future. The 'Mini-Cooper' road car had just been launched, and good publicity for one would probably be equally good for the other. To keep up with all the trends, not only did they produce another new model – the T59 – but this time it was to be sold with an enlarged, 1,095cc engine; disc brakes (now authorised by the regulations) were also standardised.

The latest power unit was absolutely state of the art as far as Eddie Maher and Morris Engines were concerned (state of the art, that is, according to the ever-expanding limits of their knowledge and experience). Not only did the cylinder block have a further enlarged cylinder bore (67.6mm), but it also had dry sump lubrication, a brand-new camshaft profile grind, a 12.0:1 compression ratio, a stiffened crankshaft, and was quoted at 95bhp at 7,500rpm.

The T59 was consequently a fine little racing car – the only problem being that the opposition, using Ford Anglia 105E engines with what, frankly, were more favourable bore/stroke ratios and better cylinder heads, seemed to have even more power. In Europe, though, Ken Tyrrell's 'works' cars, driven mainly by John Love and Denny Hulme, won a number of important International races, while in the USA Walt Hansgen once again performed well, and Tim Mayer became SCCA National FJ Champion.

By this time, of course (as we have seen in an earlier chapter), John Cooper had already inspired the first Mini-Cooper road car, and there were a number of enthusiasts who could never understand why the engine dimensions of that new Mini-Cooper road car (997cc, soon to be 998cc in 1964 with an entirely different bore and stroke) differed so radically from the Formula Junior engine (994cc) of the period – but this was mainly due to the way that FJ regulations were written.

Although John Cooper was always begging for more power, and higher revs, he knew that he could not get round the regulations without bending them a little – and that this could easily be checked by scrutineers. Accordingly, a new short-stroke 1.0-litre engine, based on the first Mini-Cooper 1071S, would not be ready for racing until 1964, by which time an entirely new formula – Formula Three – had taken over.

For 1963, therefore, Cooper made one final effort to keep ahead in Formula Junior by developing the T65, which retained the existing 1,095cc engine that had been improved in detail to its absolute limit, and was producing 98bhp at 7,800rpm, still powered by the single dual-choke Weber carburettor.

To this day, historians still get excited by the fact that the *original* version of the T65, as shown at London's

Racing Car Show in January 1963, was fitted with BMC's much-hyped new Hydrolastic suspension (as used, in production form, on the 1100 range, and on Minis and Mini-Coopers from 1964). But that was the exciting hype – the practical bad news was that extensive pre-season testing showed the Hydrolastic to be very difficult to set up and control, and such cars were never raced.

For 1963, therefore, the T65 became another totally-conventional mid-engined Cooper single-seater racer, which is to say that it had the latest iteration of the four-longitudinal-tube chassis frame and all-round coil spring independent suspension. The engine was now at its limits (whereas the Ford engine, its bitter rival, seemed still to be improving), and the Citroën-based transaxle (as modified by Jack Knight) now had six forward speeds.

This was almost the end of the era (Formula Three would take over in 1964), but the T65 still managed to take eight outright victories in major European races, though half of them were in private cars using Ford engines.

1964 and 1965: Formula Three takes over

Although Cooper records show that 20 Type 72 Formula Three Coopers were produced in 1964, a further 19 Type 76s in 1965, and a final seven Type 83s in 1966, the number of A-Series versions steadily decreased in favour of Ford/Cosworth MAE types, for the ever-practical Cooper organisation now offered both.

Compared with Formula Junior, which had been killed off in favour of Formula Three, the new models were inflicted with more severe restrictions to their engines. The latest Cooper cars – Type 72, as they were eventually listed – were simplified versions of the latest F1 chassis, and demonstrably so, but costs were cut wherever possible. The latest Type 72s had all-coil-spring independent suspensions, semi-stressed-skin chassis construction, and rocker-arm-style front suspension that allowed spring/damper units to be hidden inside the bodywork and out of the air stream.

New-for-1964 F3 regulations meant that the engine size was limited to 1.0-litre, and it had to run with just one single-choke carburettor. Although such new limitations must have been frustrating to Eddie Maher and his team in Coventry, they responded well. Basing the new power unit on the first of the more robust Mini-Cooper 970S/1071S power units (though not confirmed until

the new road car was announced), and using an SU carburettor, they evolved a new engine as follows:

Standard 1071S	*1,071cc, with 70.64mm bore x 68.26mm stroke*
1964 Formula Three engine	*997cc, with a 71.6mm bore x 61.9mm stroke.*

The reason for making changes to both bore and stroke, if only we had known it at the time, was that the 61.9mm stroke dimension was that of the still secret Mini-Cooper 970S road car power unit (it would be launched later in 1964), with the bore dimension slightly changed to make the engine as close to the 1,000cc limit as possible.

Although hampered by the compulsory use of a 36mm (1.42in) throttling inlet flange orifice, and a single SU HS6 carburettor, Morris Engines did a great job, and finalised a unit producing 88bhp at 7,750rpm. Complete with a light Hillman Imp-based transaxle, and weighing a mere 870lb (394kg), the Type 72 sold for just £1,740 complete, or a mere £1,325 if the customer wanted to supply his own engine and gearbox.

Ken Tyrrell was hired to run the quasi-works Cooper F3 team, his drivers being a youthful Jackie Stewart, and Warwick Banks. It was an amazingly successful partnership, for in that first season Stewart won no fewer than eleven F3 races, and Banks won once. As the history doyen of the Cooper team, Doug Nye, once wrote: 'The Tyrrell Racing Organisation was undoubtedly the best-prepared, best-organised and best-equipped team of that maiden F3 season, and it was to Cooper's immense benefit. Other individuals won other events in Europe, but it was Tyrrell and Stewart who made all the headlines.'

Even before the end of that season, Cooper had a replacement – the Type 76 – on the stocks. This was effectively an update of the Type 72, but unhappily it had nowhere near the success of the earlier car, for the A-Series engine was now stuck at its original power rating whereas that of the latest Cosworth-tuned Ford Anglia-based engines was still going up.

With Eddie Maher fully occupied with production car work, the Mini-Cooper S, saloon car racing and 'works' rally car operations as well, something else had to give – and this turned out to be the end of the F3 project. In the meantime Maher and a long-established contact of his – Geoff Healey – had been busy with road cars.

Sprites and Midgets on the racetracks

Until 1968, 'works' Sprites and Midgets raced all around the world – not only at Le Mans and in the Targa Florio in Italy, but also at Sebring in Florida. Through the 1960s BMC ensured that the Healey company, based in Warwick, was tasked with building, improving and developing the Sprites *and* the Midgets which appeared as 'works' or 'works'-backed cars, and that Eddie Maher of Morris Engines, at Courthouse Green in Coventry, should do much of the work on the engines themselves. Eddie's team worked repeated miracles, in offering basically production-type engines fitted with many tuning items, which lasted at high revs for improbable distances.

The Healey company regularly entered Sprites for the prestigious Le Mans 24 Hour race. This picture was taken in 1966, when a special-bodied Sprite was driven by Paddy Hopkirk and Andrew Hedges.

This is how the racing A-Series evolved in those years, and how the Healey/BMC effort at the Le Mans 24 Hour race progressed so far:

The first entry came in 1960, when a single prototype Sprite was prepared. Driven by John Colgate and John Dalton, this had a strange glass-fibre bodyshell by Falcon, and used a 996cc engine (64.5mm x 76.2mm) from Morris Engines, which produced just 63bhp at 6,300rpm. By comparison with what was to follow, that doesn't sound much, but knowledge of the engine's capabilities was still building up, and the team recognised that 24 hours of racing was a *very* long time. This effort was rewarded, with 16th place at 85.62mph and a well-earned class win.

In 1961 not one, but two different Sprites were entered – one by the Healey company, the other being loaned to the once-famous Edinburgh-based team of Ecurie Ecosse. The Healey car was a brand-new and very smart

fastback coupé, whereas the EC example was a 1961 Sebring 4-Hour race car with modified bodywork. Further development work at Morris Engines had resulted in identical engines with 73bhp, but there was no reward for this effort. The 'works' car retired with a holed piston (not even Geoffrey Healey ever discovered why) while the EC car crashed.

There was no entry in 1962, but in 1963 the team was back with a modified version of the smart coupé (a transverse rear spoiler was tried in practice), and a very special 1.1-litre engine. This was not, by any means, the standard-dimensioned 1100 type that had just been introduced to the road cars, but another carefully developed 'special' from Morris Engines. This engine had a 71.63mm bore and a 68.248mm stroke (which gave 1,100cc precisely), used a single Weber dual-choke carburettor and was actually based on the first of the Mini-Cooper 1071S cylinder blocks and heads.

By this time Eddie Maher's team had done much extra work. To quote Geoffrey Healey: 'These engines would run to high speeds with reliability, producing nearly 100bhp. They were both strong and amenable to tuning . . . In his attempts to get more power from the racing engines, Eddie Maher produced a variety of heads, including one very effective casting that had two separate exhaust ports for the middle two cylinders. We were able to fabricate exhaust manifolds with this feature, and as a result gained 3bhp.

The Healey company regularly entered Sprites for the prestigious Le Mans 24 Hour race. This picture was taken in 1966, when a special-bodied Sprite was driven by Paddy Hopkirk and Andrew Hedges.

Although this car was quick (it lapped Le Mans 30 seconds a lap faster than the 1961 example), driver Bob Olthoff unfortunately crashed it during the night while dazzled by photographers' flashing lights, and had to go to hospital for a time but soon recovered.

There was pressure to put up a better show in 1964, not only because the team cars had not finished in the previous three years but also because Triumph – the big rival in the sports car market – had entered three Spitfires, which were equipped with 98bhp/1,147cc engines. Although Triumph had no long-distance racing experience with these cars they looked efficient, seemed to be on a par with the Sprites and were in the same capacity class.

The Sprite itself was a developed version of that used in 1963, with modified coupé bodywork and with the same type of 1,100cc engine. Official figures showed that the latest car could lap in less than five minutes (101.21mph), and that it had a top speed down the Mulsanne straight of 135.5mph. The result was gratifying. Driven smoothly and sensibly by Clive Baker and Bill Bradley, the A-Series-engined Sprite finished 24th overall, a very consistent performance.

Because the Spitfires had proved to be alarmingly rapid, the Sprites had to be up-gunned for 1965. Not only was much work done during the winter in the wind tunnels (and much advice sought from aerodynamics experts), but the decision was taken to use the largest derivative of the A-Series power unit – the 1,293cc 'S', as progressively developed for rallying in the 'works' Mini-Coopers – with a special MGB-based five-speed gearbox to match. This engine was rated at 101bhp at 6,700rpm, and was fuelled by a single dual-choke Weber carburettor.

This was to be a fraught outing for the team, as there was a pre-event dispute with the organisers at scrutineering regarding the paint finish of the two cars, which were originally presented in a bright, almost fluorescent green scheme to make them more visible to faster cars but after much aggravation had to be repainted in a local workshop.

Even so, the two cars performed very well and consistently, circulating almost like high-speed trains, and although one of them broke its engine with a bang right in front of the pits, the other (driven by Paul Hawkins and John Rhodes) took 12th place, averaged 96.5mph, and roundly defeated the 1.15-litre Triumph Spitfires. Although there was no 1.3-litre class in this particular race, no such car finished up ahead of the gallant Sprite.

Although two updated Sprites (the same special coupé style, but now with twinned headlamps enclosed behind Perspex covers) were entered for 1966, their engines were really no different from the previous year, though on this occasion there was yet another transmission variation – the use of a four-speed MGB gearbox and its related Laycock overdrive, which effectively gave six forward speeds, and meant that the engine had a less hard time on the very long Mulsanne straight, where the cars could reach 130mph. Yet it was not a good year for the A-Series engine, as both power units let go after more than 19 hours, suffering broken connecting rods. The only consolation was that Longbridge, after examining the wrecked engines, concluded that they should make changes, and designed more robust rods to make sure that the problem never reoccurred, on either racing or road-car power units.

For 1967 there was just one Sprite at Le Mans, this being driven by Andrew Hedges and Clive Baker. As ever, the engine was built and prepared by Morris Engines in Coventry, and produced 105bhp at 7,000rpm with a compression ratio of 12.0:1, running with a single dual-choked Weber carburettor. Yet another variation on the transmission theme was that this year there was a five-speed derivative of the latest all-synchromesh MGB gearbox, with the fifth 'overdrive' ratio in a rear extension to the main casing.

This was the phenomenal year in which 600bhp 7.0-litre Fords were fighting for an outright win against 500bhp 4.0-litre Ferraris, so perhaps it was no surprise that at one stage Clive Baker's Sprite suffered some rear damage, a Ford being suspected of tripping over it. Even so, and in spite of needing an irritating pit stop to stabilise the damage, the gallant Sprite completed the 24 hours and finished 15th at a running average of 100.91mph – the very first time a Sprite had ever achieved this mark.

Then came 1968, the year when Healey last entered a Sprite for this classic endurance event. Although the organisers had altered the layout of the track to slow the cars down as they approached the pits, it was, of course, still advisable to have as much power as possible. Accordingly, for the last of its sleek coupé racers Healey consulted Lucas (and Morris Engines, of course), and was rewarded with a fuel-injected version of the 1,293cc A-Series engine. Not only that, but an early example of the cast iron eight-port cylinder head (as described in the

At Sebring in 1961, Stirling Moss (in the Sebring-bodied PMO200) and Bruce McLaren (in the standard-style frog-eye Sprite) took fifth and fourth overall in the Four-Hour race.

next chapter) was used, the result being that the engine produced no less than 110bhp at 7,200rpm, with more torque all the way up the rev range.

Because the injector nozzles were mounted in inlet trumpets that pointed, semi-downdraught fashion, at the cylinder head itself, it was necessary to add a 'power bulge' to the profile of the little car's bonnet. The result was an extremely effective racing power plant (which for shorter-distance races could have been super-tuned to 120bhp at around 7,500rpm). As Geoff Healey commented in one of his excellently-detailed books about the cars: 'This was a wonderful system which we should have had years before . . . This injection equipment on the Sprite engines worked faultlessly throughout some very long races. As far as the Sprite was concerned, this 1968 series of engines represents the peak of development. If we had continued racing the power would have been increased to over 120bhp.'

The proof of that pudding came in the 1968 race, when the injected car (driven by Roger Enever and Alec Poole) finished 15th, averaging 94.73mph on a slower circuit, and reaching almost 150mph when flat out. No more

proof regarding the worth of the amazing little A-Series engine was ever needed.

Apart from their regular visit to Le Mans, Healey somehow found time to send racing cars (Sprites and C-Series-engined Healey 3000s) to other classic events, notably the Targa Florio in Sicily, and the endurance races on the airfield at Sebring in Florida.

The first Sprite entry in the Targa Florio came in 1959, when Tommy Wisdom and French photographer Bernard Cahier took a Warwick-prepared car to the legendary Piccolo Circuito delle Madonie. In spite of a promising start, the unlucky duo's car suffered from a fuel spillage (from a spare can carried in the car!) and a broken throttle cable, but still managed to finish sixth in class: one development tweak to come out of this was that Healey never again used a standard cable, but instead substituted a modified motorcycle clutch cable to do the same job.

Five years later Healey went back to Sicily with a much more highly developed Sprite, this having a smoothly-shaped and lightweight body which would eventually form the basis of the Le Mans cars already described. Unhappily it broke an axle half-shaft partway through the first session. A year later a similar though further developed car, complete with a 1.3-litre A-Series engine and twin-choke Weber carburettor, went to Sicily, where it was allocated to Rauno Aaltonen and Clive Baker. This time there was a problem with a sticking front brake caliper, but the little

Sprite still managed 15th and second in class.

A year later again the same car became a coupé (registered EAC 90C), looking rather like the Le Mans machines, but faltered after Rauno hit a rock and deranged the rear suspension: third in class was no reward for a sterling effort. Then came 1967, when a brand-new 1,293cc-engined car was prepared, but Clive Baker crashed while trying to avoid a spectator who was running across the inadequately-policed road.

Two more Targa Florio entries followed, the 1968 event being contested in a brand-new car complete with Le Mans-type dry-sump 1,293cc engine, and five-speed gearbox (which boiled its engine), while the 1969 race was contested by another new car, which looked effectively like a Le Mans but rebuilt in strictly open style. Constructed for the very last of the 1,293cc Le Mans-style A-Series race engines, complete with a cast-iron eight port/ crossflow cylinder head, a dry sump installation and Lucas fuel injection, it had been ready for the 1969 Le Mans event but did not actually make the start, because Lord Stokes' hierarchy slashed the British Leyland motorsport effort to ribbons.

Healey also enjoyed regular trips to Florida for the races on the bumpy ex-airfield racetrack at Sebring during March every year, though fortunes were mixed. The first attempt, in 1959, for the Twelve-Hour race, was with three lightly-tuned (57bhp) 948cc-engined cars, which carried basically standard bodywork and used front-wheel disc brakes. To everyone's delight they took first, second and third in their class.

For 1960 there was a four-hour race for smaller-engined cars, which Geoff Healey was convinced the Sprite could win; so Stirling Moss was duly hired to drive a much-modified version of the 1959 Targa Florio machine. Without the need to change tyres, and to refuel, Stirling might, indeed, have won, but he actually finished a very close second to a very special Abarth. In the Twelve-Hour race a special Falcon fibreglass-bodied Sprite eventually won its class, in spite of blowing a cylinder head gasket at one stage, this having to be replaced by hard-working mechanics in front of the pits.

An even bigger effort was mounted for 1961, with two Sprites in the Twelve-Hour and three cars in the Four-Hour. In the Four-Hour, Sprites took third to eighth places inclusive, and in the Twelve-Hour one car managed 15th. It was a similar story in 1962, when four 998cc-engined cars contested the Four-Hour, and one started the Twelve-

Hour, with Stirling Moss' car third in the Four-Hour while the Twelve-Hour car suffered an engine failure (main bearing cap broken).

For the rest of the 1960s Healey made regular visits to Sebring, always having to labour against more specialised, low-production opposition. In 1963 and 1964 1,098cc-engined cars won their class; in 1966 and 1967 Le Mans-style 1,293cc cars also won their class, as did standard-style cars in 1968 and 1969. This was the point at which British Leyland's financial support dried up, and the Sprite's racing career came to an end.

Abingdon race and rally Midgets

While Healey worked its own magic, the 'works' competitions department at Abingdon was so busy with its larger cars, and later with its Minis, that it had little time or money to lavish on other A-Series-engined machines.

Even so, the Abingdon story really began in mid-1958, as soon as the Austin-Healey Sprite had been launched, when the company loaned out three new cars for use in the gruelling French Alpine rally, which were in virtually standard mechanical condition. Driving a car whose registration number (PMO 200) would soon become famous, John Sprinzel and Willy Cave won their capacity class, with team-mates Tommy Wisdom and Ray Brookes backing them up. The same car let the side down on the Liège-Rome-Liège marathon when a front stub axle failed, and the errant wheel made a bid for freedom in a nearby river! All three cars then tackled the 1959 Monte, when Sprinzel achieved 14th overall, but that was really the height of it all until the end of 1960, when Pat Moss finished second in the ladies' category of the end-of-year RAC rally.

Once Stuart Turner took over from Marcus Chambers as competitions manager in 1961, there was a change of emphasis. One of his first decisions was to order the building of three brand-new MG Midgets (this new model had been revealed earlier in the year), which were to be rallied in FIA Group 3 tune. This limited them to the use of 948cc engines, though their power outputs were progressively improved.

Two cars started the RAC rally in November, and although this event was totally unsuited to the cars (it was the first to see the use of long, rough and loose-surfaced Special Stages), one car (YRX 727, driven by Derrick Astle and Peter Roberts) won its class and finished a spirited eighth overall, with Mike Sutcliffe's sister-car close behind him.

Paul Hawkins and Timo Mäkinen shared this special-bodied Sprite in the 1966 Sebring Twelve-Hour race, winning their capacity class in spite of having to deal with a sub-tropical rainstorm at one point.

Peter Riley then drove the third car (YRX 747) in the 1962 Monte Carlo rally, winning his capacity class – and if the Mini-Coopers had not themselves looked so promising this might have been the signal for an even more ambitious programme. A year later the 'rallying Reverend' (Rupert Jones) won his class in the Monte Carlo rally, but that was really the end of the programme.

This is surely the right time to also mention the three extremely smart and successful Midgets built at Abingdon, two of which were prepared for London-based MG dealer Dick Jacobs' organisation for use in British and some European events, and one of which was raced by John Milne in Scotland. Not only was it the ever-improving technical specification that caught one's eye, but also the very attractive style of the closed coupés that evolved around the standard Midget bodyshell.

Jacobs, reputedly a great fan of the current Aston Martin DB4 body style, sketched up a similar fastback shape on the Midget, and somehow persuaded MG's John Thornley to approve the building of the cars at Abingdon. To quote my historian colleague Peter Browning: 'The new shape was

wind-tunnel tested, and with its lightweight construction contributed much to the cars' performance. Some 13bhp less was required to propel the little cars at 100mph.'

Many of the exterior body panels were fashioned from hand-beaten aluminium panels, along with the smart sweeping fastback coupé style (no opening boot lid, but who cared?) and an extended nose, the result being an extremely pretty little machine which weighed 342lb less than standard.

In that environment, a race-tuned A-Series engine could really perform well. In 1962 the cars ran with 948cc-type engines which were over-bored by 0.040in (as much as the Group 3 regulations allowed), this resulting in 972cc. Along with all the established state-of-the-art race equipment, this engine ran with a single horizontal dual-choke Weber 45 DCOE carburettor and produced about 75bhp. That, though, was only the beginning, for in the coming months the engines were enlarged again to 996cc (like those being used by the 'Warwick' cars). Soon after the Midget had progressed to Mk II (in October 1962, with a standard long-stroke 1,098cc engine), the Jacobs team got their hands on what were still rare, strengthened versions of the new engine, running with 1,139cc and unstated horsepower which must, nevertheless, have been around 85bhp.

There was yet more to come, though not in homologated

form, as the Midget did not receive another engine size boost until the end of 1966, by which time these pretty little cars were obsolete. However, once the Mini-Cooper S engine (already described) had reached 1,275cc, and all manner of astonishing horsepower figures were being achieved at Abingdon and at Morris Engines, the Jacobs team found many opportunities to run their cars in 'prototype' classes with race-tuned 1,293cc power units. Not only that, but in the later stages of development they were revamped to run with dry sump lubrication, which not only made them more reliable on very undulating circuits but also seemed to liberate a little more horsepower.

Once complete, the two new machines – 770 BJB and 771 BJB – started an intensive British racing programme, where they were invariably successful at class level, for even the 972cc-engined types could almost reach 120mph at 7,750rpm. One thing a race-tuned A-Series was never short of was revs!

In the next three seasons the Jacobs cars in particular were extremely successful, before being returned to Abingdon for refurbishment and for use as genuine 'works' cars in international motorsport in 1965. In that one season their outstanding performances were in the Targa Florio (Sicily) and the Bridgehampton 500 (USA).

Minis and Metros – A-Series for ever

Even as the 1970s opened, the A-Series' racetrack successes had not yet come to an end. However, because this was so closely connected with what had already been achieved in rallying I have added that particular story to the end of the next chapter. As we are about to see, in motorsport it took only five years for the Mini to progress from being hopelessly fragile and underpowered as an 850, to become a winning car in 1275S form and for that particular model to finally become a worldwide success – formidably fast, versatile and rugged, even though often seriously maltreated by teams and drivers expecting it to be reliable.

John Sprinzel's hard-working Sebring Sprite, PMO 200, with a highly-tuned A-Series engine, competed in the 1961 RAC rally, where it was driven by Vic Elford and Paul Hawkins. Incidentally, it's a small world: the co-driver in the 'works' Sunbeam Rapier standing behind the Sprite at this control is the author of this book . . .

CHAPTER 7

Minis: the all-conquering front-wheel-drive cars

ould the A-Series engine have been anything like as famous if it had not powered all the Minis that were produced from 1959 to 2000? Further, would it have been anything like as famous if the tiny front-wheel-drive car had not been so successful on the racetrack or in rallying, worldwide? I doubt it very much, and it is for this reason that I believe the motorsport exploits of the 'works' Minis (there is no space to cover every Mini, everywhere . . .) deserve a chapter all of their own.

The story began in 1959, as soon as the original Issigonis marvel appeared, and did not end until 1970, when the 'works' motorsport department was so brutally closed down by Lord Stokes' British Leyland regime.

In the early days few people thought that the original Mini would be successful in motorsport, for with just 34bhp from an 848cc A-Series engine it was not very fast, nor did it seem to have much potential. Clearly it was too slow to be an outright winner, and although its handling was quite superb this could not make up for the lack of power. Minis soon appeared in British rallies, where their handling and traction sometimes helped make up for their low-70s top speed, but clearly they couldn't cope with high mountain passes or with flat-out circuit racing.

Not that the 'works' motorsport department at Abingdon was really interested in the new car. As team manager Marcus Chambers later noted in the book *BMC Competitions Department Secrets*: 'A Mini 850 was delivered . . . It stayed in the car park for several days,

nobody rushed to drive it. Indeed, Dougie Watts recalled that one lunchtime he needed to pop into town, and looked around for a car. Dougie walked over to the Mini . . . and then changed his mind. He took a Healey instead.'

Even so, BMC's sales departments urged Abingdon to develop 'works' cars, which, though reluctantly at first, they duly did. Although the newfangled front-wheel-drive transmissions (the A30-based cluster which effectively lived 'in the sump' of the transversely-mounted A-Series engine) proved to be infuriatingly weak after the engines had been power tuned, the frailty of the original-spec steel wheels was another hazard.

Because FIA homologation rules meant that the existing Mini-type single-SU carburettor and cast manifolds had to be retained, and even though Weslake (and later Don Moore) modified heads were employed, it was difficult to extract much more than 50bhp from the 848cc engine, though this was often enough to chew up oil seals and clutches in the transmission. With tiny Dunlop racing tyres fitted to standard wheels on race circuits it was soon obvious that the front wheels would crack up around the studs, and this duly happened in full view of the public in the 750 Motor Club's Six-Hour Relay race!

The very first 'works' rally entry was by Marcus Chambers (a large man in a small car!), with engineer/ex-racing driver/ex-test pilot Peter Wilson alongside him, in the Norwegian Viking rally of September 1959, where it finished 51st overall. There was really no shame in this performance, for

Probably the first-ever Mini rallying victory came in late 1959. Enthusiasts like when David Hiam drove this 850 – registered 16 BOJ – to great success.

the 848cc engine probably put out no more than 40bhp, Marcus could charitably be called 'portly', while Peter Wilson was a rangy 6ft 3in tall. In fact the first home win went to Pat Moss/Stuart Turner in the Knowldale CC's Mini Miglia rally in the same year (where much of the success was due to Turner's navigational skills), and it took time even to gain class wins at International level.

There was no success in any of the first entries – 1959, RAC or Portugal, 1960 Monte, Geneva, Tulip or Acropolis – mainly because the little Minis were quite outpaced by the 'works' Saab 96s. Tom Gold then broke the ice with a plucky class win in the French Alpine (high passes and all), while in November David Seigle-Morris and Mike Sutcliffe finished sixth and eighth overall in the RAC rally. That, though, was almost the height of it, for in 1961 there was only one more class victory (by Peter Riley, in the Tulip rally) to add to this score.

Even so, the point had been made – that no matter how valiantly these nimble little cars were to be driven, the combination of lower power and torque, limited ground

clearance (which didn't help on rough rallies) and the problem of getting enough traction from the ten-inch diameter wheels was always going to be insuperable.

It was also a fact that the regulations surrounding motorsport (especially those connected with the 'homologation' – or official approval – of the cars which could be used) was a real limiting factor with these 848cc-engined machines. Marcus Chambers' deputy, Bill Price, has repeatedly pointed out that his job, as the man who had to deal with the homologation of every BMC car, was closely limited by the standard specification of the cars being produced at Abingdon, Cowley and Longbridge at the time. It was all very well, for instance, for a private owner to suggest that *his* 848cc-engined car could go much faster than the 'works' machines, since he was probably using an engine with twin SU carburettors, different manifolds and a different type of camshaft, none of which were allowed by the regulations that applied to International events.

Although the 'works' Abingdon Competitions Department gave no direct financial support to the original Mini 850 racing cars there was definite support, technical advice, a supply of engine tuning parts and the latest heavy-duty chassis components for those privateers who wished to race.

Although it was quite unexpected, Sir John Whitmore used his own ex-works 850 to win the BRSCC British Saloon Car Championship outright in 1961 – not by winning races, but by consistently winning the 1.0-litre capacity class and using the marking systems to his best advantage: this, don't forget, was *before* the Mini-Cooper was launched. It was at this time that the legendary Whitmore sideways-driving technique was first seen.

All this, of course, was small beer compared with what was to follow. When the Mini-Cooper arrived, Abingdon's interest in the little front-wheel-drive car perked up considerably.

Cooper and Cooper S in motorsport: 1961 to 1964, the learning years

Two important events changed the motorsport scene at Abingdon in the autumn of 1961. One was that the original Mini-Cooper was announced; the other was the arrival of a new, young and ambitious competitions manager, Stuart

Turner. Not only was the Cooper eminently suitable for use in races and rallies (its 997cc A-Series engine at the upper end of the capacity class), but Turner was ruthlessly ambitious and determined to make it so.

Almost immediately Turner decided on a two-prong strategy – that Abingdon would concentrate entirely on rallying (which, because he had been a successful co-driver, was Turner's first love), while works-assisted motor racing of Mini-Coopers in saloon car events would be contracted out, originally to the Cooper Car Co and later to Ken Tyrrell as well.

'Works' rally cars

Starting in 1962, and in spite of the fact that it used a long-stroke engine, the 997cc Mini-Cooper immediately became a winner. Though Rauno Aaltonen's entry in the

The 'works' competitions department at Abingdon was full of a range of cars in the early 1960s. In 1962, A-Series engines were to be used in the Mini-Coopers and the 1100 being prepared at this moment.

Monte ended in a fiery crash, that formidable young lady Pat Moss fell in love with her new car (737 ABL), not only by winning the Tulip and German rallies, but also winning the European Ladies' Championship too. By the end of the year Turner had decided to build up a new fleet of Mini-Coopers in place of the hotchpotch of 850s, Austin A40 Farinas and Minor 1000s that his predecessor had favoured, and the strategy worked well. By that time, of course, he and John Cooper had already persuaded Sir George Harriman to back the introduction of the very special series of 'S' engines, starting with the 1,071cc car.

Using 997cc-engined Mini-Coopers, Rauno Aaltonen took fifth on the 1962 RAC rally, and then a magnificent third in the 1963 Monte, with Paddy Hopkirk sixth. Paddy then took second overall in the Tulip (only a monstrous and very special 4.2-litre Ford Falcon could outpace him), but it was

in the hot, often high and always demanding French Alpine rally that Rauno got his hands on the very first 1,071cc-engined Mini-Cooper S and astonished the rallying world by winning the entire Touring category outright.

Three months later Paddy Hopkirk and Henry Liddon shared another brand-new 1071S (33 EJB) to finish third overall in the Touring Car Category of the ten-day Tour de France. The French were livid, for up to that time this high-profile event was almost understood to be the shop window for their own products. Almost from that day forward, in fact, Abingdon lost all interest in improving the 997cc car any further and would never even take a later 998cc car on to the strength.

They were wise. Not only did Paddy finish fourth in the RAC rally (in 1071S 8 EMO) but two months after that, in the never-to-be-forgotten Monte Carlo rally of 1964, he won the event outright in 33 EJB. Although, on the treacherous ice and snow of Southern France, his wasn't quite the fastest car of all he was consistently nearly there, and a favourable 'handicap' (where engine size was a factor) helped him beat the 4.7-litre Falcons which might otherwise have prevailed.

The Mini-Cooper S was already a successful rally car in 1963, but when Paddy Hopkirk took it to an unprecedented third place overall, on handicap, in the Tour de France of that year, it caused a sensation. The self-same combination – Paddy plus 33 EJB – went on to win the Monte Carlo rally, outright, in 1964.

Is this the most famous A-Series-powered car of all time? Paddy Hopkirk's 1964 Monte-winning Mini-Cooper 1071S on show after its famous victory.

Paddy Hopkirk and Henry Liddon stand proudly with their Mini-Cooper 1071S, 33 EJB, as they collect their prizes for winning the Monte Carlo rally in 1964.

Famous faces – five of them human, and one of them a motor car: 33 EJB, the Mini-Cooper 1071S which had just won the 1964 Monte Carlo rally, being admired by (left to right) Bill Appleby, Daniel Richmond, John Cooper, Charles Griffin and Alec Issigonis.

In 1964 the Mini-Cooper S was already a well-balanced little rally car, the 1,071cc engine helping it to be torquey, responsive and ideal for every condition, especially the snow and ice of the Monte Carlo rally.

Two views of a rally-prepared 1275S engine from the mid-1960s, showing the special HT leads and the 16-bladed cooling fan. Those were still the days when an old-style dynamo, not an alternator, provided electricity.

This was the first of a string of Cooper S outright victories in International rallies that would make the little car immortal. Nevertheless, the avalanche of Cooper S rally wins was only just getting under way, and there was still more to come from the valiant A-Series engine. Not only that, but A-Series race experience could be used in rally engines, and vice versa. It was the perfect way for an engine to reach its maturity.

Abingdon then entered its very first 1275S-engine car (AJB 66B) in the Tulip rally of April/May 1964, where Timo Mäkinen gave it a memorable debut victory. Fourth overall for Rauno Aaltonen in the French Alpine rally, and fourth for Timo in the 1000 Lakes, added to the success of the 1275S in its first season – but the best was yet to come.

'Works'-supported racing cars: rapid progress, 1962 to 1964

No sooner had the 997cc Mini-Cooper been put on sale, and gained FIA homologation, than BMC contracted the Cooper Car Co to campaign cars on its behalf in the BRSCC British Saloon Car Championship. Recognisable from the very start by their glossy green finish, and the two broad fore-aft stripes painted on the extremes of the bonnet, two smart and very agile cars (one driven by John Love, the other by Sir John Whitmore) dominated their 1.0-litre class, though Christabel Carlisle, driving a privately-financed car which had been prepared by Don Moore, astonished everyone else with her pace and flair.

Daniel Richmond

Although much more is written elsewhere here, especially in the section covering the A-Series' successes in motorsport, it is worth separately summarising Daniel Richmond's career before and during his links with the A-Series engine.

Born of well-to-do parents in 1927 (his father, Sir Daniel Richmond, worked in the Indian Forest Service, and his mother was the daughter of Sir James Davy), he originally worked with British European Airways, then set up a tiny garage business in Downton, a village in Wiltshire, close to Salisbury. It was there that he started working on various exotic cars – Rolls-Royce, Bugatti and Lagonda among them – which were owned by his chums in the Vintage Sports Car Club.

Notably eccentric in his lifestyle (his general appearance was of the 'unmade-bed' variety) and habits (which seemed to revolve around sloth, strong drink, and fishing), he also became an acknowledged genius in the black art of cylinder head breathing and combustion chamber design. By the 1950s he seemed able to extract unlikely amounts of power from any engine put in front of him, but it was his work on the little A-Series, allied to the Mini, which eventually made him world-famous.

First with the Mini, then the Mini-Cooper, and finally with the 1275S, he helped to make the little front-wheel-drive cars faster and more capable than seemed credible. His friendship with Mini designer Alec Issigonis led to him becoming an official consultant to BMC at Longbridge for years up until 1970. He also worked his very successful magic not only on the A-Series but on other engines in the BMC range, and some of his suggestions were later applied to mass-production power units. By that time, too, he was supplying performance conversions to customers all around the world, so that Downton Engineering grew to employ up to 80 staff.

Unhappily for Richmond, he became one of the victims of the notorious Stokes/British Leyland cull of 1970, where several famous consultants (who also included John Cooper and Donald Healey) were fired to save on royalty payments and fees. This was a doctrinaire and stupid decision that not only cost British Leyland much credibility, but denied them access to much valuable engineering and marketing expertise.

Thus rebuffed, Richmond gradually withdrew from business reality, fished and sulked much more than he worked, and was felled by a heart attack in 1974. He was only 47 years old.

She said she didn't know how fast she was going, and played the wide-eyed novice to perfection.

In 1962, although a fleet of Jaguar 3.8-litre Mk IIs were habitual outright race winners, John Love's 997cc 'Cooper Cooper' comfortably won his class enough times, for no other 1.0-litre competitor could match the pace of this little front-wheel-drive car. Although it was not quite the same story again in 1963 (by that time Ford had latched on to the 'homologation special' business, producing the Lotus-Cortina), John Whitmore used 997cc, then 1,071cc Minis to win his capacity class on most occasions, and to take second in the Championship; Paddy Hopkirk backed him up all the way.

Things then got even more serious in 1964. In Britain, not only had Ford rolled out a mass of Lotus-Cortinas (F1 World Champion Jim Clark drove one) and 7.0-litre Galaxies, but BMC had reacted with the formidable little 100bhp-plus 1275S Minis for the 1.3-litre class. Clark's Lotus-Cortina was powerful enough to win several races outright, but John Fitzpatrick's 1275S easily won the 1.3-litre category and took second in the Championship.

Meantime, BMC had also hired Ken Tyrrell's team to run two works-supported Mini-Cooper S types in the European Saloon Car Championship, once again with an eye to winning their class and taking best advantage of the favourable class marking position. Warwick Banks, John Rhodes and the Belgian driver Julien Vernaeve all drove them. The result was that Warwick Banks easily won his class *and* the European Championship. The Mini racing phenomenon was really on a roll.

High tide in motorsport: a winning streak

Between 1964 and 1967 the A-Series-powered Mini-Cooper 1275S became the most successful competition car in Europe. No matter how its rivals tried to measure success by their own standards, the fact is that front-wheel-drive Minis won more races and rallies than any of their rivals. Whether these were 'works' rally cars or 'works-backed' racing cars, and often if they were well-prepared and supported privately-owned cars, a Mini could keep up with, and often defeat, some of the most powerful competition cars in Europe.

'Works' rally cars – 1964 to 1966

After 1964, and when the 1275S had gone into series production – more importantly, after the 'works' team and serious engine builders had learned how to super-tune the engines *and* keep the much-improved transmissions in one piece – this was an incredibly capable machine.

By 1965, when Abingdon had brought a rival sports car, the Austin-Healey 3000, to the peak of its development, it was astonishing to see that the 1275S could often outpace even that car on special stages. The 2.9-litre 'Big Healey' (as it was always affectionately known) was certainly faster on tarmac stages, or on a racetrack, but the fully-developed 1275S was often faster on all but the roughest of loose-surface special stages. Not only that, but if it broke (or, whisper it softly, if the driver damaged it . . .), mechanics found that they could re-fettle it faster and more effectively than the Healey.

Even so, Abingdon had to treat these cars as consumables, for in the hands of their superstar drivers – Paddy Hopkirk, Timo Mäkinen, Rauno Aaltonen and Tony Fall – they were usually driven so hard that they took a terribly battering. Between 1964 and 1967, fleets of Mini-Cooper S types were prepared and re-prepared to do battle. Peter Browning's excellent book *The Works Minis* shows that no fewer than 37 brand-new, and different, identities (by registration number) were employed. Not only that, but (as is well known) any rally car that had a particularly hard time was re-shelled more than once. I have no doubt that more than 100 different 'cars' were used in that period. Sometimes more than one example of a particular 'identity' is claimed to have survived – and all their latter-day owners may have a point.

Over time, incidentally, there seemed to be no settled policy to cover the use of 'Austin' or 'Morris' identities, which reflected the conflict that still existed within BMC between the historic Austin and Morris factions. Along with the geographic location of some events, this conflict sometimes depended on the influence and importance of the importer or dealer chain in that country. Some particular 'works' cars changed their individual badge identities at least once during their lives, and there are recorded instances of matters being in such chaos that

'Austin' and 'Morris' badging (at front, rear and on the steering wheel horn push) *both* appeared on the same car, at the same time, on the same event.

Except on very rare occasions (when there was particular kudos or valuable class and financial bonuses to be gained), the 970S was not used in rallying. Once the last of the 997cc Mini-Coopers had been pensioned off, almost every Abingdon entry was a 1275S. Although it was BMC marketing policy to push the merits of Hydrolastic ('wet') suspension at this time, a surprising number of these 'works' Minis were still used in old-style rubber/'dry' form, or had suitable screw-down taps placed out of sight (under the rear seat cushion) so that the fore-aft transfer of Hydrolastic fluid could be arrested.

Team manager Stuart Turner once described Timo Mäkinen's great Monte victory of 1965 as the 'drive of the century', for the way in which he dominated the event in blizzard conditions.

As with the policy on badging, a 'works' car might be 'wet' at one point of its career and 'dry' at another, for both layouts were homologated, and there was no important packaging problem in swapping one system for the other. A driver's own preferences were always taken into account when cars were being prepared or allocated, and since there was no such thing as a dedicated 'Paddy' or 'Timo' car this could make preparation and re-preparation even more complex.

Rally regulations, too, had an influence on how a car was prepared. Some events (like the notorious Monte of 1966, where the Minis were blatantly cheated out of a deserved victory by chauvinistic organisers) were run for Group 1 – showroom standard – machines, which meant that very few improvements were allowed. Others ran to Group 2 rules, where all the team's homologated extras, including 100/110bhp 1,293cc engines, straight-cut gearboxes, Minilite wheels, special seats and a host of special pieces could all be employed.

Where there was any advantage to be gained, the same cars might be entered in Group 3 (Grand Touring) or even in Group 6 (Prototype) guise, where exotic and non-homologated items such as aluminium or glass-fibre body panels and Perspex side and rear windows could all be employed, and where surplus weight could be ruthlessly pared away. For all these reasons, therefore, it is quite impossible to respond to the question 'What goes into a "works" Mini?' – and it also makes it difficult to identify or authenticate the hulk of a neglected old 'barn find' that may be claimed as a long-lost, now-rediscovered 'works' rally car.

Some of the famous victories have become legendary among Mini fans – Monte Carlo in 1965 and 1967 being

perfect examples – but Timo Mäkinen's disqualification from the 1966 event (after he had won it 'on the road') also has its own corner in the Mini Hall of Fame. That was an occasion when the organisers were widely accused of favouring French cars to win the 'showroom' category event by devising very constrictive regulations, and when the scrutineers clutched at any straw (in this case the use of single-filament quartz-iodine headlamp bulbs) to make sure that the Minis were excluded.

Each and every superstar driver won several major international events outright, though it was only Rauno Aaltonen who was suitably stage-managed by BMC to win the European Rally Championship of 1965, with five outright victories in that season alone. Timo Mäkinen was widely accepted as the world's fastest driver in this period, but was also hardest on his cars, which explains a number of his retirements. Aaltonen, on the other hand, was the most analytical, and would sketch out desired

We wuz robbed . . . Timo Mäkinen and this showroom-tune 1275S completely dominated the 1966 Monte Carlo rally, but were later disqualified on trumped-up charges regarding headlamp specifications.

modifications to his car on any white surface available – which on one famous occasion was the white tablecloth of a restaurant where he was having dinner!

The 'works' Minis deserved to win more than one RAC rally (Aaltonen in 1965, defeating Mäkinen's Healey 3000 in a straight fight on snowy stages) and more than two French Alpines (Paddy's win in 1967 was a famous victory in a Group 6 car), though it was surely asking too much for Aaltonen to tackle the incredibly demanding 1967 East African Safari in a 1275S (supplied with its own on-board pump-up kit for the Hydrolastic suspension).

During his time at Abingdon, it was team boss Stuart Turner who helped bring these cars to the peak of their powers, and when he moved on in January 1967 it was Peter Browning who so capably took over until the last-

ever 'works' Minis were rallied in 1970.

'Works-supported' race cars – 1964 to 1967

After the 1964 European Saloon Car Championship success which, frankly, was not expected, Abingdon's contracted teams found themselves coming under more and more pressure from rivals driving the 'homologation specials' which had been introduced by teams that saw how the regulations could be exploited. Such cars, whether in the Mini-Cooper classes or not, were also built with class domination in mind, and often had very different engines from their standard relatives – usually much more special that the S-derivative of the long-established A-Series.

Revenge is sweet – after the disqualification of 1966, BMC returned to Monte Carlo in 1967, where Rauno Aaltonen won the event in this 1275S. It was the Mini's third success – really its fourth in four years.

John Rhodes was one of the most spectacular of all Mini-Cooper racing drivers. His Cooper Car Co machines had a phenomenal appetite for front tyres, but he never seemed to use any brakes.

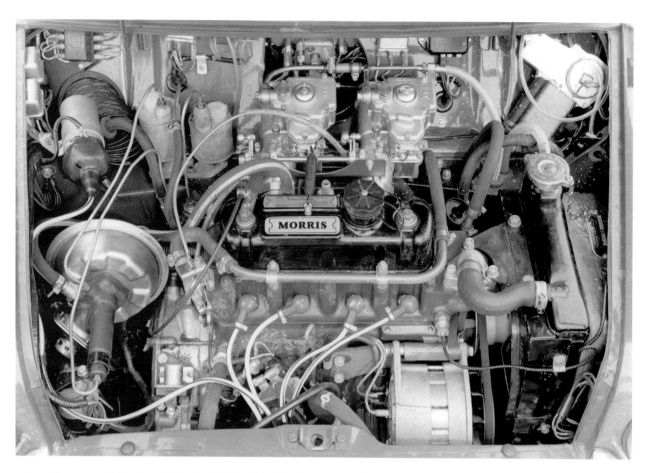

For this reason Abingdon decided to husband its funds, and to concentrate on the British series, with occasional forays to important overseas events. This explains why three 'works' Mini-Cooper S cars were sent out to Sebring in Florida in March 1965, where Warwick Banks/Paddy Hopkirk (whose car had fuel feed problems) finished closely behind a class-winning ex-Broadspeed car.

In Britain, in 1965, the Cooper Car Co cars were driven by John Rhodes (1,300cc class) and Warwick Banks (1,000cc class), whose main class opposition came from the privately-financed Broadspeed machines (driven by John Fitzpatrick and John Handley). After a ding-dong battle with the Superspeed 1.3-litre Ford Anglias, Rhodes won his class that year, while Banks easily won the 1.0-litre category and took second place overall in the series. This was a season, incidentally, when the Broadspeed cars sometimes proved to be faster than the Cooper Car Co machines, which was embarrassing. Fortunately for the factory, this situation did not persist into 1966 as Broadspeed then defected, to campaign Ford Anglias instead!

For 1966, and under pressure from manufacturers who

In an effort to squeeze the last bit of power and torque from a rally-prepared 1,275cc engine while still complying with international rally regulations, the 'works' team at Abingdon evolved this power unit, where two much-modified Weber carburettors (using only one of the twin venturis in each case) were employed on the 1968 Monte Carlo rally. Although it was a successful experiment there was controversy, so they were not used again. (*Jon Pressnell*)

were rivals to BMC, the BRSCC changed its Championship regulations completely, in effect relaxing all manner of restrictions. Henceforth the racing would be under FIA Group 5 regulations, which was effectively a free formula in that the original bodyshell and the original engine cylinder block had to be retained, but almost everything else on or in the cars could be changed. This meant that poorly specified cars like the Ford Anglia and Anglia Super 1200 could benefit enormously, while well-developed road cars like the 1275S had little to gain.

In 1966, as it happens, the 1,300cc class featured a season-long points battle between John Rhodes' Cooper Car Co 1275S and John Fitzpatrick's 1.0-litre Broadspeed

Somehow or other, it was just possible to modify the familiar twin-choke Weber carburettor so that only one venturi was working, then fix two of them to a 1275S engine for rallying. The gain, they say, was not more than 5bhp – but worth having.

Ford Anglia. At the end of the year both cars ended up at the top of the listings with the same number of points, but the 1275S, whose engine used a single twin-choke Weber carburettor (instead of twin SUs) and had about 120bhp from its Downton-tuned power unit, was clearly close to the peak of its development in that form.

By this time Rhodes' driving methods – which seemed to be to ignore the brake pedal almost completely, to throw the car sideways before the corner, to lay a dense smoke screen from the spinning front wheels as he negotiated the corner, and to blind his rivals – was becoming legendary. Nothing that Dunlop could do would reduce the tyre smoke, but as Rhodes only wanted a cover to last for about one hour of racing (and he wasn't paying the bills . . .), he wasn't at all worried about tyre wear.

A year later Rhodes still retained his mastery of the 1.3-litre class, helped along by the use of Lucas fuel

injection instead of a carburettor, but with the Group 5 Superspeed Anglias now developing about 145bhp it was beginning to be a real struggle. Even so, he triumphed by sheer consistency, won his capacity class and took third overall in the Championship. Lucas certainly knew a lot about fuel-injecting A-Series engines, as has also been made clear in connection with the experience of Austin-Healey Sprites in circuit racing. For 1968, though, it really would be 'deep breath' time, for Broadspeed was expected to be running new-generation, state-of-the-art Escort 1300s.

Even so, when BMC merged with Leyland Motors in January 1968 to form British Leyland, Abingdon could have had no idea of the huge impact it would have on their race and rallying activities. Soon after the merger was formalised British Leyland set out on a rationalisation programme, and it was made clear that *all* the corporation's marques – including Rover and Triumph – should be considered for future motorsport programmes.

Fortunately for Peter Browning and the Cooper Car Co, by the time this edict came down plans for the 1968 season were already in place. It was pure coincidence, however,

The joint enterprise of Eddie Maher at BMC's Engines Branch at Courthouse Green, and Harry Weslake, produced this fuel-injected cast-iron crossflow eight-port head, which was eventually homologated and used in BMC cars as various as 'works' Mini-Cooper S and Austin-Healey Sprite Le Mans racing cars. Very few of these heads now survive.

that this was the year in which the 1275S was gradually overhauled by new opposition, principally from Ford. In 1969, with British Leyland's antipathy to competing anywhere in which they could not almost guarantee success, all 'works' programmes would be slashed.

Although there were no more outright rally wins to celebrate in 1968, the 1275S was still ultra-competitive. Third on the Monte Carlo (Aaltonen), third on the Tulip (Vernaeve) and second on the Scottish (Ytterbring) all proved this, but with Abingdon concentrating on preparing 1800s for the Safari and the London-Sydney Marathon this was a restricted programme.

Apart from Paddy Hopkirk's second overall in the Circuit of Ireland, and a fine class win in the Tour de France, there would be no 'works' rally entries at all in 1969. Lord Stokes' advisers made sure that Abingdon committed itself instead to racing and rallycross, where the crowds were larger and the expenses were reduced.

Invented in the late 1960s to help TV fill its schedules on wet Saturday afternoons, rallycross – a cross between autocross (cars competing on loose surfaces on their own) and racing (small grids on mixed surfaces) – was soon attracting large audiences. Where traction and handling mattered, stripped-out 1275S types driven by heroes like Hugh Wheldon and 'Jumping Jeff' Williamson

became very popular.

As part of Lord Stokes' 'win where the public can see you doing it' policy, Abingdon was directed to enter cars in the ITV Winter series of 1968–69. At first handicapped by a total lack of preparation experience in this fledgling sport, the team provided John Rhodes and John Handley (racing drivers on dirt – whatever next!) with ever-improving cars. The first victory came in April 1969, and in the end Rhodes' consistency provided second overall in the Championship series; but this was an experiment which was not repeated in the future.

In and around all this, Eddie Maher's inventive little development team at Morris Engines in Coventry (along with some advice from Weslake) had tackled the one basic problem that still afflicted the A-Series racing cars: the layout of the original-shape five-port cylinder head. Working within the parameters of the existing 1275S cylinder block, they developed a brand-new, cast-iron, crossflow eight-port cylinder head – in which four inlet ports exited to the other side (in other words, facing forward in the Mini installation) – and linked this to the use of Lucas fuel injection.

Because FIA Group 5 regulations applied in the British Touring Car Championship series (where such alternative, non-homologated, cylinder heads could be used) in 1968, for the first time, this was an encouraging period for the

In the late 1960s, Jim Whitehouse of Equipe Arden designed and developed a phenomenal eight-port crossflow cylinder head in cast aluminium, which allowed the 970S race engine to produce up to 115bhp. This engine, in this car, brought the British Saloon car Championship to Alec Poole in 1969.

racing teams. As ever, the Cooper Car Co ran the 'official' 1275S racing team (John Rhodes and Steve Neal were the drivers), while there was also support for John Handley's British Vita-prepared 970S in the European Championship.

Handley's experience, allied to British Vita's preparation skills, saw this friendly little team not only win their class but – due to the marking system – also win the European Championship outright, though they could not use the eight-port heads as the rules were different. For the Cooper Car Co, however, it was more of an uphill struggle. Even though they had been equipped with the Lucas fuel-injected 1,293cc eight-port engines, which produced about 130bhp, Rhodes and Neal had to fight a running battle with Broadspeed's 145bhp/1.3-litre Ford Escort GTs. If the Fords had been more reliable the battle would have been even tougher, but the good news for Abingdon was that John Rhodes once again won the 1.3-litre Championship class and finished third overall in the series.

This was the point at which Lord Stokes' management team withdrew all financial support from contracted teams, and from Downton Engineering. Not only was Abingdon (which specialised in rallying) then directed to go motor racing – something it had never done with Minis, and which it would therefore have to learn from scratch – but it was also obliged to compete head-on with the Cooper Car Co team, which had been reborn as Cooper-Britax-Downton.

Still using eight-port-headed cars (and occasionally larger bore/shorter stroke 'specials') throughout 1969, John Rhodes and John Handley (Abingdon) fought head-to-head against C-B-D (Gordon Spice and Steve Neal) *and* against the Broadspeed Escorts. Honours were split between the teams, with the most successful driver (Spice) finishing second in the 1.3-litre class. It took Abingdon until late summer to make up for a total lack of previous experience, but it all came right at the Austrian Salzburgring in October, when Rhodes and Handley took first and second overall in a tightly contested 1.3-litre race.

Amazingly, however, while all this brotherly fighting was going on a private team, Equipe Arden, had built up and developed its own variety of eight-port 970S, which had their own privately-developed design of aluminium eight-port/crossflow cylinder head designed and developed by Jim Whitehouse and Norman Seeney, and used TJ

(Tecalemit-Jackson) fuel injection. This was stretched to 999cc, and by the standards of its 1.0-litre class produced quite phenomenal horsepower – claimed at 115bhp – and had the ability to reach 10,000rpm if pushed.

Alec Poole drove this car, to concentrate on the British Touring Car Championship, where he completely obliterated his opposition and won the series outright. In a 12-round series, where class, as opposed to outright, performance mattered so much this nimble, shrieking little Mini won its capacity class seven times, and finished second three times more.

It all looked very promising for the early 1970s, except that the RAC then changed its own rules and effectively banned such ultra-special machines from the circuits in future years. Alec Poole recalls that the Equipe Arden car was eventually turbocharged ('it produced about 190bhp, and was seriously quick'), but it could only be used in club racing.

In the end both the eight-port cylinder heads (cast iron and aluminium) were made available, and sold at high prices. Though they were homologated as from 1 January 1970 this was really too late, as the front-wheel-drive Mini was no longer quite competitive enough against its more modern rivals.

1970: The last 'works' Minis in rallying

Before the motorsport department at Abingdon was abruptly closed down (by diktat of British Leyland management) in the autumn of 1970, there was time for a final handful of Mini-Cooper rally entries to be made. However, because the department was otherwise almost completely bound up with the preparation of Triumph 2.5PI and Austin Maxi cars for the monumental 16,000-mile *Daily Mirror* World Cup Rally, these did not even begin until April.

Even so, and first of all in the 'Mini season', for the World Cup rally Abingdon prepared a highly-tuned and very non-standard A-Series-engined 1275GT. Realistically, no one thought that a Mini could possibly survive such a rough-and-tough six-week test, so the intention was always for the Handley/Easter car to be a 'hare', and to take a few headlines before it expired. Unhappily, that breakdown duly came in the first few days, in Italy, when the highly-tuned engine began to suffer from fuel supply problems and blew a piston.

Weeks later, and having been re-prepared to run in 'prototype' form in the Scottish rally, the same 1275GT was urged into second place overall by Paddy Hopkirk, this actually being the last ever rally finish to be recorded by a 'works' Mini of any type in the UK.

The management axe fell later in the year, and the last 'works' Mini of all – a 1275S driven by Brian Culcheth – started the Australian Rally of the Hills in November 1970 and finished fourth overall. Thereafter it was private owners who carried on using Minis for some years, both in rallies and on the circuits.

A-Series rallying in Marinas

Although the idea of competing for outright victories in rallies in the Morris Marina fell into the 'high hopes' category, Abingdon eventually made sure that A-Series- or B-Series-engined 'works' cars, driven by Brian Culcheth, were at least credible. Such Marinas won their 1.3-litre capacity class in Britain's RAC rally of 1971, and even managed an excellent second overall in the hot, rough and tough Cyprus rally of 1972, but they could not be expected to beat the 'homologation specials' of the day.

One intriguing 'might-have-been', which (as far as the author can gather) never got beyond the testing stage, came from Eddie Maher's enthusiastic team at Courthouse Green, who produced what must be the ultimate in Weslake-type eight-port-head engines for use in the Marina, though test-bed work was carried out at Longbridge.

The base engine was a 1,293cc unit, complete with a cast iron eight-port head (as homologated for the Mini-Cooper S), with a 12.5:1 compression ratio. The camshaft was an AEG 599 type, with 320° profiles (and 60°-55°-80°-95° opening and closing points), and carburation of the most effective version was by four motorcycle-type Amals. Peak power was 116bhp at 7,150rpm (Amals) or 118bhp at 7,250rpm (twin 45DCOE Webers).

Metros in touring car racing

In the 1970s and 1980s, success in Britain's premier racing series for saloons depended on the regulations that were being applied. From 1974 to 1982 FIA Group 1 rules were followed, but with so many performance-raising allowances that they were nicknamed 'Group 1½'. Since Championship points were also awarded on a capacity class basis, it also meant that an A-Series-engined Mini racing car might (just might) be competitive.

Because British Leyland allocated all its budget to

After a great deal of development, Eddie Maher's team at Courthouse Green concluded that the combination of an eight-port cylinder head with four motorcycle-type Amal carburettors gave the most power ever developed in the 1,275cc A-Series engine. With more than 120bhp recorded, this was a formidable little power unit.

Triumph Dolomite Sprints and Jaguar XJCs, no corporate money was available for a Mini programme – and in any case, the Cooper S had dropped out of production and was no longer eligible. However, by 1977 Richard Longman (an ex-Downton engine builder who had started his own business, and was also a successful racing driver)

had found enough backing to race a Mini 1275GT, even though that production car only had an engine fuelled by a single SU carburettor.

Because there was such vigorous competition in all the classes, the destination of the 1977 Trophy was in doubt up to the very last round at Brands Hatch. If Longman had had the use of a Mini-Cooper S things might have been different, but even so, his battles with Bernard Unett's 'works' Avenger GT1300 were stirring. As commentator/journalist Robin Bradford later commented (having watched the ongoing contest throughout the season): 'Time and again the green-and-white Avenger and the blue Mini would come out of a corner with

Before the turbocharged Metro became available, several entrants raced normally-aspirated MG Metros in the British Touring Car Championship. Car number 77 was driven by Richard Longman, the ex-Downton employee/engine builder who probably knew more about A-Series power-tuning than anyone else in the business.

less than a coat of paint separating them, and these two provided some of the most exciting racing of the season, away from the top class struggles.'

Even so, the iniquities of this Championship's point-scoring system was never so apparent as in 1978, when Ford Capris won ten races outright, yet it was Richard Longman's snub-nosed Mini 1275GT that won its class 11 times in 12 races and accordingly lifted the Championship too, which was a hugely popular result. It was the same story again in 1979, for although one of a fleet of Capris won 11 of the 12 races it was Richard Longman's Mini 1275GT – which won its class ten times – that easily won the Championship. It was typical of

the apathetic BL publicists of the period that they made nothing of these successes.

This was all too much for the administrators at the RAC MSA, who reshuffled their rules again for 1980 and made higher minimum weight limits compulsory, which suddenly made the A-Series-powered 1275GT uncompetitive. Even so, in 1982 – the last season in which the Group 1 rules applied – Richard Longman saw his opportunity and, by using an MG Metro 1300 (which was much more powerful, in standard form, than the old-type 1275GT had ever been), once again won the 1.3-litre Championship class. However, he then went off to drive Ford Escorts and continuity was lost.

Metro Turbo climax

As far as the BTCC was concerned, from 1983 it was all-change time, for the RAC MSA dropped obsolete regulations (Group 1 in this case) and imposed new ones (Group A) in their place. At the time they can have had no idea of the power race they were about to unleash. The story of the first, 1983, season is quickly told, though its technical manoeuvrings could take up an entire chapter: Tom Walkinshaw's TWR organisation built three 'works' Rover 3500s, which won every one of the 11 qualifying races.

Unhappily, there was personal animosity between Walkinshaw and Frank Sytner (who ran a BMW 635CSi), for Sytner seemed determined to find homologation irregularities in the Rovers. The dispute went on for months, all the way up to an official inquiry led by Lord (once Sir Hartley) Shawcross, and it was not until June 1984 (eight months after the end of the Championship) that Rover (and TWR) washed its hands of the whole business and 'disassociated' its team from the Championship – this unhappily sweeping away a spirited attempt by Roger

In 1983 and 1984 the Austin-Rover 'works' motorsport department prepared several ferociously powerful MG Metro Turbos for saloon car racing, where they proved to be dominant in their capacity class. The Group A turbocharged race engines produced a consistent 200bhp (with up to 220bhp available for qualifying), but it had a ferocious appetite for transmission drop gears, which had to be changed before every race outing.

Dowson Engineering (on behalf of Austin-Rover) to produce a class-competitive MG Metro Turbo.

It is worth going into more detail about this short-lived programme, for it concerns an engine which was basically 30 years old, and which (as far as is known) had never been turbocharged before. The racing car, don't forget, was a front-wheel-drive machine, so the fact that it was eventually tuned to produce up to 200bhp at 7,200rpm, still using the five-port cylinder head and a single SU carburettor, meant that traction was likely to be a problem. Although the shared oiling system was maintained, in addition to the existing oil pump, the racing engine had an extra external pump along with a massive engine oil cooler under the floor pan, behind the seats.

This all meant that getting the power down to the ground was always a problem. Because of the turbocharging 'factor' of 1.4 applied by the regulations, the RAC saw it as a 1,810cc car, and it had to run in the 2,500cc class. Looking back nearly 30 years, Roger Dowson still smiles at the development problems involved:

'BL commissioned my new company to take on the Metro Turbo project – they were getting too busy with the secret Metro 6R4 project. The first car was

built in John Davenport's "works" department at Cowley, where Richard Hurdwell was the designer, and Phil Humphries was the development engineer. Fuel came from Esso, and major sponsorship came from Computervision.'

The new car was homologated in February 1983 – very enterprisingly, too, for somehow coil springs, as opposed to Hydragas units, were specified for the suspension – and started racing in May.

'Tony Pond drove those cars, as did Patrick Watts and Robin Brundle. We had a lot of head gasket problems, but we got that sorted with Wills Ring gaskets. Tom and Phil Howley then took over engine work, and by the end of 1983 we were getting 180–190bhp: we were getting about 8mpg! The cars were so light that we had to run with 80kg of ballast, but they were seriously quick.

'We ended up with a special stiffened casing, and with a special four-speed gearbox developed by Jack Knight. With so much power, that was the weak link on the car, for the turbo A-Series engine would break the drop gears on the end of the crankshaft. We started with 13in wheels, but later we were playing with 15in wheels, which put the gears under even more strain.' It seems that the strain on the drop gears was so serious that these were habitually renewed between qualifying and the race – and that even this was not always enough to keep the cars in one piece for the weekend.

'In the original concept, we should have had 12 engines in the system – most of the time we would go to do practice, take the engine out overnight and put a fresh engine in for the race (mainly because of the gearbox problem) . . . At first, the major problem was keeping the Avon race tyres alive – so in the last race, all three cars ruined their tyres, all three needed changes, and all three lost a lot of ground.'

Even so, Tony Pond won his class once, and was on the class pole three times, sometimes beating the Championship winner Andy Rouse's Alfa GTV. For 1984 RDE built two new cars ('which were tidier and better'), which proved to be extremely competitive. Tony Pond had gone off to drive the 6R4 in rallies, but Watts won

Except for its lurid Computervision colour scheme, the Group A Metro Turbo racing car of 1983 looks very standard indeed. With up to 200hp in racing trim, this was definitely the fastest A-Series-engined car in the world at this time.

three classes (and Robin Brundle once), the cars leading all six races in which they started (engine and fuel feed problems accounted for the rest). But then 'Mr Davenport pulled everything out of the Championship, and we had to withdraw . . . and that was the end of the programme.'

If only company politics had not got in the way of this promising racing car programme, this might have been a fitting climax to the A-Series' motorsport career. As it was, the engine then faded rapidly into the sporting background, for although the Metro Challenge series and one-make racing at club level has continued, the headline glamour of international motorsport was no more.

With 200bhp up front, the 'works' MG Metro Turbo racing cars of 1983 and 1984 were formidably rapid little saloon-car racing machines when driven by heroes such as Patrick Watts and Tony Pond.

Chapter 8

High tide: into the 1970s

As far as the A-Series engine was concerned, by 1968 there had been two major developments: one was that the 1,275cc version of the engine had been turned into a mainstream derivative, and the other was that British Leyland had come into being. For reasons that now become obvious as this story unfolds, both made the A-Series an even more important 'building block' than it already was in the old BMC empire.

Basically, the fact that a mass-produced version of the 1,275cc engine was available meant that it could be used in heavier cars (those requiring more power and torque than the 1,098cc version could provide), while the growing rationalisation of models propounded by the new British Leyland made its long-term future problematical – or fluid, to say the least.

Even by 1965 it was clear that the development of the 1,275cc Mini-Cooper S engine had been a breakthrough, a great advance within the confines of a power unit which had appeared to be running out of potential. Put in very simple terms, the reshuffling of the internals of the cylinder block, to provide relocated cylinder centres and a much larger cylinder bore, while leaving the outside casting 'envelope' alone, was the work of genius – and much credit for this goes to Eddie Maher (and to John Cooper!) rather than to mainstream engine designers at Longbridge.

It was at about this time that a decision must have been made to 'productionise' the 1,275cc unit – not, that is, to detune the existing and rather special 1275S engine (which was, and whose future was, based at Courthouse Green), but to evolve a mass-production derivative to be built at Longbridge. In many ways, the two 1,275cc types were rather different.

However, just to confuse everyone – historians, enthusiasts and spare parts managers alike – before this could be done BMC also introduced a much-changed, much-detuned version of the Courthouse Green-built 1,275cc engine, for use solely by the twin Austin-Healey Sprite/MG Midget sports cars (earlier versions of these models had always had their engines manufactured at Courthouse Green anyway). Like the 1275S, it had the re-cored block and the ten-stud cylinder head, but it had a tuftrided instead of a nitrided crankshaft, a different camshaft profile, a lowered compression ratio and smaller inlet and exhaust valves. All this reduced costs considerably, but the power output also dropped, from 76bhp (1275S) to 65bhp (1967 model Sprite/Midget).

To add the 1,275cc engine to the range of power plants would, as already described in Chapter 5, involve taking every advantage of the enlarged, rejigged and reinstalled A-Series mass-production facilities in East Works. It is worth noting that in 1966 East Works was already producing 848cc, 998cc and 1,098cc engines, sometimes changing machine settings and assembly procedures to make more, or less, of the engines as demand fluctuated. Two years later, the 1,275cc engine had been added to that list, this particular unit having a revised cylinder block, different from that originally phased in for S-Type engines in 1963, and distinguished by having a solid wall rather than a removable panel close to the camshaft and tappets.

Clearly the work at Longbridge, both in modifying the build facilities, and in finalising the 'mass-production' specification, was carried out very briskly, for the first evidence of all this labour appeared during 1967. It was typical, however, of the rather chaotic manner in which BMC introduced new models at this time,

South African engines

It all took time, but no sooner had the front-wheel-drive Mini been announced in the UK than BMC's South African subsidiary in Blackheath began an ambitious 'local component' production programme. This would come to maturity by the end of 1965, when the company started using locally cast and machined cylinder blocks and cylinder heads. This, incidentally, was done by concentrating on the later type of 'solid block' (which is to say that there were no access panels for easy attention to the valve gear), a casting that was substantially more rigid than the original A-Series power unit.

At first, and as in previous years when imported A-Series engines (or components) had been used in locally-built BMC cars such as the Austin A35 and the A40, the South Africans had concentrated on the 848cc engine and a specifically redeveloped version of the 998cc engine, and once the UK business had introduced the long-stroke (Austin/Morris 1100 type) 1,098cc engine this was also adopted.

Then, in the mid-1960s, under Phase Two of this ambitious programme, the South Africans decided not only to develop and manufacture their own A-Series engines but also to evolve a new-type 1,098cc power unit, which would have entirely different bore and stroke dimensions, unique to this power unit, and never adopted by the 'Home Country'.

Since the South Africans were determined to use their own lightly-modified version of the modern 1,275cc engine, they had to make all manner of decisions when two engines were needed for a plant which was only to build up to 12,000 cars a year. Having concluded that they needed two engine sizes – 1.1 and 1.3 litres – to equip their various models, they analysed all the options of common bores/different strokes, common strokes/different bores, and two different engines on parallel assembly lines – and made what sounds like a sensible and most pragmatic decision.

In the end they retained one cylinder block, one version being the UK-standard 1,275cc dimensions for the larger engine, then produced their own short-stroke 'South African' 1.1 by reducing the stroke from 81.28mm/3.20in to 69.85mm/2.75in. Not only was this a very cost-effective method of doing the job (a new crankshaft and new pistons were needed, but little else, for the same connecting rods were retained), but it very conveniently produced a capacity quoted as 1,098cc – the same as the long-stroke Longbridge 1.1-litre engine, though an accurate calculation puts it very slightly different. Interestingly enough the South Africans preferred to do this rather than to take up the 'standard' dimensions of the 1071S engine (which had a stroke of 68.26mm/2.69in), concluding that they wanted to go their own way.

This was not a totally simple, or unthinking, design/development job. With the blessing of a renowned and expert South African historian, Ryno Verster, I am able to quote the following: 'The bottom end was kept as a three main bearing set-up, since the A-Series block is too short to warrant a five main bearing design, yet the Leyland engineers decided to increase the main bearing surfaces to much bigger proportions, namely 50.8mm/2.0in. The big-end bearings were also increased to 44.45mm/1.75in.'

And there was much more, in detail, including new oil circulation arrangements (including a screw-on type of filter), more robust piston gudgeon pins, different connecting rods and pistons, a more solid camshaft which incorporated a mechanical oil pump drive, and other important improvements.

Prototype testing of this 'short-stroke' engine began in March 1969, and the new unit was made available in the latest Mini models in 1971. Series production ended, it seems, in 1979, the last cars of all actually being delivered in 1980. This particular 'short-stroke' engine was never fitted to cars produced and sold in Britain and Europe.

that the productionised 1,275cc engine edged into the limelight rather than being relaunched with a flourish. First it was admitted that 1100 models to be sent to the USA would have the bigger engine, and then, from June 1967, customers were invited to order a 58bhp/single SU carburettor version for their MG 1100/Riley Kestrel/ Vanden Plas Princess and Wolseley 1100 front-wheel-drive cars. Not as standard equipment? Why not? Presumably because existing 1100 versions were still in the pipeline, or even sitting, unsold, in the showrooms.

BMC dealers, however, had learned not to be complacent at this time, for further changes (some of them looking positively panic-stricken) were already on the way. From the summer of 1968 all of these models got a 65bhp/twin-SU version of the engine, and only months later the MG and Riley derivatives got a further upgrade, to 70bhp; and a year after that both Austin and Morris types spawned 1300GTs of their own. If you ordered automatic transmission, the rating was usually reduced, and if you preferred Wolseley or Vanden Plas types you never got the chance to run 70bhp versions either. There was never a shortage of variety, not to say outright confusion, in the new British Leyland's marketing offices at this time.

1,275cc into the mainstream

Numerically at least, although the 848cc and 998cc versions of the A-Series were still to be the most significant of all the engines being built at Longbridge, the newly productionised 1,275cc unit would gradually take on more and more marketing significance as the 1960s progressed.

Compared with the ultra-special 1275S engines which had been built at Courthouse Green, the latest Longbridge-built versions were neither as complex, nor as expensive, to build. In spite of the production engineers' reluctance to make changes to the rapidly ageing facilities in North and East Works at Longbridge (this will be covered in more detail further on), money was spent on new cylinder block coring, and machining (to take account of the specialised centre line spacings essential to having such a large cylinder bore), along with similar investment made on new but non-specialised cylinder heads and all the other details needed to rationalise this layout. When launching its new-for-1968 range, BMC made it clear that the new block *was* a new block, made on new tooling, that it had a narrower centre main

bearing, and that the extra cylinder head holding-down studs used in S-type engines were not carried forward.

Even before British Leyland was formed (in January 1968), BMC had thoroughly reshuffled its pack, and made the A-Series even more vital, all-important even, to its line-up. It was at the Earls Court Motor Show that the entire Mini range became 'Mk II', and the entire 1100/1300 also became 'Mk II'. Visually ('style-wise', as our American cousins would no doubt dub this) there was little to note, but in each and every case the all-A-Series engines line-up was made more far-reaching and more complicated.

This signalled the fact that the productionised 1,275cc A-Series was now well and truly available at Longbridge. This is how Longbridge planners had to juggle with all their resources by the end of 1967:

Mini and derivatives 848cc and 998cc
Mini-Cooper and S 998cc and 1,275cc S
1100/1300 family 1,098cc and 1,275cc
Austin-Healey Sprite/MG Midget 1,275cc
Morris Minor 1000 1,098cc

A -Series fitted where?

In the UK alone, series production A-Series engines were fitted in numbers to cars, trucks, vans and even tractors in five different factories – Abingdon, Adderley Park, Bathgate, Cowley and Longbridge – not forgetting the principal overseas assembly plants in Australia, South Africa, Belgium, Chile, Holland, the Republic of Ireland, Italy, New Zealand, Peru, Portugal and Spain.

In the meantime there had been another reshuffle in the technical ranks. Immediately after British Leyland was founded, Alec Issigonis was discreetly sidelined and given a long-term research position (which meant – as I note in detail later – that he concentrated on finalising his 9X replacement-Mini project). The post of technical director was taken up by Harry Webster, the distinguished engineer who had led the Standard-Triumph technical team from the mid-1950s until 1968, when British Leyland's Sir Donald Stokes had moved him swiftly to Longbridge to run the Austin-

Harry Webster

Once Standard-Triumph's celebrated technical chief, Harry Webster had only a marginal influence on the fortunes of the A-Series engine, though he encouraged the design of replacement power units (all of which were cancelled on finance/investment grounds). Originally a Standard apprentice in the 1930s, he worked his way up through the engineering departments, first becoming chief chassis designer, then chief engineer and a director of Standard from 1957.

It was Webster who discovered the mercurial Italian stylist Giovanni Michelotti, the two jointly inspiring a series of successful Triumph cars in the 1960s. Clearly Leyland, who had rescued Standard-Triumph from bankruptcy in 1961, liked what they saw, so when British Leyland was formed in 1968 Webster was speedily moved across to Longbridge to sideline the unfortunate, unworldy Alec Issigonis, and to revitalise the Austin-Morris engineering operation.

Like most people who arrived at Longbridge at this time, Webster was appalled by the lack of coherent product planning that he found, and by the lack of investment capital which was available to develop new models and engines. Although (as explained on page 152) Alec Issigonis was already scheming to dump the A-Series in favour of his new overhead-camshaft engine for the 9X project, a lack of money soon consigned it to oblivion.

No matter what Webster and his team could propose in the next six years, there was either a great deal of inertia, a lack of vision or a plain lack of capital to enable an A-Series successor to be brought to market. Several projects, including the original overhead-camshaft conversion, were proposed, but none made it beyond the experimental stage. Webster finally became terminally frustrated by the difficulty of pushing new projects through the byzantine 'system' which persisted at British Leyland, and, accepting a lucrative and prestigious offer from Automotive Products of Leamington Spa, he moved out in 1974.

He was sorely missed.

Morris design and development empire. Issigonis' vastly experienced deputy Charles Griffin became chief engineer, directly responsible to Webster, and seemed to relish his new post.

The father of the A-Series, Eric Bareham, chose this time to move on, so by 1969 Austin-Morris was suddenly looking for a new top engine designer. Although it was not specifically spelt out at the time, after the new-generation 1.5-litre E-Series had been unveiled (initially for the Maxi, but it would eventually go into several other British Leyland models) the urgent need was to update and improve, but not necessarily replace, the existing A-Series and B-Series ranges.

It was at this point that a noted young engineer, Geoff Johnson, joined the team. This, however, was an unexpected appointment, for Johnson had spent most of the 1950s and 1960s with the BRM Grand Prix team, where he had been responsible for the design of the successful V12 3.0-litre engine. After Tony Rudd had left BRM to join Lotus, Johnson felt that he also needed to make a change, and when he saw a rather vague advert in the *Daily Telegraph* seeking an engine designer 'in the West Midlands', he reacted to it, and to his amazement found that it was to take up Eric Bareham's old job at British Leyland.

'The first interview was quite formal,' Geoff told me, 'but the second was much more technical, for Harry Webster and Charlie Griffin were present. They wanted to rejuvenate the design side: I was eventually offered the position of chief engineer, petrol engines, and started work in November 1969.'

It is worth noting that by this time three one-time Standard-Triumph engineers – George Jones (the gruff but extremely capable transmission specialist), Stan Holmes and Ray Bates (who the author has always considered as one of Webster's 'hit men', for he could tackle almost every challenge) – had also arrived.

It was a big change for Johnson, and a culture shock for his new team: 'I had come from BRM, with a total number of employed at 100 maximum, but now I was taking charge of more than 100 talented people on the design and engine development side alone. I don't think I would have been successful without great colleagues like John Barnett, Wes Hunt, John Monument and others. It's fair

Sir Donald Stokes was the dynamo behind the expansion of Leyland in the 1960s, and became British Leyland's managing director at the very beginning of 1968 and its chairman from the end of that year. It was he, more than any other individual, who persistently vetoed the approval of an A-Series replacement in the 1970s. (*BMIHT*)

Before Alec Issigonis was removed from a position of authority at British Leyland, he was still a useful figurehead at public occasions. Here he is shown with Lord Stokes and photographer Lord Snowdon. (*BMIHT*)

Sir Donald, later Lord, Stokes, ran British Leyland from 1968 to 1975. His ideas and his sentiments were good, but he was often frustrated by the truculent attitude of his workforce, particularly those at Longbridge.

British Leyland always took every opportunity to celebrate anniversaries or major achievements. (Left to right) Alec Issigonis, George Turnbull, Harry Webster and a model make much of the completion of the five-millionth front-wheel-drive car. That is a Mini Clubman, but most of the five million had been classic short-nose Minis and the 1100/1300 range.

This was the new E-Series engine, launched to power the Austin Maxi in 1969. It was British Leyland's first overhead-camshaft power unit, predating a whole stream of overhead-cam A-Series replacements developed in the 1970s. (*BMIHT*)

to say that I was received with a bit of suspicion at first. From then on, of course, I was to be a manager, and never again drew a line on a piece of paper.'

Ray Bates, who arrived from Standard-Triumph in April 1968, well before Johnson, was similarly nonplussed: 'Harry [Webster] had moved to Longbridge, and shortly came the telephone call – "Ray, I want some help, can you please come over and join me?" There was no specific job really, but I believe I was called technical manager. I went to see Harry and asked him what he would have me do? He said: "Well, there doesn't seem to be any planning in place. And I'm very concerned about the proliferation of engines that we've got. Could you have a look-see, and tell me what we have got?"'

The fact is that the A-Series and B-Series types were dominant parts of the Longbridge scene, while Issigonis' 9X engine 'family' was coming along, the new E-Series was almost ready to be launched, the much-revised C-Series was being built and there was talk (but no more, at that point) of providing an overhead-camshaft

George Turnbull took over as managing director at Austin-Morris in 1968, when the priority was to keep producing 'more of the same', rather than go for innovation. It was under Turnbull that Longbridge turned out record numbers of A-Series engines in the 1970s.

conversion for the A-Series. Outside the factory gates but central to the evolution of new British Leyland cars, there were also Triumph's new slant-four (already being built for Saab), the recently launched Rover V8 and the still secret Triumph Stag V8.

'I was just an investigator at first,' Ray Bates recalled. 'I asked a lot of questions, of a lot of people, then went across to the machine shops and the tracks at Longbridge and had a chat with the foremen. It all seemed to be rather casually arranged, uncoordinated even . . .

'Then I "discovered" about Eddie Maher and his specialist team at Courthouse Green. They didn't seem to want to come over and work at Longbridge . . . Anyway, they had clearly done a good job there, they had developed the Cooper S . . . so that all seemed to work well.'

This was the point at which Ray made his boldest proposal: 'I put together a plan to rationalise on the 1275 block, because the cylinder head pattern on the 1275 was different from the 998. We put together a plan – we didn't do any design work at that point, it was just a matter of looking at drawings and things. That, I thought, gave us a chance to develop a standardised cylinder block, and a standard cylinder head. I prepared this plan in great detail.

'But then I thought, what do I do now? Was there a committee? No, nothing like that – I was told that I would have to go to see people in Production Engineering, and a chap called Joe Greatorex. He was a very severe-looking man, typically what I would call an ex-military man.

'He refused, point blank, to do what I suggested. And because no one else seemed to want to back us up, it had to be left like that. Then we went through a B-Series investigation, and got the same response . . . We were getting nowhere. It was obvious that Longbridge was production-led, and whatever Joe Greatorex said, went. It continued to be like that for some time.

'There was obviously some need to get some planning. Even so, it was not until 1972 that they [British Leyland top management] decided to set up a Product Planning department. Mark Snowdon, Nick Stephenson and others were involved.'

Although Ray Bates eventually become intimately involved in new engine design, he also had many other responsibilities as Harry Webster's 'eyes-and-ears' man at the time, and left Geoff Johnson to his own devices.

As I will shortly describe, Johnson's team enjoyed (or should I say 'suffered'?) a very productive, but ultimately frustrating, time at Longbridge. However, because little that he and his team proposed ever reached the public, British Leyland was often accused of neglecting the A-Series throughout this time. If only people had known just how much work went into idealising the A-Series for cars as diverse as the Allegro, the MG Midget, a series of MG design proposals and the first of the Metros they would have thought differently.

This meant that when the A-Series reached maturity in the Metro, which was introduced in 1980 (where it was already seen to be at its peak), there was no shortage of loud-mouthed criticism about this. Pedants who knew little about the depth of the financial problems that Longbridge-based engineers had faced in the 1960s and 1970s had no idea of the true behind-the-scenes story. That fact is that in the 1970s and 1980s all manner of attempts were made to replace the A-Series, but all had fallen away, swallowed in a morass of so-called corporate planning and financial forecasting.

For example, some years ago when I was writing about the birth of the new-generation (BMW) Mini, I quoted that car's original project engineer from Longbridge, Chris Lee, who told me that: 'It became quite amusing to see just how many people there were who would draw up a product plan showing the demise of the Mini'; to which another BMC/British Leyland stalwart, Fred Coultas, retorted: 'Some of us have been trying to replace the Mini since about 1964!'

Somewhere at Longbridge people were always trying to replace the A-Series. It didn't seem to matter that often there was a management edict against such projects, drawing boards and even test beds would be full of schemes, ideas and 'why-don't-we . . .?' projects. The first of these took shape in the 1950s, Alec Issigonis backed new engines in the late 1960s, and in the indecisive years of British Leyland there were several more.

Not that such replacements always took the same path. Sometimes there might be proposals to change the architecture without changing the details – two- or three-cylinder types, perhaps; sometimes there might be proposals to change the overhead valve layout; sometimes thought was given to producing overhead-camshaft conversions; and (increasingly) sometimes schemes for all-new engines took shape.

The miracle (or the tragedy, depending on which side one's sentiments lay) was that none of these engines ever took over. It was not until 1989, when the all-new K-Series was launched, originally to power the Rover 200/400 and eventually the Metro ranges, that the venerable A-Series could see its own obsolescence looming.

Even so, as many people as there were trying to get rid of it and replace it with something new, there were others ready and willing to keep it going at all costs. It was the 'replacement' faction, however, who seemed to have the big guns and the most prominent reputations, at first including, most notably, consultant Harry Weslake and Alec Issigonis himself.

As already explained in some detail, the limitations of the original A-Series were well known. They had been realised, of course, almost from the day that the first line was drawn on the first piece of designers' paper. Basically, although the bottom end was strong enough, or could be made strong enough, it was the capability and development potential of the cylinder head which was the limiting factor. The first proposed updates, therefore, concentrated on the cylinder head and its replacement. Geoff Healey's book *More Healeys* described what was probably the very first proposal, which dated from the late 1950s, less than a decade after the A-Series had been revealed:

'Harry Weslake came up with a suggestion for producing a special head, that would give us [Austin-Healey, for competition cars] the power we required. He designed a single overhead camshaft unit that could be bolted to the standard 948cc block. Naturally the inlet and exhaust ports and combustion chambers were very special. However, just when the design was completed and pattern equipment was about to be made, someone at Austin got to hear about it. Both we and Harry were politely told not to go ahead, and that was the end of the matter. Just why this was done I never understood, but as both our companies were small, we could not afford to go too far out of line.

'Tim Fry, then with Rootes [later Chrysler UK] designed another interesting head with separate ports. This improved output with very little development, but was never very reliable . . .'

Early in the 1970s Innocenti of Italy (which was controlled by British Leyland) commissioned Bertone to develop this smart new hatchback car, which was based on the platform and running gear of the Mini 1275GT . . .

This was also the time when another engineering team at Longbridge, led by Duncan Stuart, was working on a new engine family which, though larger in scope and capacity, would inevitably have affected the largest-capacity A-Series' future. This, of course, was the ambitious V4/V6 family, which ran with a tiny vee angle of only 18°, and used a single cylinder head to cover both cylinder banks, with one centrally placed overhead camshaft, which actuated two valves per cylinder, and which had SU carburettors on both sides of the cylinder head, one providing fuel/air mixture to each bank. In general layout it seems as if Stuart had looked at what Lancia had already proved, for they also had vee engines of this type.

The reason for the very narrow vee angle was to restrict the overall bulk of the power units, so that they could be used in-line, or transversely, depending on the range of BMC models to be equipped. All engine design engineers will confirm that a narrow-angle vee-4 is roughly square when seen in plan view – it is as wide as it is long.

Full details of this engine have never been released, though engine drawings have been shown, but it seems that the smallest capacity V4 would have been approximately a 1.3-litre unit, which would have been in direct competition with the 1,275cc A-Series. When they were originally designed space was certainly allowed in the engine bay of the 1100/1300 models (which otherwise use A-Series throughout), though few prototypes seem to have been built.

Although this was a serious project, with a cast iron block and head, SU carburettors, and a limited-expense camshaft and valve gear layout (the drawings make

. . . but the style became less pure as the years passed.

this clear), in the end Sir George Harriman's colleagues decided that it would have been too costly to complete, for the potential capital tooling bill was colossal, and much of Longbridge's machining capacity (or the factories in which new tools had to be installed) would have had to be torn up and rebuilt. In addition, though little was made of this at the time, the small-capacity V4 looked as if it would have been significantly heavier than the existing A-Series, which made it less desirable.

In the meantime, as his total domination of the BMC engineering and product planning hierarchy continued to grow, Alex Issigonis had his own ideas. Because he was totally committed to the concept of building front-wheel-drive cars – whether Mini, 1100 or 1800 size – not only did he want to replace the A-Series with a new, small straight 'four', but he also wanted to link this to

the master plan (in other words, an Issigonis master plan) involving fours and straight sixes, all of which could be transversely mounted, and which would have capacities which spanned 750cc to 1,500cc. It is worth noting that at this stage he did not have the approval of the BMC board of directors, even though he was a member of that board.

This was the first of many small-capacity engine projects that took shape between 1967 and 1980, and was conceived when the Great Man was at the height of his power and influence at BMC. Unhappily, no sooner had British Leyland been formed in 1968 than Issigonis was briskly sidelined, and a more pragmatic engineering team, headed by ex-Triumph man Harry Webster, took over at Longbridge.

This Issigonis 'master plan' began to take shape in 1966–67, as he retreated from routine technical director duties to concentrate on the 9X – the replacement Mini project which was finally unveiled in the early 1970s when it had been irrevocably cancelled. The newly-formed British Leyland's supremo Sir Donald (later Lord) Stokes officially learned of this when he asked Issigonis to provide a report on his current activities. Responding to this on 18 April 1968, Issigonis wrote:

'I enclose a short résumé of work that I am currently engaged on . . . Management approval or rejection of these projects is still to be determined . . . The greatest need in combating increased production costs over the year is the development of a new engine for a small car of this [Mini] type. The present A-Series engine offered a quick way of getting the car into production in 1959, but has now outlived its purpose both for weight and cost compared with European competition.'

His five-part list of projects started with these two items:

'1 Design and development of a 750/998cc 4-cylinder engine and transmission system for transverse or normal drive applications, for a new small car. In addition to this work, we are doing a design study, in conjunction with Automotive Products Ltd [of Leamington Spa] for a 4-speed automatic transmission unit.

'2 Development of a six-cylinder version of the above engine to give capacities from 1300 to 1490cc, using as much common tooling as possible, including the same transmission system . . .'

However, these proposals were quickly kicked into the long grass by British Leyland, who were not interested in technical excellence or innovation at a time when they

If Alec Issigonis had got his way in the late 1960s, the A-Series engine would have been replaced by a family of compact, straight 4/ straight 6 overhead cam units. This, believe it or not, was a straight 6 – count the plug leads for confirmation.

After George Turnbull left Austin-Morris, Ray Horrocks was appointed to run the entire cars side of British Leyland, which was renamed BL at this time. Originally, Horrocks thought that not enough had been done to replace the A-Series, and was astonished to learn just how much had been tried, designed, done and proven – but always cancelled – in previous years.

wanted Austin-Morris to return to profit-making and to financial stability. Issigonis was sidelined in favour of Harry Webster, his influence on BMC/British Leyland's cars all but over. Amazingly two examples of the proposed 9X prototype (complete with 850cc four-cylinder engines) were built in 1968–69, one survives to this day, and details of the engine (including cross-section drawings) also survive . . .

The 9X engine range

A detailed 'Review of Major Projects' which was prepared in January 1979 for study by the newly-appointed managing director, Ray Horrocks, shows that the 9X engine subscribed to a strong Issigonis theory, which he once explained to a business colleague as follows: 'I have researched the machine tool industry, and enormous savings can be made by buying standardised machines which can only operate at 90 degrees.'

All the manufacturing operations that were required to make the engine's block, crankcase and cylinder head were to be driven by three-axis spindles, but all at 90° to each other, and they only went vertically and horizontally. Issigonis had the 9X engine designed to be made only by these. The resulting engine was not only simple looking, but one which had a somewhat austere aspect. An 850cc example is fitted to the surviving 9X car, which is one of the BMIHT's most prized possessions.

In accord with the well-established Issigonis/front-wheel-drive layout, the engine featured a transmission in the sump, and with the final drive/differential and driveshafts positioned behind that transmission.

So far, so conventional, but every component of the

One of Alec Issigonis' final projects was to design a new series of engines, hopefully to replace the A-Series. This was fitted to the 9X prototype in 1968.

9X engine was different from the A-Series, not only in layout but in construction. Not only did the cylinder head feature single-overhead-camshaft valve gear, but the cylinder head was to be of aluminium, while the cast iron cylinder block sat atop an aluminium crankcase, which itself then sat on top of the aluminium transmission case. Five crankshaft main bearings were provided (as compared to three on the A-Series).

The overhead camshaft drove a line of eight valves that were totally vertical, in line and in the centre of the line of cylinders. The combustion chambers were to be

located, Heron-style, in the piston crowns themselves, and the camshaft was to be driven by an internally cogged belt. This was a non-crossflow head, but as there was no forest of pushrods to be avoided it meant that individual inlet and exhaust ports could be accommodated on what (in transversely-mounted form) would be the side of the engine closest to the passenger bulkhead. Fuelling on the prototype was by a single semi-downdraught SU carburettor, and the distributor was mounted on the end of the cylinder head, driven directly by the camshaft and located, in space, above the clutch housing.

The designers kept the engine as short ('narrow' really, for this was to be transversely mounted in cars!) as possible by arranging for cylinders 1-2 and 3-4 to be siamesed. Because the cylinder bore could not, therefore, be enlarged, this meant that the larger capacity of the 998cc derivative would have to be achieved by a long-stroke crankshaft. The bore and stroke are not known, but the 850cc engine appears to be almost 'square' in its dimensions.

All in all this was a very compact, very well-reasoned and very thoughtful design which, in happier and more expansive times, would surely have found favour. Not only was it smaller, physically, than the A-Series, but lighter too, and manufacturing estimates showed that it might have cost £68, instead of £74, to manufacture.

The F-Series

Even before the 9X was cancelled, BMC – the mainstream engine design team, this time – had started work on a new four-cylinder engine project, which was christened the F-Series. This choice of lettering was logical, for A, B, C and D had all been in use for some years, while E-Series was applied to the all-new 1.5-litre engine which was about to be standardised in the still secret Austin Maxi, and for which expensive tooling already existed in East Works (the ex-'shadow' factory near Cofton Hackett).

However, although 'F' followed 'E' there appeared to be no link between the two engines, for their layouts were completely different, as the auxiliaries were in entirely different locations, the camshaft drives were different (that of the E-Series was by chain), and the E-Series valve gear layout was unique to BMC/BLMC in that the valve layout – inlet versus exhaust – was slightly 'knock-kneed' in the combustion chamber.

The F-Series did not have a dedicated or already chosen destiny, though it was an obvious contender to replace the ageing A-Series. Surviving documentation shows just how much change, or experimentation, took place in the period while it was active. Although it was always certain that a single-overhead-camshaft layout would be chosen, 'various valve operating layouts, ranging from inclined rockers, hinged fingers and bucket tappets were considered'.

The F-Series was meant to encompass the 1,100–1,300cc capacity range. Prototypes had equal bore and stroke of 74mm, which equates to 1,273cc, and it seems that just two such engines were built, and test run for a total of 200 hours. Without engines being fitted into cars, it seems, the project was cancelled in 1970/1.

Compared with 9X this was a much more conventional engine, for although it had five crankshaft main bearings

it centred around a cast iron cylinder block and cylinder head, and was always intended for use in both transverse and in-line installations. One important packaging feature was that all auxiliary units (distributor, oil pump and fuel pump) were mounted in a single 'capsule', carried on the side of the cylinder block – the side remote from the carburettor(s) – at the front end of the engine, and driven by the same toothed belt that would drive the single overhead camshaft.

The toothed belt itself was lengthy, and traced a complex path. This was novel for the period, but once high-performance engines like Cosworth's Ford BDA had proved capable of reliability in a similar fashion, British Leyland was more relaxed about this.

The H-Series

After the F-Series had been cancelled the design team took time out to work on other, larger engines. Notably, these included one which was the overhead-camshaft derivative of the B-Series that finally (after some years of development) matured as the O-Series four-cylinder family of 1.7-litre and 2.0-litre engines, which powered cars as diverse as the Morris Ital and the Princess and was at one time also scheduled to power developments of the MG MGB and Triumph TR7 sports cars. These, at least, showed how British Leyland's collective minds were working, for there were features in the O-Series that were recognisably related to those of the so-called Mini-replacement units that followed. It was an engine of which Geoff Johnson was proud when it was conceived, but which frustrated him in the time it took to get it into production.

The first of these, which originated in about 1971, was the H-Series, which incorporated every lesson learned in designing the F-Series. It was, however, a more specialised power unit, in that it was originally dedicated as a 998cc engine, with no thought (theoretically at least) of further expansion.

'Harry directed that it should be a 1,000cc unit,' Geoff Johnson told me, 'and if the engine could be stretched any further than 1,000cc, then I hadn't done my job! Pictures of the head gasket show that there was no way of increasing the bore, and the stroke was pretty well constrained too. The H-Series would only have been fittable to Mini cars, but the first K-Series would have been a 1,300cc unit, which could have gone into a car like the Allegro.'

Geoff Johnson's team developed this very smart and compact new H-Series engine in 1972, which was designed around a single overhead-cam cylinder head, with a belt-drive for the camshaft and an integral casing for the final drive unit.

However, as we shall see, the layout itself was expanded in a later design. Originally laid out for vertical installation in the engine bay of a Mini-replacement car called ADO74, it would eventually inspire the birth of the first (but not definitive) K-Series. Later in its development, it was tilted sharply back towards the engine bay/passenger compartment bulkhead. Clearly George Jones, in charge of all transmission development, was also closely involved.

The single-overhead-camshaft layout of the iron cylinder head, allied to cogged belt drive from the crank, now seemed to be a 'given'. The combustion chamber was located in the crown of the pistons, which meant that the cylinder head face could be machined flat, with no recesses for the valves, but because this new engine was designed as an integrated engine-transmission unit, many changes to the layout were obvious. Although it was to be an 'over-square' engine (the bore was 72mm, the stroke just 61.2mm and the capacity 998cc), it was a somewhat squat arrangement, but as a classic bucket-tappet layout had also been chosen the power unit fitted easily into the ADO74 (which was, in fairness, somewhat bulkier than the Mini that it was meant to replace in the mid-1970s).

Even so, the cylinder block featured a row of siamesed cylinder bores, which meant that once settled and tooled up there was absolutely no scope for the cylinder bores ever to be enlarged in future years. This 'squeeze' on the length of the engine meant that there was no space for intermediate main bearings, which ensured that there would only be three crankshaft main bearings. General arrangement drawings show that there was, indeed, scope for the stroke to be lengthened to the 78mm which would be needed to provide the 1,270cc of a '1300' version, but only in original-type K-Series form.

The H-Series of 1972 was a very compact little overhead-cam engine, which would have been cheaper to build than the A-Series, and would have been significantly more powerful.

On this occasion the distributor was placed at the end of the cylinder head/camshaft housing, and above the clutch housing, while the alternator and the water pump were to be driven by a vee-belt directly from the rear end of the crankshaft, and the oil pump was crankshaft mounted. Once again this was a non-crossflow head, and once again fuelling would be by a single SU carburettor.

Clearly the design team had been thinking hard about maintenance, for an internal document (written after the engine had been cancelled) pointed out that: 'Engine and transmission were readily serviced by the removal of a single sump, and the clutch by the removal of its end cover. This effectively overcame the servicing criticisms of A, B and E-Series transverse power units without

sacrificing the packaging advantages of the engine-over-transmission configuration.'

This and its lineal descendant, the first-generation K-Series, were very serious projects, both of which only died when the ADO74 project itself was cancelled (due to a financial calculation that the tooling costs for the new model would have been a monumental £130 million, money which British Leyland did not have at the time or, indeed, for years afterwards). As it was, just four prototype 998cc H-Series engines were built, which ran for 200 test-bed hours and (significantly) for 25,000 miles on the road in heavily-disguised Minis.

Much agonising, navel-gazing and redesign (one is reminded of a famous remark made by Jaguar's supremo William Heynes, 'Paper is cheap, it's cutting metal that's expensive') then took place before 'H' became 'K'; incidentally, no one now seems to recall what happened to 'G', 'I' or 'J'.

From a highly confidential source I have now been able

The H-Series of 1972 was a dedicated 1,000cc 'small car' engine and – as can be seen from this layout display of components – had its cylinder bores at maximum, even as designed. Carburation was by a single SU.

to consult a discussion paper (which I think came from Geoff Johnson's ongoing thoughts) written in February 1971. The discussion centred on the H-which-became-K-Series, and shows how opinion was hardening regarding replacement of the increasingly venerable A-Series, but – and this is important, both technically and commercially – purely for the Mini. I am able to quote extracts from this significant document:

'Design Parameters of the Dedicated Power Unit for Mini Replacement.

'The object is to design a dedicated engine/transmission unit of minimum overall cost such that its swept volume cannot be increased.

'In order that the Mini replacement engine will be fully competitive when introduced, possibly in 1975, it is considered that a minimum capacity of 1000cc will be required. The power unit of the engine will have to be 60bhp . . .

'To achieve a power output of 60bhp/per litre from a small-capacity engine, it is an essential requirement that the unit should be capable of breathing efficiently . . . On

this basis, a large bore is necessary, and consequently an over-square engine is the result. It is considered that the stroke/bore ratio should be between 0.75:1 and 1:1. A further consideration, to enhance the performance figures in BHP-per-lb power unit weight, must also be given to the weight of the combined power unit.

'In view of these important factors, it is necessary that a dedicated engine design is achieved. This automatically means that the cylinder bores are fully siamesed . . . the crankcase and transmission are tailored so that it is not possible to increase the throw of the crankshaft without a major modification. Should a smaller capacity unit be required, then a "short block" could be designed to this effect with a reduced throw crankshaft.

'To achieve a reduced height the new engine has its gearbox and final drive mounted alongside, and integral with, the cylinder block casting. In addition, it is also intended that the unit be installed at an angle between 15 deg and 30 deg to the horizontal to assist with gear change, exhaust pipe runs and lowering of the installed height.

'In the interests of marketing a smooth modern engine in the mid-1970s, the decision to design a five-bearing crankshaft was taken.

'Consideration has been given to the possibility of a future requirement to convert the engine to an in-line version. The design is such that this will be possible by means of an alternative cylinder block, by deleting the differential housing . . .'

Much more detail was included in this discussion document, and there was a specification summary which defined a cylinder bore of 72mm, a stroke of 61.2mm and a swept volume of 998cc. It was interesting to see that the distance between (siamesed) cylinder centres was only 78mm, which meant that enlarging the cylinder bore would have been quite impractical.

All this, of course, confirms just how fluid the thrust of A-Series replacement engineering was at the time;

but it also confirms just how much deep thinking was going on at Longbridge. Even so, the speed at which vertical engines gave way to angle-installed engines and five-bearing cranks gave way to three-bearing cranks, consideration of both aluminium and cast iron cylinder heads and capacities of 1,000cc and/or 1,300cc, all went into the melting pot.

What we do know, however, is that all this thought, and the actual physical design, testing and road work which went into the H-Series, was then concentrated on the original-type K-Series, which was very different from that eventually put into production:

The K-Series

Without question, the original K-Series was a lineal development of the H-Series, was also intended for

By 1975 British Leyland's team had brought the idea of producing an overhead-camshaft version of the A-Series engine, by retaining the standard cylinder block, to its ultimate stage. This was the 'in-line' version, complete with a normal wet sump and a conventional four-speed gearbox. The forest of belts includes drive for the original A-Series camshaft position, which would have been retained as a 'jack shaft' for the original distributor drive.

fitment into the ADO74 'SuperMini' and incorporated many of the features mentioned in the discussion paper of 1971 *and* proven in the H-Series of 1971–73. This time, however, the goalposts had moved a little, for the K-Series was now taking shape as an 1,100cc/1,300cc power unit.

First of all, to basics. Once again it was to be a single-overhead-camshaft engine, with two valves per cylinder, mounted in line with the cylinder bores and actuated by bucket-type tappets, all being operated by an internally-cogged rubber belt. As before, there was to be a Heron-type head, with all the combustion chambers in the top of the piston crowns, and with flat-face machining to the head itself, which was to be aluminium, but non-crossflow. There would be individual inlet and exhaust ports. This time around, too, a three-bearing crankshaft was back in favour, this being made possible – desirable, even – because the cast iron cylinder block had completely siamesed bores.

Meant to do everything that the H-Series had proved possible, it was a dedicated transverse-mounting engine, arranged to have the cylinder block leaning 30° backwards towards the passenger bulkhead. This time it was meant

to accommodate a two-shaft five-speed transmission carried in a substantial housing cast integrally with the rear transverse face of the cylinder block; and (unlike the Mini or 1100/1300 range) there would be a simple, though large, pressed steel sump pan.

Was it a success? We do not know, because here was another engine that enjoyed a very limited lifespan. Although five such engines were built, and run for a total of 800 hours, the project was shelved as soon as the ADO74 programme itself was cancelled in 1974.

An overhead-camshaft A-Series conversion

Now, perhaps, it was time for a bit of pragmatic make-do-and-mend engineering, for if management could not be persuaded to invest in an all-new engine, perhaps they might approve of a much-modified A-Series instead. But *how* modified?

Throughout the 1970s (up to and including the rushed adoption of the A-Plus for the Metro project in 1978–80), it was conceded that if British Leyland could not afford to invest in an entirely new engine, then maybe there

The 1975 overhead-camshaft version of the A-Series, as seen from the left side of the cylinder block, shows that the original A-Series block would have been retained. Only a single SU carburettor was proposed, and of course the manifolding was completely novel.

was a case for a redesign which centred on the existing A-Series cylinder block and crankcase, along with its three-bearing crankshaft layout. Even by 1971 a single-overhead-camshaft conversion was already running (archive paperwork and photographs prove this), one which was arranged so that the updated unit might still mate with the front-wheel-drive transmissions still used in cars as various as the ADO20-type Mini, the last of the 1100/1300 types and the Allegro range.

'When the H- and K-Series didn't make their way properly,' Johnson said, 'we looked at how we could improve the existing A-Series. It had reached the limit of size by then, and it had already been around for 20-odd years.'

The result, in the author's opinion, was the evolution of an extremely practical redesign that could, and should, have been put into production, and would have extended the A-Series' high-profile life for several seasons. Basically, it involved the design of a new cylinder head in aluminium, with a single overhead camshaft driven by an internal cogged belt.

All this took shape because of the successful (and parallel) development of the O-Series engine, which was a considerable, though linear, overhead-camshaft evolution of the long-lived B-Series engine, as used in many BMC and British Leyland models. After finalising this and coming to terms with the constraints on capital spending and the ageing facilities at Longbridge, the design team learned a lot from the O-Series and then turned their attention once more to the smaller A-Series, to do the same resourceful conversion job again.

The engines shown in this section (which are of units developed by Johnson's team at the time) define a neatly-detailed engine which is clearly based on the existing, and definitive, mass-production A-Series 1,275cc cylinder block, complete with fully siamesed cylinder bores (which meant no cooling water between them) and a three-main-bearing crankshaft. The single-overhead-camshaft non-crossflow head operated the line of valves through inverted bucket tappets, for the designers had long concluded that this was the most simple and reliable way of doing such things. The ports were located so that four inlet ports were in a line, high up, with the four exhaust ports also in a line, offset and below them.

The camshaft was driven by an internally-cogged/ reinforced rubber belt, this being actuated by a jackshaft mounted in the normal camshaft location in the cylinder block itself. The jackshaft also operated the oil pump and the distributor driveshaft, which remained in the usual A-Series position. As with other, earlier, overhead-cam project engines, the combustion chambers were located in the piston crowns themselves, which meant that the cylinder head could be completely flat and machined all over.

The intention was that this comprehensive redesign would sweep away the need for any of the old-type pushrod overhead-valve A-Series types, and for that reason it was to be built in 970cc, 1,097cc and 1,275cc sizes, all with the existing Cooper S-size cylinder bore of 70.6mm. Two of those capacities, of course, already existed, while the third one could be 'created' by providing a new crankshaft throw of 69.85mm (the same dimension as used in the South African 1.1-litre A-Series which was manufactured in that country for domestic use).

If the 1975 overhead-camshaft evolution of the A-Series had been fitted to a front-wheel-drive British Leyland car of the day, it would have looked like this in single-SU form, or perhaps . . .

. . . like this, with a twin-SU installation. In both cases the original 'overhead-valve' cylinder block was retained, as was the familiar gearbox-in-sump transmission layout.

Incidentally, anyone wondering why such esoteric stroke dimensions (in mm) were chosen should be reminded that the 'Imperial' ethic, and the desire to continue using good old British feet and inches, was still alive and well at Longbridge. To explain:

Engine size	Bore x stroke (mm)	Stroke, measured in inches
970cc	70.6 x 61.91	2.43 or 2$^7/_{16}$in
1,097cc	70.6 x 69.85	2.75 or 2¾in
1,275cc	70.6 x 81.3	3.20in

The initial engines clearly had quite sporty characteristics, with a lot more torque than before but developed at much higher engine speeds. Clearly this type of engine was breathing very freely, as test figures taken in mid-1975 demonstrated, but this shape of torque curve could certainly have been eased as development progressed. The following chart shows just what a substantial improvement was gained:

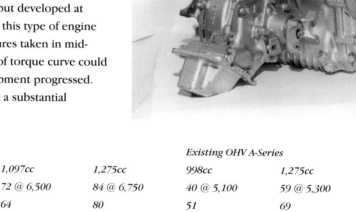

Unit	OHC A-Series			Existing OHV A-Series	
	970cc	1,097cc	1,275cc	998cc	1,275cc
bhp @ rpm	59 @ 6,750	72 @ 6,500	84 @ 6,750	40 @ 5,100	59 @ 5,300
Torque (lb/ft)	51	64	80	51	69
@ rpm	5,250	5,000	4,500	2,600	3,000

This was a substantial and very serious programme. No fewer than 11 prototype units (examples of all sizes among them) were built, and completed 3,200 hours on test beds and 2,200 vehicle miles.

This was a compact redesign that held a great deal of promise, and if only British Leyland (which had become a nationalised concern while the work was going ahead) had been able to commit the necessary investment capital it would surely have done a great job. We now know, of course, that BL was always a loss-making company at this time, and such funds were not made available.

As Johnson and Ray Bates both confirmed, the main stumbling block was the Production Engineering department, who convinced the powers-that-be that they should not take such big steps.

'We had a director of production who was a man called Joe Greatorex,' Johnson recalled. 'I never got on with him, and he never got on with me. As far as that particular type of engine was concerned [meaning any and all of the overhead-camshaft layouts], he simply didn't see eye to eye with what we were doing.'

Three cylinders – who needs four?

Although it never got beyond the making and test-bed running of cut-and-shut prototype engines, in the late 1970s there was also a flirtation with the idea of building a three-cylinder engine, based on the engineering of the E-Series range (which had been in use since the launch of the Austin Maxi in 1969). In a way this would have been

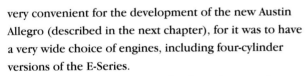

The 1975 OHC conversion featured belt drive to the overhead camshaft, and a choice of single SU or twin-SU carburettor installations.

The 1975 OHC conversion retained all the familiar A-Series features, such as the starter motor, generator (alternator in this case), distributor and sparking plugs on the same forward-facing side of the original cylinder block.

very convenient for the development of the new Austin Allegro (described in the next chapter), for it was to have a very wide choice of engines, including four-cylinder versions of the E-Series.

Not only did it appear, superficially, to be a good way of providing a modern engine at limited capital cost, but it also looked as if it might be valuable for packaging purposes. For all those reasons, studies began in 1975 using the 1,748cc E-Series engine as a starting point.

The E-Series production engine, of course, was a single-overhead-camshaft unit with a cast iron head, and camshaft drive by chain, but a unique valve gear arrangement. Inlet and exhaust valves shared the same camshaft but were then slightly splayed so that they were no longer in line when they reached the head/block face (which meant that the valve heads could be larger without coming into contact with their neighbours). Not only that, but the E-Series block had totally siamesed bores, and a

cylinder bore of 76.2mm/3.00in.

As there were to be two four-cylinder E-Series capacities – 1,485cc and 1,748cc – this meant that the original three-cylinder version could either be 1,114cc or 1,311cc, though only the larger of these two units was investigated at first. An even smaller capacity could have been developed by using a short-stroke crank derivative of what was, of course, a long-stroke four-cylinder engine.

As is the tendency in such ad hoc programmes, further changes (at least on the drawing board) then took place, to consider not only a cogged-belt camshaft drive but also a different type of cylinder head, with opposed valves operated by finger tappets from the camshaft, all allied to part-spherical combustion chambers. Yet another version might have allied three valves per cylinder to a Heron head arrangement. And if that was not all, similar technical somersaults were carried out on the Standard-Triumph 'slant four' engine (the unit fitted to Dolomite

1850s and Triumph TR7s, and originally supplied to Saab for the 99 model). None of these engines, in fairness, were pressed too far towards conclusion, for at about the same time the cash-strapped BL combine decided to develop the A-Plus engine instead.

Irreplaceable?

After all the travail which had led to such frustration for so many multi-talented engineers in the 1970s, one is tempted to suggest that the valiant little A-Series could survive anything. Or is that an exaggeration? Considering the way that British Leyland struggled, staggered, crashed-and-burned, came back from the dead, changed its name and hid under the wing of various owners during the next decade, probably not.

Quite literally, without the A-Series one cannot see how the wounded colossus could have survived at all.

Below the cylinder head face of the block, every feature of the 1975 overhead-camshaft conversion will be familiar to A-Series users.

CHAPTER 9

Marina, Allegro, Metro, Maestro and Montego

Everyone knows, surely, what happened to British Leyland in the 1970s? Here was the classic business school case study of a massive, overmanned, poorly managed colossus which should never have been formed. Its foundation was more of a statement of policy, of dogma even, from the left-leaning British government of the day, than one inspired by industrial, marketing or financial logic.

There is no doubt that Prime Minister Harold Wilson, and colleagues who included the Rt Hon Anthony Wedgwood-Benn (Tony Benn, as he preferred to be called), had much to do with events leading up to the merger, which was publicly announced in January 1968. However, the reader may now relax, for no political diatribe is going to follow. It goes to prove, however, that dogma often takes no account of common sense.

The bare facts are that at this juncture, British Motor Holdings (which included BMC) finally got together with the Leyland Group, leading to the birth of the British Leyland Motor Corporation. Although this was repeatedly trumpeted as a merger of equals, it rapidly became clear that Leyland would have the upper hand. Accordingly, for the first year BMC's current chairman, Sir George Harriman, became chairman of the new group, while Leyland's Sir Donald Stokes became deputy chairman and chief executive. Thereafter Sir George retired – this was a genuine withdrawal, for he was no longer a fit man – and Sir Donald (soon to be ennobled as Lord Stokes) become the Corporation's outright ruler. He would remain at the pinnacle of this colossal business for the next six years.

The immediate result was that the Corporation inherited a product line that must have been a marketing man's nightmare. Although only one major element of this line-up included the A-Series engine, in terms of numbers being built these were very significant. It is worth listing the British car brands that suddenly found themselves under the same ownership:

Austin*
Austin-Healey*
Daimler
Jaguar
Land Rover
MG*
Morris*
Riley*
Rover
Triumph
Vanden Plas/Princess*
Wolseley*

Of equal significance, the principal commercial and military vehicle brands were:

AEC
Albion
Alvis
BMC*
Leyland
Scammell

For interest, I have marked with asterisks the brands that partly relied on A-Series engines for their motive power.

The shotgun marriage that created British Leyland (it

was certainly not made in heaven) broke cover suddenly in January 1968, when I clearly recall working up a chart for my then employers at *Autocar* which clearly showed that, at this time, the existing range of British Leyland private cars included no fewer than 23 different families, in terms of chassis platforms (or frames), and a plethora of engines spanning 848cc (Mini A-Series) all the way to 4,561cc (a Daimler V8). Although A-Series engines currently found a home in just three of those existing platform/chassis frames, they were all best-sellers at the time.

Commercially and financially, to let this situation persist for any period was madness, pure madness, but such was Sir Donald Stokes' sympathy with the government – and their politics – of the day, and their collective desire to protect employment, that no sensible amount of streamlining took place for many months to come; nor, as far as I can see, were any such measures even proposed. Puzzling – for one of the main economic arguments in favour of a merger like this would have been to rationalise on facilities, factories and model lines.

The reverse, in fact, seemed to be the case, for no sooner had the marriage been legitimised than Donald Stokes drafted in a 'hit squad' of Leyland managers, finance staff and engineers to bring about the changes to the old BMC organisation which he thought to be necessary. Just as soon as he could arrange it, therefore (and as already described in the previous chapter), Stokes made sure that Alec Issigonis' overall control of BMC engineering was decisively ended, that the very practical BMC engineer Charles Griffin was confirmed as engineering director of Austin-Morris, and that Harry Webster was brought in over his head (from Standard-Triumph) to take complete technical control of the design and development activities of the Austin-Morris Division.

Although Webster's reputation preceded him – he took much of the credit for the restoration of Standard-Triumph's engineering reputation to eminence during the 1960s – in later years he readily acknowledged that at first he knew very little about the new empire which he came to control. Although there had already been one front-wheel-drive Triumph – the much-respected 1300 saloon of 1965 – this had an entirely different layout from that of the Issigonis-inspired Mini/1100/1300/1800 (and, soon, Maxi) pedigree, and Harry later admitted that neither he nor his immediate staff knew much about any of these cars, or their engines, when they arrived.

Webster, however, already held several aces – one being

that he was used to engineering conventional (*ie* front engine/rear drive) cars, the other being that his Coventry-based Standard-Triumph team had been successfully developing their own small four-cylinder engine (the SC range), which had already been in production for almost 15 years. That engine had already proved itself in many different road cars, and also on the race and rally tracks of the world (most noticeably in the Le Mans 24 Hour races of 1964 and 1965).

Incidentally, in spite of a few biased and ill-informed comments to the contrary, the Standard-Triumph SC did not, and never had to, rely on the A-Series for any of its architecture and detail layout.

'We need to match the new Fords'

Even before Webster arrived at Longbridge, BMC (Sir George Harriman and Charles Griffin, rather than the other-worldly, blinkered Issigonis) had perceived that its entire small-medium range of conventional rear-wheel-drive cars was dying of old age, and losing its market. Issigonis did not seem to care, but the dealerships most certainly did, as they were having to fight very hard to sell the Austin A40 'Farinas' (launched 1958), Morris Minors (1948) and Austin-Morris B-Series 'Farinas' (1958–59). In the case of the A40 and Morris Minor, where those cars were suffering so was the demand for A-Series engines.

Not only that, but what we later came to describe as the British 'fleet car market' was booming. More and more companies began to award individual members of their management with a 'company car' as part of the salary package, and such cars tended to be of the conventional front-engine/rear-drive variety. Ford in particular, with its wide range of Cortinas and with a fresh new range of Escorts announced in the very week that British Leyland was formed, led the lists.

'I distinctly remember,' Ray Bates told me, 'that Leyland's John Barber insisted that what we really needed was a direct competitor to the Ford Escort. Charles Griffin tried to explain to him that we, on the other hand, believed in front-wheel-drive and that we didn't have a rear-wheel-drive model.

'Barber then said, effectively, "Well, get one."

'Well, the only existing car we actually had was the ancient Morris Minor, which was dying, if not altogether dead, so we had to resurrect that and have another look at it, complete with its lever-arm front shock absorbers, and leaf springs at the rear – and that's really where the Marina came from.'

It was with all this in mind that in 1968 Longbridge's first, pressing, priority was to develop a new but conventionally (for which read 'old-fashioned') engineered car to replace its old models, the sort of cars that Issigonis had deliberately ignored for a decade. On the basis of 'the impossible we do at once, but miracles take a little longer', the design team set about producing a new front-engine/rear-drive car which would be ready for launch within three years.

Once British Leyland's sales force were consulted, they wanted a new car at once, even though they did not apparently understand the realities of mass-production tooling schedules, for they hoped to get it on show at the Earls Court (London) Motor Show in October 1970. That

was never really going to be possible, and the new car – eventually badged as the Morris Marina – was launched in April 1971.

Here was a car developed at breakneck speed, so it simply *had* to be engineered in a conventional no-risk 'we've all done this before' manner. Right away, the new car, coded ADO28, was to have a complex product-planned line-up of two body styles (two-door coupé and

By the 1980s Longbridge had reached the limit of its industrial expansion, for there was no more land on which new buildings could be erected. This aerial view, taken from the south, shows how the two CABs (Car Assembly Buildings) dominated the site. West Works and North Works are at the top of the shot, the multi-storey car park and the 'Flight Shed' are closest to the camera, while East Works is actually underneath the plane from which the photograph is being taken. (*BMIHT*)

four-door saloon, with a third, the estate car, to follow), and two engines – one of which was to be the A-Series. As originally planned the new model was to have a choice of A-Series and E-Series (Austin Maxi-type) engines, and a new manual gearbox which was an evolution of the existing Triumph GT6 variety (tooling for this was to be installed in Longbridge's historic 'Flight Shed', close to East Works).

After a brisk styling competition, in which British Leyland's own team (led by ex-Ford personality Roy Haynes) fought off proposals from Pininfarina and Michelotti, the themes were accepted before the end of 1968, and all the detailing was settled within a year. Assembly, it was decided, would be at the rejigged (Morris/BMC) factory at Cowley – which automatically

doomed the much-loved Morris Minor to extinction – and would also involve the construction of a massive bridge over the public roads to allow bodyshells to be transported from the Pressed Steel Fisher complex. Not only that, but with British Leyland hoping to produce up to 5,000 Marinas every week the truck 'pipeline' from Longbridge to Cowley (there was no M40 motorway at this time) would be a vital element in the production process. In the words of one experienced BL publicist of the day, 'We really *owned* the A44, you know . . .'

There was never any doubt that the A-Series engine would be a very important part of the product planning jigsaw for this model, though at first it was thought that it would have to struggle to deal with the weight of the new ADO28's structure. Because the new car was to face up to the Ford Escort and Cortina, the Vauxhall Viva and (though this was not known in 1968) the new Hillman Avenger, ADO28 would be significantly larger than the Minor 1000 had ever been. For comparison, this is how it eventually lined up:

Love it or hate it, you'd have to admit that the Morris Marina sold well enough in the 1970s to return good profits to troubled British Leyland. Around half of the Marinas built – like this coupé – had 1.3-litre A-Series engines.

ADO28/Marina 1.3	96in wheelbase	1,825lb unladen weight
Morris Minor 1000	86in wheelbase	1,735lb unladen weight
Austin/Morris 1300 (FWD)	93.5in wheelbase	1,780lb unladen weight

For that reason, for the price 'entry-level' it was decided only to use one type of A-Series engine – the Longbridge-built 1,275cc derivative – in single-SU carburettor guise, when it was rated at 60bhp at 5,250rpm (almost identical with that being used in the newly-launched Mini 1275GT). With Longbridge geared up to produce as many as possible of the same type of A-Series, all that was needed to tailor it to this 'north-south' alignment was new manifolding and a new sump, along with suitable carburettor and air-cleaner installations.

At that rating, incidentally, the A-Series provided the new Marina with a top speed of 85mph, 0–60mph acceleration in 17.3 seconds, and overall fuel consumption of around 30mpg, which made it completely competitive against its rivals – and it is worth noting that in 1971, when the Marina appeared, the A-Series was already a 20-year-old design and was producing twice as much power as its 1951 ancestor.

By this time, of course, almost every engineer, planner and manager in British Leyland could virtually ignore the A-Series – and many of them did so – because it had become so unfailingly reliable, so adaptable and (if one could give a piece of metal sculpture a character) so faithful too.

Ray Bates, however, recalled ADO28 without pleasure: 'The original plan was to have a 1,300cc A-Series version, and a 1,500cc or 1,600cc E-Series alternative. That was what we went ahead with in Engineering, until my "friend" Joe Greatorex said "No way" – his production plant did not have the capacity. So that's why we had to put the "load of concrete" at the front instead – which was our name for the old 1.8-litre B-Series.'

What happened in the next few years has little bearing on the A-Series story, but it is worth noting that the Marina (suitably rejigged as the Ital in 1980) ran through until 1984, and that, in total, no fewer than 808,381 were produced. Not only that, but as already mentioned in the analysis of events concerning motorsport activities (Chapter 7), in Brian Culcheth's hands the 'works' Marina rally cars were competent and credible, if not outright winners, for some years during the 1970s.

By any standards, even those of hard-nosed financial accountants, the Marina had been a success.

Mini: still going

Through all the traumas, the strikes, the financial bombshells, the nationalisation of British Leyland and the financial reconstructions which had to be made in the 1970s, the Mini kept going on . . . and on . . . and on. Without the Mini, it seems, the entire Longbridge complex sometimes looked as if it would grind to a halt. The fact that it rarely made any money for the company during that decade is not of major influence on this part of the A-Series story – except that a shortage of investment capital for new products meant that it just had to continue, little changed but everlastingly popular. It was for that reason that none of the new engines designed under Geoff Johnson's supervision at this time (see Chapter 8), some of which would have been ideally suited for use in a rejuvenated Mini, ever had a chance of making their way into production.

Although assembly of Minis at Cowley ended in 1968 (to make way for the all-new Maxi, which took its place in those ageing buildings), overall Mini production continued to be vital to the company's survival. As an example, in the financial year 1971–72 (with the Marina also already in mass production), this is how the production of cars with A-Series engines stacked up:

Mini	283,113
1100/1300	137,046
Marina	85,000 approx (many B-Series-engined types were also built)
MG Midget	16,247
Morris Minor	8,447

– along with many 'knocked down' kits for which individual production totals are not available.

Each and every Mini was powered by an A-Series, though the sub-type, power output and detail specification changed subtly as the years passed.

After 1968 and the foundation of British Leyland, one of the first decisions made by Sir Donald (soon to be Lord) Stokes was to make 'Leyland' much more up-front, to get rid of a number of what he considered obsolete brands, and to fire the technical consultants who, in his opinion, were milking the company of fees and of royalty payments.

Hindsight now tells us that this was a disastrous and stupid move. On the one hand, he got rid of 'badge-engineered' cars like the slow-selling Riley Elf and

Wolseley Hornet, which was reasonable (although the dealer chain did not agree). On the other, 'Mini' suddenly appeared as a brand instead of a model name, yet at the same time four renowned and world-famous consultants – John Cooper, Donald Healey, Daniel Richmond (of Downton) and the Weslake concern – were swept aside.

The consequence was that brands such as Austin-Healey and Mini-Cooper were speedily killed off, and Daniel Richmond's undoubted tune-up talents were dismissed. Stokes' problem, apparently, is that his henchmen (who knew far less about the motor car, as opposed to the commercial vehicle, industry than they would have him believe) convinced him that there was enough talent within his new empire to do the job for themselves. The result was that the MGC was introduced to take over from the 'Big' Healey 3000 (it failed, technically), the new Mini 1275GT took over from the Mini-Cooper (in marketing terms that failed, too), and the Mini-Cooper S suddenly stopped winning races and rallies as it neared the end of its ongoing development programme. For the real enthusiasts, the insult was the British Leyland tag line, which tried to convince them that the 1275GT 'Carries on where the Cooper left off . . .'.

As far as the A-Series engine was concerned, the murder of the Mini-Cooper (which came in 1969), the Mini-Cooper S and the Austin-Healey Sprite was a triple blow. From that time, there was no conceivable future for the very specialised 1,275cc Mini-Cooper S engine (which was still manufactured only at Courthouse Green in Coventry); and since Mini-Cooper and Sprite engines had also always been built at Courthouse Green, the Coventry factory began to look underused. It was, indeed, one more chink in its armour – one which led to Courthouse Green being closed down in the late 1970s.

The rationale in introducing the newly-badged long-nose Mini 1275GT in 1969, effectively as a replacement for the Mini-Cooper 1275S (which died in 1971) but with a mass-market Longbridge-built A-Series, was to improve the range's profitability. In the UK, although the last of the Cooper S types retailed at £1,008, at a time when the 1275GT cost £894, the S had always been inherently costly to build.

Maybe, just maybe, that was justified – but the fact is that the A-Series engine fitted to the Cooper S produced 76bhp at 5,800rpm, whereas that of the 1275GT produced just 59bhp at 5,300rpm. Not only that, but the

sturdy S engine, complete with its special cylinder head, twin SU carburettors, fabricated exhaust manifold and sporty camshaft, could be power-tuned considerably if needed, whereas the engine fitted to the 1275GT had one SU, a cast iron exhaust manifold, and was virtually the same as that fitted to ADO16s of the period.

For the rest of the 1970s, therefore, the Mini range carried on, with a myriad of minor changes taking place, but with nothing major ever being done to the ever-faithful A-Series engine which powered it. New paint jobs, new fascias, new run-flat tyres, 12in wheels and a host of special/limited editions all made an appearance, but under the bonnet very little changed.

Even so, there was a steady stream of reshuffling, to take account of minor regulatory changes and to keep the ageing car well clear of new models being launched all around it – not least the controversial Austin Allegro in 1973. Throughout the 1970s the Mini range started with the 848cc version of the A-Series, which was no more powerful and no more torquey than it had been in 1959, but an increasing number of Minis were fitted with the 998cc version, where peak power gradually (almost imperceptibly) improved from 38bhp to 41bhp. The long-nosed Mini Clubman started life with the same 998cc engines, but from mid-decade this was enlarged to 45bhp/1,098cc.

By the end of the 1970s, when the Mini Metro was finally ready to be introduced, more than 150,000 cars a year were still being produced, though the range had contracted significantly. From 1981 the Mini City and the Mini 1000 (both with 998cc versions of the A-Series) were continued, but for how long? No one knew, but at the time it looked as if the Metro was all about BL's future, and the dear old classic Mini was the past.

How wrong we all were.

Allegro: the ugly duckling

In the meantime, British Leyland had spent four years bringing ADO67 – aka the Austin Allegro – to the marketplace, where it was to become one of the most heavily criticised new cars in the nationalised concern's range throughout the 1970s. Conceived as an all-things-to-all-men replacement for the well-liked (and very successful) 1100/1300 range, it was not a success.

Indeed, it was almost mission impossible to expect any new car to do better than the Pininfarina-styled

Although the Allegro was a controversial car it sold well at first, with nearly 90,000 assembled in its best-ever year, 1975–76. This was the scene at Longbridge at that time. (*BMIHT*)

1100/1300. Throughout the 1960s and into the 1970s this range had often vied with Ford's Cortina as the fastest-selling car on the British market. No fewer than six different 'badge-engineered' types had been marketed, and by the time it retired in 1974 no fewer than 2.2 million had been built, each and every one of the British-built examples with a 1,098cc or 1,275cc A-Series engine.

With a new model required, and with everyone agreed that it should have a transverse engine and front-wheel drive, this was the point at which 'product planning' got in on the act. Product Planning, which was relatively new to British Leyland (previously the sales force and lobbyists from the dealer chain had defined their own imperatives),

concluded that the new car – coded ADO67 – should not only fill the price and marketing gap between the Mini and the Maxi, but should overlap those two cars. Not only that, but British Leyland decided that, being front-wheel-drive, it should be an Austin, and not a Morris, and that only one other badge – the Vanden Plas Princess – should be added to the nose.

However, this is not the place to analyse every controversial area of the design – such as the style, which was bulbous and definitely inferior to the car that it replaced; the fact that the proportions were affected by the enforced use of a bulky new 'corporate' heating/air-conditioning system; or the lack of refinement and elegance which the old 1100/1300 had most certainly had.

It is worth mentioning, too, that the new car did not have a hatchback, at a time when every one of its rivals (and a growing proportion of the world's new models) had such a feature. The most bizarre item of equipment, at first, was that the cars were equipped with what was known as a 'Quartic' steering wheel, which was more square than round, and which was roundly despised by everyone except British Leyland's blinkered management.

The Allegro/ADO67's one saving grace, however, was that the fully-developed range was eventually sold with a wide choice of 1.0, 1.1, 1.3, 1.5 and 1.7-litre engines. The smaller engines were all derivatives of the long-running A-Series, whereas the 1,485cc and 1,748cc engines (entirely different, including the use of totally different transmissions) were larger E-Series types as normally found in the Austin Maxi. Both types, of course, were being manufactured in the same massive East Works part of Longbridge, but with a difference: the E-Series facility was drastically underused (and would continue to be so), while the A-Series plant was always bursting at the seams.

For the record, the multifarious A-Series types were all of the single-SU carburettor variety, and over the years they were produced as follows:

998cc	*44bhp*
1,098cc	*45bhp and 48bhp*
1,275cc	*59bhp and 62bhp*

Between 1973 and 1982 the Allegro stumbled on, never selling in anything like the volumes hoped. In its peak year (1975–76), 89,933 such cars were built at Longbridge, which was only half of what its sponsors had intended, and by the time it was dropped in 1982 a total of 642,350 had been produced, more than half of these being A-Series types.

Metro: the 'make or break' car

Millions of words, and several worthy books, have been written about the tortuous way in which the car we eventually knew as the Metro came to market in 1980. Throughout the 1970s a variety of projects were started, then abandoned, reinstated, renamed, re-engineered, and once again abandoned. Everyone could be – and usually was – blamed for this farrago, but a lack of investment capital or a loss of priority in the British Leyland development cycle was always a root cause.

Earlier in this book (see the previous chapter) I detailed how Alec Issigonis had conceived the 9X project to replace the Mini, and how Geoff Johnson's engine

design team had worked tirelessly on a series of ground-up revisions, and even overhead-camshaft conversions for the A-Series engine, but had found all such projects persistently killed off, sometimes after a great deal of test-bed and experimental road-car running had taken place.

There seems to be little doubt that this was one major reason for Issigonis' eventual 'retirement', for Harry Webster's decision to resign in 1974, and for his successor Charles Griffin to follow him out of British Leyland's 'revolving door' in 1978. It also explains why the gallant A-Series engine carried on, and carried on, still the most prominent of all 'building blocks' at Longbridge, yet still most urgently in need of modernisation – or retirement.

It was not until the late 1970s, however, that a Mini-replacement finally began to emerge. A new small hatchback, coded ADO88, gradually emerged after fighting its way through the thicket of Product Planning, Financial Strategy and Corporate Plan proposals. At this time, no question, it was intended to replace the classic Mini completely: many months were to pass before ADO88 was seen as a car which was somewhat larger than the ageing Mini, and that the two types could carry on side-by-side.

Although the engineering and packaging of the ADO88 was most ably directed by Charles Griffin, the Longbridge-based styling took ages to come to fruition. The new car was somehow seen as too 'Plain Jane', and when it was finally exposed to limited public view at a series of styling clinics in 1977 and 1978 it fared very badly indeed. The story of how Sir Michael Edwardes, the newly-appointed and pugnacious chairman, agreed to a complete surface facelift (even though some of the tooling for the floor pan and inner structure had already been commissioned) has often been told. ADO88 became LC8, and the launch was set for October 1980.

In the meantime, work went ahead on an improvement programme for the A-Series, for the old engine was now expected to carry on into the 1980s. Because of the now familiar constraints on investment capital spending, and on the time available, the work had to be done at breakneck speed. In 1978, when a number of development threads came together, there was precious little time to spare, but this time no less than £30 million was made available for new tooling and manufacturing facilities for the A-Series at Longbridge.

No single person was responsible for what was done, for much individual expertise and knowledge was

Allegros were powered by A-Series or the altogether larger E-Series power units. This explains why the A-Series installation here seems to have a great deal of space to spare. (*BMIHT*)

involved. As Ray Bates commented: 'There was a lot involved in going from A to what we called A-Plus. On the HLE version we raised the compression ratio to about 10.0:1 . . . Then came the MG version, and it was obvious to me that quite a few people in my development area had raced old-type Minis, and knew a lot. I had a round-table meeting, challenged them all to produce a more powerful version for the MG Metro, and told them to get on with it.

'Well, about an hour later we had decided on the spec using their know-how. There was already a lot of information out there, so it was just a matter of collating it, and deciding what we were going to do.'

The improvement was not in outright performance

figures, but in the quality of the product. Though the 998cc engine was improved from 38bhp to 41bhp – that was only an 8% improvement – it brought together a number of enhancements. Not only that, but the 1,275cc engine, which had been rated at 54bhp in the latest Mini 1275GTs, would be re-rated to a much more stirring 72bhp in MG Metro form. These were all the results of what BL claimed to be major uprating – from A-Series to A-Plus-Series.

The new 'Metro' engine actually broke cover in July 1980, when it was applied to the Morris Ital, itself a much reworked derivative of the Marina, though it was only in its Metro iteration that it got much attention. Central to the whole package was a stiffened-up cylinder block, complete with external ribs in the revised casting, and although the five-port cylinder head was much as before it was now mated to a new inlet manifold for the single

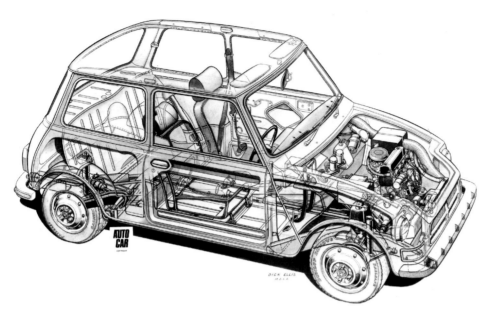

As the move to look more closely at a series of experimental, high-tech safety cars intensified, BL developed this A-Series-powered Mini SRV4 in 1974. Note the front-mounted radiator, and the Dunlop Denovo tyres.

Because of all the new regulations, and the fact that it would have to overcome 30mph barrier crash tests, the Mini Metro of 1980 was significantly larger than the old Mini. As this cutaway drawing confirms, this meant that there was more space for the A-Series engine.

SU carburettor, and a twin-outlet exhaust manifold. Incidentally, although it was almost a decade since he had had any influence on the way A-Series engines were evolving, it is known that Daniel Richmond of Downton had originally recommended such upgrades.

To add to the package, the inlet manifold casting was arranged to suit the use of larger HIF-type SU carburettors, there were revised camshaft profiles, higher-temperature cooling thermostats, and the compression ratios were raised to 8.3, 9.6 and 10.3:1, depending on the tune. Hidden away were features which had evolved from the now-obsolete 1275S-type engines including

The arrival of the new Metro – officially known as the Austin Mini Metro at first – in 1980 was BL's most hyped launch of all time. Until 1990, each and every Metro was powered by the ever-willing A-Series engine. (*BMIHT*)

nimonic exhaust valves, a crankshaft torsional damper, a hydraulic timing chain tensioner, Stellited exhaust valve seats and fillet-rolled crankshafts.

All this, and other facets of the new Metro, were pushed through ruthlessly by Austin-Rover MD Harold Musgrove, who reported to Ray Horrocks, the two bringing a new urgency to the way that new BL products were being developed. Charles Griffin had tired of the way that some things were being done, and retired, leaving Ray Bates to become engineering director:

'We worked our backsides off with that car', Bates told me. 'Everybody there did. We used to go out with Harold Musgrove from Gaydon, with Metro prototypes, wait until it was dark, drive them like maniacs all round Edge Hill and the local roads. Then have a debriefing meeting at Gaydon at about one- or two-o'clock in the morning. Harold would then say: "Right, we'll have a meeting in

To power the new Mini Metro, announced in late 1980, BL uprated the A-Series to what they called A-Plus. Though fundamentally not changed, it was a better engine in many details, including the use of a stiffer cylinder block and more efficient, free-flowing, inlet and exhaust manifolds. Within two years there would be an uprated 'MG Metro' derivative, and even a turbocharged type for the 'MG Metro Turbo'.

my office at eight in the morning, to decide what is to be done." In fact we had chaps who would go back to the office then, and work through the night to get ready for that meeting.'

The effort, for sure, was all worth it, and the Metro was launched in a haze of patriotic fervour in October 1980, surged ahead on the crest of an amazing amount of gung-ho advertising, and began to sell just as rapidly as BL could produce the cars at Longbridge. With all the bodyshells produced at Longbridge, along with all the transmissions, and with every car powered by an A-Plus engine (and, yes, from this moment I will revert to calling them mere A-Series types) this was definitely Longbridge's finest hour, especially as management under Sir Michael Edwardes finally faced down the strike-prone, trouble-seeking elements of the workforce and got rid of the ringleaders.

This glossed-up display engine/transmission assembly of the original 'A-Plus' of 1980 shows just how compact and nicely detailed this engine was. The use of an alternator (instead of a dynamo) was a relatively recent development.

As far as the Metro was concerned, a great start – in its first full year (1981) no fewer than 165,745 cars were produced in the much-revised CAB buildings, with a peak of 180,763 achieved just two years later – was to be followed up by more and more successful derivatives. In 1982, not only did a 'pensioners' special' (the Vanden Plas type) go on sale, but so did the so-called MG Metro, which

was the first of the BL cars used to revive the famous old badge after the ancient MGB had finally been killed off.

Both those cars used the same amazingly effective version of the 1,275cc engine, which produced no less than 72bhp at 6,000rpm, although to do this only a single SU HIF44 carburettor was required. This, above all, proved that BL's engine specialists had not been asleep in recent years, for it compared extremely well with the 76bhp that had once been produced by the now-obsolete 1275S power unit, though that had needed twin-SU carburettors, a special cylinder head and many other expensive components to do the job.

Even so, Ray Bates' Longbridge team had worked away at many details, which included a new and rather sporty camshaft profile, larger-diameter inlet valves, modified port profiles, a 10.5:1 compression ratio and a water-heated inlet manifold, all of which proved his point that a great deal of development and tuning knowledge had built up behind the scenes at Longbridge, and had only been waiting for the opportunity to be added to production engines.

The so-called A-Plus engine of 1980 was no more than a solid update of the A-Series engine itself, and the 'Plus' part of the title was soon forgotten.

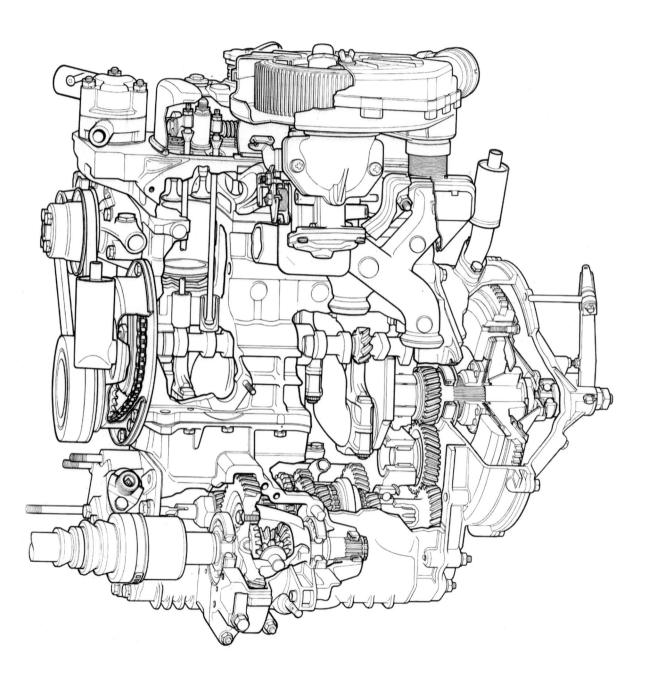

The basic packaging difference between the Mini and the Metro was that the Metro (shown here) was fitted with a front radiator. The Mini would not follow suit until the mid-1990s.

Harold Musgrove managed the Austin-Morris business in the late 1970s and early 1980s, and was the main driving force behind Metro development, in which the A-Series engine played such a big part.

Turbocharging

Even so, this was not the end of the road. Until BL's Product Planners got round to inventing the Metro Turbo no one at Longbridge had thought much about turbocharging the A-Series engine, for the pedigree of the power unit was now so lengthy that it was not really considered appropriate.

Not that forced induction of an A-Series was unknown. Way back at the end of the 1950s, when Healey were developing the Austin-Healey Sprite as rapidly as they could, a few supercharged versions had been produced; but these had been built primarily as engines for use in 'record cars', and had been privately tuned by Shorrock, who provided the supercharger itself.

Austin-Rover's first and only turbocharged A-Series engine was fitted to the MG Metro Turbo, which was announced in 1982.

In 1959, in EX219 (see Chapter 6), a 948cc engine prepared for a car to attempt to break endurance records of up to 12 hours was rated at 70bhp at 5,400rpm, whereas the same car, when trying to set short-distance sprint records, could have a similar engine producing 86bhp at 6,000rpm.

At the same time, as BMC's publicity handout made clear, 'So that we may also attempt a short distance sprint record at maximum speed, a spare engine is available . . . developing 98bhp at 6,500rpm' – all of which proved that the basic architecture of the A-Series engine was sturdy, to say the least.

It was only when BL decided to develop a complete range of Metros, and to 'push the barriers', that turbocharging was even considered. Although it had become fashionable in the European motor industry, forced induction like this was still developing fast.

Turbocharged F1 engines had only begun to win races at the end of the 1970s, and the first real road car (the BMW 2002 Turbo) had only appeared in 1973, followed by cars like the Porsche 911 Turbo and the Saab 99 Turbo. In 1979–80, when Product Planning got its way, no other of Britain's largest car-makers – not Ford, not Vauxhall and not Peugeot (ex-Chrysler) – had yet taken the plunge. Lotus, however, was known to be at the forefront of such innovations, and was working on a turbo version of its own Esprit sports car.

Once inspired to take the lead, however, BL wanted to do the job quickly, and for that reason they hired the consultancy arm of Lotus to do the job for them. Lotus, by this time, not only built cars but carried out a lot of basic work for client manufacturers, and even though they had become heavily committed in preparing the DeLorean project for series production in Northern Ireland, they took on the task.

Although it would have been easy enough to boost the A-Series' peak power to well over 100bhp, BL had to put a limit on Lotus' ambitions. The limit was not in the gallant little engine's crankshaft, or its other vital organs, but in the transmission drop gears that transferred the torque from the end of the crank to the gearbox 'in the sump'. Without spending squillions of pounds, and making changes which could not be accommodated in East Works, where the engines were to be built, those drop gears would have to remain in place.

For that reason, therefore, all manner of electronic limitations (up to the technical standards of the day but, of course, rudimentary compared to what would be achieved in later years) were applied to the turbocharging installation itself. Nor was there any need to find space, or any sensible packaging solution, for the fitment of an air-air intercooler. Somehow or other Lotus managed to squeeze most of the new kit behind the cylinder block, and ahead of the bulkhead/firewall of the Metro bodyshell. It was so neatly done that even Alec Issigonis (who was not, of course, involved) would have approved. A 'dustbin' type air cleaner was mounted high and to one side of the engine, which fed fresh air to the Garret AiResearch T3 turbocharger itself, which was at cylinder-head level and was fixed directly to a new shape exhaust manifold, driven by the engine's exhaust gases, and therefore channelled compressed air to the finned inlet box which surrounded the single SU HIF44 carburettor. Amazingly, the combustion chamber retained the 9.4:1

compression ratio normally seen on a Metro 1.3S – which was much higher than would normally be found on rival turbo engines of the day.

So far, so simple, but in order to restrict the boost (and therefore, to restrict the stress on the transmission drop gears), the turbo's performance was restricted, to provide peak torque of just 85lb/ft at 2,650rpm; this speed was one at which most other turbo installations were just beginning to work, not reaching their peak! Maximum power was 93bhp at 6,130rpm – more than three times what had been developed by the original 803cc A-Series engine, all those years ago, but not nearly as high an output as could have been tolerated if the Metro transmission had allowed it.

To limit the torque, the waste-gate (effectively the 'boost limiter') was set at a mere 4psi, and was controlled by a Lucas-developed piezo-electric sensor, though this installation gradually slackened its control at higher revs, with no less than 7.3 psi being allowed at 6,000rpm. Hidden away inside the engine was a nitrided crankshaft, strengthened pistons, reinforced big-end bearing caps and sodium-filled exhaust valve heads.

All in all, this seemed to work well, particularly as the car itself was endowed with an engine oil cooler up front, with wide-rim alloy wheels, firmed-up suspension, bigger brakes with ventilated discs and an even more capable handling package. It went on sale at £5,650, which was £851 more than the 72bhp MG Metro model, and immediately began to sell well, but not close to the potential capacity of 10,000 Turbos a year.

Incidentally, although there was no functional intercooler, BL elected to give that title to the finned airbox around the carburettor. The Motorsport department (which wanted to develop this car for saloon car racing) had a hand in this, as the then motorsport director John Davenport recalls:

'We had good connections with Product Planning, especially guys like David Bloom, Nick Stephenson and Steven Schlemmer . . . thus we knew about the MG Metro Turbo from almost its earliest beginnings.

'One interesting story from that time was that David Wood (our engine design guru) went up to the Longbridge design department when everything was still on the drawing board, to have a look at the engine. The Metro Turbo had no separate intercooler but, if you had one at all, Appendix J at that time allowed it to be replaced by one of unlimited size.

'David cunningly suggested that the word "intercooler" should be inserted into the name of the design of the slightly finned casting that fed the compressed air into the SU. I am pretty sure that this was done and we were thus able to race with a full-sized air-air intercooler.'

At this time, road-testers sometimes affected an air of slightly puzzled embarrassment, that A-Series-engined cars could still be around, but in the case of the MG Metro Turbo they were, at least, welcoming in their remarks. When *Autocar* finally tested a car in March 1983, they discovered a top speed of 110mph and 0–60mph acceleration in 9.4 seconds, which was extremely competitive for that period. In addition they found a very smooth and linear power delivery, and that: 'The progression of power is much smoother and less stepped than usual for a turbo, so much so that drivers used to normal turbo cars can be heard complaining that the MG doesn't "really go" . . .' When the car's character was being summarised, the conclusion was that: 'In engine terms, the turbocharged car is more acceptable than usual because of its unusually wide, less stepped, power band.'

Although the A-Series engine was much the oldest feature of the Metro range, it did not disgrace it. Before it was re-engined (with the K-Series unit, and renamed with a 'Rover' badge at the end of 1990), no fewer than 1,518,932 Austin Metros, 120,206 normally-aspirated MG Metros, and 21,969 Metro Turbos had been produced, which made it a profitable car by any standards.

Maestro and Montego: yet more A-Series applications

Amazingly, and more than 30 years after it had originally been launched, the now fully-matured A-Series found itself pressed into service in larger (specifically medium-sized) cars. Technically, this never made much sense (for the cars chosen were very significantly larger and heavier than the Mini/1100/Metro models for which the engine was ideally suited, which meant that the A-Series would always struggle to deliver competitive performance); but the truth was that the A-Series fulfilled a worthy task, when asked to provide power for the closely related Austin Maestro and Austin Montego models.

Although not actually put on sale until 1983 and 1984 respectively, these two closely-related cars had been conceived well before the Metro went on sale in 1980,

when they carried the project codes of LC10 and LC11, which eventually became LM10 and LM11 respectively. In fact, if the truth be told, BL had once hoped to start building LM10s *before* the Metro came along, though company politics and – guess what? – matters of high finance made this impossible. LM10 was, effectively, a replacement for the Allegro and Maxi models, whereas LM11 catered for a larger and more costly market sector.

Every student of product planning, and especially of styling, could immediately see that the basic engineering and styling of these two cars was closely related. Both were front-wheel drive (with the familiar transversely-mounted engine layout), they shared some elements of their structural bodyshell and styling, and in many ways they shared the same engine, transmission and suspension packages.

Although both were to be assembled at Cowley (with bodyshells provided by Pressed Steel Fisher, just across the road), the basic difference was that the LM10/Maestro was a five-door hatchback model, whereas the LM11/Montego was a four-door notchback saloon, eventually to be joined by an estate car alternative. Technically, the big advance was that these were the very first BL-designed front-wheel-drive cars to be developed without a 'gearbox-in-sump' feature; for the first time, and in line with all future BL/Austin-Rover models, they would be fitted instead with the more conventional 'end-on' gearbox, a layout which had already been adopted by most of their industrial rivals. Not only that, but their suspension was by steel springs, all thought of using Hydragas or even Hydrolastic having been dropped. The simplicity of the complete design was the hallmark of Spen King, who had been technical director at the time the twin cars were first schemed up but had since moved on to become deputy chairman of BL Technology at Gaydon.

We must never forget that BL was still a nationalised company, a situation that affected almost everything that was going on in the business at this time. Nor can we forget that the tortuous story of how the LM10 came to be conceived, delayed, designed, rejigged with more than one different line-up of engines and transmissions, then affected by pitiless scrutiny from those in government who had to be persuaded to provide the investment capital to re-equip the Cowley assembly lines, has been told before, so that what follows is a mere summary.

LM10/Maestro had to replace not one, but two different existing models: the Austin Allegro, which had been

Even though there was ample space to 'package' an A-Series engine in the Maestro bodyshell of 1983, all manner of carburettor electronic controls, to monitor the emissions, were beginning to bulk up the power unit.

launched in a storm of controversy in 1973, and the Austin Maxi of 1969 (though with several updates along the way). Through this protracted period – and it took at least five years – it was always clear that a small and cheap-to-build engine, which ought to have been an A-Series successor but (as I have already made clear in Chapter 8) did not work out that way, should have been included in the entry-level versions.

When launched in March 1983, therefore, the five-door hatchback Maestro had power outputs ranging from 64bhp to 103bhp, and by the time the range was fully developed there would be a turbocharged 152bhp model too. A-Series versions (all, naturally, of 1,275cc) produced 64bhp or 68bhp, depending on the trim package chosen, and all of them were mated to 'end-on' four-speed VW Golf gearboxes. Clearly the A-Series engine was going to have a hard time, for the most basic Maestro weighed 1,929lb, which was yet another significant increase compared with, say, that of an Austin Allegro 1300, which had weighed just 1,850lb.

To suit the new 'end-on' gearbox arrangement (this VW transmission/final drive unit was always mounted on the left side of the engine bay – *ie* the right side when looking in from the nose of the car), the A-Series engine had been rotated through 180°, so that the ignition side of the unit was located 'behind' the engine (close to the passenger bulkhead), with the carburation and manifolding at what had become the front side, immediately behind the front-mounted radiator. This, therefore, was the first time that an A-Series engine had ever been mounted in this way in a production car. With more under-space available than ever before, this also allowed the engineering team to provide new and more efficient manifolds; there was a higher (9.75:1) compression ratio, and the most highly-tuned version of this installation produced 68bhp at 5,800rpm. In almost all other respects, however, the 1,275cc unit was as before.

Amazingly, the 1,275cc engine proved to be not at all unsuitable for the big job which it was asked to take on, for independent road tests showed that a Maestro 1.3 was capable of 96mph, and could get up to 60mph from rest in 12.3 seconds. That both these were improvements on equivalent Allegro figures proved that the engine was still a lusty machine, and that the aerodynamics of the Maestro were considerably more 'slippery' than the Allegro had ever been.

The sales figures (approximate, for full and final figures were not made available to me) prove their point. Although more than 600,000 Maestros were produced in the next 12 years, at least half of them were thought to be powered by A-Series engines.

The second part of this story belongs to the Montego model, which appeared a year later and, although clearly derived from and related to the Maestro, was a larger, longer, heavier and more upmarket car – a four-door saloon rather than a five-door hatchback. As with the Maestro, there was an extensively product-planned series

In 1986 Canadian businessman Graham Day was drafted in by the British government to run BL. Day, a great Mini enthusiast, made sure that this fading model was continued, and that the A-Series engine therefore survived.

of specifications, with the venerable A-Series engine used to power the entry-level version of the range.

Austin-Rover, the new name (yet another new name!) for BL, can surely not have expected to sell many A-Series-engined Montegos, especially as these cars weighed in at 2,094lb, but at least it gave them the opportunity to quote a super-low price for the new range. And so it transpired. Although subsequent tests suggested that a 1.3-litre-engined Montego might approach 90mph, the buying public was not impressed, and only 26,841 A-Series-engined types (of more than half a million Montegos) were ever produced.

The end in sight: or was it all premature?

Cynics were now ready to write off the A-Series, affectionately perhaps, but to write it off nevertheless. After all, the last major technical update had been with the turbocharged unit used in the Metro Turbo of 1982, the last new model launch had been in the Montego of 1984, and surely the wonderful old Mini was about to die too?

By the early 1990s almost all of the cars that had been assembled at Cowley and Longbridge in the 1970s and 1980s had died, in favour of new, Honda-inspired machines that made use of the K-Series power unit (described in the next chapter). Here is a comparison between A-Series users in 1985 and those of a decade later, in 1995:

1985
Mini
Metro (Austin and MG)
Maestro (Austin and MG)
Montego (Austin and MG)

1995
Mini
Mini-Cooper

In that decade, not only had the Honda influence spread far and wide within the Rover Group (the name had changed yet again . . .), but at long last a new small engine – the technically advanced K-Series – had finally gone on sale.

There was, however, to be one final hurrah for the A-Series, and it came in the shape of the rebirth of the Mini-Cooper.

CHAPTER 10

1989, and the K-Series arrives at last

In May 1989, Mini enthusiasts greeted one modest piece of news from the Rover Group almost as reverently as the Second Coming, though as far as the company's accountants were concerned the impact was less shattering. For the first time since 1971, Longbridge had once again given official approval for the name 'Cooper' to be linked with 'Mini'. Although at first this approval was only for a performance kit, more important developments were already on the way.

When British Leyland's much-loved Mini-Cooper 1275S had been killed off in mid-1971, most of us thought it was the end of a distinguished career for that sort of car. Out there, however, Mr Customer – yourselves – wouldn't let it die, and kept on nagging for a return. Even so, it was nearly 20 years before a new generation of Longbridge managers was persuaded to dig out the old files, blow off the dust from the old marketing profiles and relaunch the Cooper badge.

In the meantime British Leyland had died, discredited, in the late 1970s, Austin-Rover had followed, and a company called the Rover Group had then taken its place: not only that, but since 1988 Rover had been owned by the British Aerospace Group. Most of Longbridge management's old Mini-Cooper enthusiasts had moved on, and the Mini – though still using A-Series engines, on the same old assembly lines – had become a marginalised model.

Personal interest from British Aerospace's chairman, Graham Day, had much to do with its survival, but management had to be very canny. This explains why the very first batch of 'new' Mini-Coopers would be officially-approved conversions of ordinary Minis, twin-carburetted 64bhp/998cc-engined cars to be built by John Cooper at his Worthing premises in 1989. That conversion, incidentally,

was only available on manual transmission cars, which had no catalytic converter fitted.

When Britain's *Autocar* tested one, it headlined its feature 'Return of the White Roof', and (although this car only had 64bhp) cooed over the increase in performance,

After many years of nagging, John Cooper got his way and saw the 'Mini-Cooper' brand reinstated. First there was the carburetted A-Series type of 1990, which was followed by this fuel-injected derivative, the Mini-Cooper 1.3i.

This was the A-Series sub-derivative that relaunched a brand. Mainly for sale in Japan, John Cooper's private business developed this 998cc twin-SU version of the A-Series engine for use in Minis. Austin-Rover approved, soon put their own version of the reborn Mini-Cooper back on the market, and the rest is history.

and character. Maybe a top speed of just 85mph, and 0–60mph in 13.2 seconds merely put this car back on a par with the Mini-Cooper of the 1960s, but who was counting? Cast alloy wheels, a three-spoke alloy steering wheel, a bit of wheelspin if and when you were lucky, the white roof *and* the special livery (which included stripes along the side, and rear decals) made it all worthwhile, though it came at a rather stiff price – for the conversion cost £1,466.

Series-production Mini-Coopers – and fuel injection at last

That, though, was only a start, for with plenty of A-Series capacity now available (the Metro was just about to be re-engined with the new-generation K-Series power plant) there was every reason to promote the Mini brand once again, so Rover planned to start building Cooper-badged Minis at Longbridge once again. The very first of these new-generation 1,275cc-engined cars was launched in July 1990.

However, although the name was the same as in the 1960s, the technical specification was very different and much less specialised. Not only that, but everything from the engine to the transmission, the suspension, brakes and body equipment, had 'grown up' in the intervening years.

Because of the need to meet the latest noise and exhaust emission regulations, which were by now proliferating and becoming more severe all over the world, the new cars had to be fitted with single-carb 1,275cc engines so that they could produce acceptable performance *and* a clean exhaust. This was most critical in Japan, where the cult of the Mini remained strong.

The reborn Mini-Cooper engine only produced 61bhp (the same as the contemporary MG Metro), which rather disappointed enthusiasts who had been expecting more. Rover originally suggested that only 1,000 of the highly-specified, highly-decorated first limited edition cars (which cost £6,995, and included facsimiles of 'John Cooper' signatures on the bonnet stripes) would be produced, but in the end no fewer than 1,650 were made before the standard spec was introduced, its features somewhat slimmed down.

Then, within months, John Cooper's latest officially-approved Mini-Cooper S conversion went on sale – not built at Longbridge, but converted at Worthing in Sussex – this adding 17bhp, and 10mph to the top speed, all helped along by the use of twin SU carburettors and a reworked five-port cylinder head. With a top speed of 97mph, it was the fastest 'official' Mini so far put on the market.

Because of the way that exhaust emission regulations

The Mini-Cooper brand was officially reborn in July 1990, with the special limited edition that included 'John Cooper' signatures on the white striping on the bonnet.

Coopers all around – with John Cooper, his son Michael, and two examples of the reborn A-Series-engined Mini-Coopers of the 1990s.

When the Mini-Cooper 1.3i was introduced in October 1991, the A-Series engine was virtually submerged under a plastic cover ahead of the distributor and ignition wiring, and by a large injection air cleaner.

were becoming ever more severe worldwide, the specification and equipment of the A-Series then had to be upgraded yet again for the 1992 model year. From October 1991, the Mini-Cooper 1.3i therefore took over on the production lines at Longbridge, that magic letter 'i' showing that the engine had been fitted with single-point Lucas fuel injection.

As far as the 30-year saga of the Mini was concerned, this was a first (other less-powerful Mini models would follow suit a year later), especially as space had somehow been found underneath the virtually flat floor pan for a three-way catalytic converter. The quoted peak power even edged up to 63bhp, and the top speed eased up to over 90mph.

Amazingly, this kept the A-Series – and the Mini – alive, and fleetingly in the headlines, for several more years to come, though at Longbridge fewer and fewer of these appealing cars were being assembled. Although the five-millionth Mini had been built in 1986, annual production had since fallen to less than 40,000, and by 1996 it fell to

less than 20,000 for the very first time. The reason, simply, was that this time – well over 40 years after production of this gallant old engine had begun – the A-Series was starting 'The Long Goodbye'. Not only that, but after more than 20 years of starts and stops on such projects, a successor to the Mini was finally on the way.

To emphasise this, an all-new engine, coded the K-Series, had arrived in 1989 and, in its own way, would become as successful and as controversial as the A-Series had ever been.

The K-Series – an A-Series replacement at last

By the 1980s there must have been engineers and managers at Longbridge who thought that they would not live to see the A-Series replaced, or even sidelined, that it was somehow immortal. Time and time again, as I have detailed in earlier chapters, dedicated teams had set out to change, improve or even replace the A-Series. Time and time again they had designed new engines that showed every promise of finally being better – more powerful, more economical, lighter and cheaper to manufacture – but time after time their efforts had been frustrated by short-termism, inertia, company policy changes or (most persistently) a lack of investment capital to make it all possible.

Accordingly, it was not until August 1989 that the Rover Group finally revealed its new small-car engine. No less than 38 years after the A-Series had made its bow (that had been in October 1951), and after a number of false starts, changes of management, changes of strategy and constant reshuffling of corporate alliances, the all-new K-Series arrived, supposedly ready to take over.

Let us not get too confused, however, by the K-Series title, for this was not even an evolution of the original engine which Geoff Johnson's team had devised in the 1970s (which I described in Chapter 8), but an entirely different engine, both in concept and layout. Neither was it to be a direct replacement for the ageing A-Series, as it was generally agreed that no modern engine could possibly do that, and in any case it would provide a choice of larger cylinder capacities, and much more potential power.

Compared with the A-Series – and logically so, because it was being developed 40 years later – it was to be much more technically advanced, more upmarket, and in fact was a statement of what an engine for a new small Austin-Rover Group car should be and should look like. Of vital importance was that it would not, could not, and had never been planned to, fit into an existing Mini, though it would fit into every other engine bay at Rover that mattered.

Nor was it a direct development of the advanced three-cylinder engine unveiled in BL Technology's ECV3 research vehicle of 1982, though conspiracy theorists would suggest that it was. After Spen King had moved from Longbridge to Gaydon, to become BL Technology's deputy chairman, he and his team spent much time working on advanced machines intended to be super-economical. Announced at the end of that calendar year, ECV3 (ECV stood for Energy Conservation Vehicle, by the way) was the third such project, a transverse-engined front-wheel-drive car of Allegro/Maestro size, with a smoothly-detailed five-door body style that had been inspired by Harris Mann.

The engine in this car was a 1,114cc three-cylinder unit, with E-Series (not A-Series) bore and stroke dimensions, but with an entirely different head, a single overhead camshaft and four valves per cylinder. In later years there were suggestions that this was a direct ancestor to the definitive K-Series, though as every significant feature of the K-Series was different, this looks difficult to prove. BMC guru Ian Elliott reckons that the only way such a

link could be drawn is by referring to the K-Series launch booklet, circulated in 1989, which suggested that: 'Work on a three-cylinder, twelve-valve ECV3 project at the company's research and testing centre at Gaydon had already given some early leads in low emission, multi-valve, lightweight engine technology' – but nothing more concrete than that. It was the knowledge, rather than the hardware, which provided any inspiration.

Accordingly, when the new power unit appeared it created a wave of technical and marketing interest in the industry, and in the media. If it wasn't to be a direct replacement for the A-Series, for what cars could it be used? If it would not, or could not, be fitted to Minis, then what were the implications for the Mini? Was it, therefore, to be the end for the A-Series, which now qualified as a vigorous but nonetheless definite engineering pensioner?

Hesitant K-Series beginnings

As I have already made clear, even in the mid-1980s Austin-Rover's reliance on the A-Series seemed to be as firmly entrenched as ever. Even though the company was growing closer and ever closer to Honda, at that time the A-Series engine still featured in the Mini, the Metro, the Maestro and the Montego. The sharing of Honda engines with other models, some of them indeed inspired in Japan, had only just begun, and was still confined to the Rover-badged 200 series, while larger Honda V6 engines were destined for use in the still secret Rover 800.

Even so, as the events described in the previous chapter have made clear, BL's top management (the cars side being led by Ray Horrocks and Harold Musgrove) had big plans for their company's future. Unhappily, not only were those plans regularly disrupted by the farce of chaotic labour relations, and the company's continuing financial losses, but it was also clear that there seemed to be no long-term future for the A-Series engine.

More than once, as had happened so persistently in the past, the A-Series' prospects were talked down with gloomy relish by motor industry pundits; yet on each occasion the robust little engine seemed to bounce back, as its continuance seemed to be essential to the company's survival. Most front-wheel-drive cars being assembled at Cowley and Longbridge in the early and mid-1980s continued to feature at least one derivative of the A-Series engine, and none could have survived without it.

Even so, and although the design personalities involved had changed considerably, the thought of replacing the A-Series completely was never abandoned altogether. By then Geoff Johnson had finally tired of producing great idea after great idea (and seen them vindicated on the test beds, and in test cars) and left the company; Ray Bates had moved out to his old stamping ground at Canley; and Spen King had moved on to become BL Technology's deputy chairman at their newly-developed HQ at the former RAF V-bomber base at Gaydon, south of Warwick. By the early 1980s, Roland Bertodo, as director of power train engineering, had effectively taken over where Geoff Johnson had left off, and yet another attempt was being made to revive a K-Series project.

Within a year of Sir Michael Edwardes vacating the chair of BL in 1982, his successor, Sir Austin Bide, formulated an ambitious (but costly) plan to restore the company to glory. Not only did this envisage the hiving off of Jaguar into the private sector (which did, indeed, take place in 1984), but it requested the government to provide up to £1.5 billion to underpin development of the next generation of cars and engines. Of that, no less than £250 million was earmarked for the design, development and tooling for a brand new small engine – which soon became known as the K-Series. The fact that any one of the engines designed by Geoff Johnson's team in the 1970s could have done the job earlier, just as well and for a much reduced investment was never mentioned.

Initially, the government (especially Prime Minister Margaret Thatcher) was not impressed, and suggested that there must be a suitable Honda engine which could do the job instead. Indeed there was – but the latest Bide-Horrocks-Musgrove management team was neither ready nor willing to cede even more control of its destiny to the Japanese. Musgrove, in particular, spent much time nagging away at Trade and Industry Secretary Norman Tebbit to approve the K-Series project, and his persistence eventually paid off, for by the mid-1980s approval had been given to go ahead with the K-Series project.

What, when and where?

There was, of course, no way that such a new engine could be brought to the marketplace in less than about four years, and there were several good reasons for this. No one at Austin-Rover, especially the engineers, wanted to see such a brand-new engine slotted into a long line of old models (and, by the time it was made ready, cars like the Maestro and Montego would be looking old), though they were eventually persuaded that the ageing Metro was a prime candidate for such an upgrade.

The new engine would have to be much more powerful, more compact, lighter *and* much 'greener' than the A-Series, able to produce much lower exhaust emissions and to be quieter in operation. It would have to meet all existing and proposed safety and emission requirements, especially as Austin-Rover was determined to get its products into new market territories where such laws were strict.

Technically, of course, all this was feasible – most of the potential hurdles had been cleared (theoretically, at least) several times in the past. Space to build such an engine could certainly be found at Longbridge, for as the demand for the A-Series gradually fell away, so did the need for such extensive production facilities (particularly in North Works and East Works). But surely this could not be a direct replacement for the A-Series?

Way back in the early 1970s, technical chief Harry Webster had wanted Geoff Johnson to produce a dedicated 1.0-litre engine (one which would *only* have suited the Mini, and which would therefore have replaced the A-Series), but in the mid-1980s Austin-Rover's product planners, led by Mark Snowdon, had abandoned that idea for a more ambitious scheme. There were other considerations too. Although the 1.7-litre and 2.0-litre O-Series (another Johnson-era design, new in 1978) had been well received, this was after all only a thorough updating of the B-Series, so a replacement for that power unit was also required within the group.

The result was that not one, but two new engine families were proposed, approved, designed, and eventually put into production at Longbridge. After decades of famine (and Len Lord's insistence on the adoption of not more than three engine families – A, B and C – for use in a host of models) this change of pace, emphasis and technical progress was remarkable.

This, in fact, led to a further change of priorities. Because what we may now call the 'Honda connection' was becoming more and more established, this meant that a larger new-generation engine would need to be fitted to the front-wheel-drive 800 range which was coming along in 1986: the result was that what was known as the M16 (a 2.0-litre, twin-overhead-camshaft, 16-valve evolution of the O-Series) took first precedence.

Almost by default, therefore, the new K-Series had to wait its turn, then to cater for several existing and planned ranges, and was provisionally laid out to have a capacity which would be based on 1.4-litres but could be shrunk to 1.1-litres (which was relatively straightforward) and stretched up to 1.6-litres. It would be a 16-valve twin-cam unit, and would be detailed to meet every possible piece of legislation (noise and exhaust emission) that fate could throw at it. That was the initial theory, but not only did management decide that it also needed a single-cam 8-valve version (which would only be seen in 'entry-level' models), but eventually it also wanted to see the engine stretched up to 1.8-litres.

The A-Series engine, therefore, was still safe – or was it? Was this a full reprieve, or merely a stay of execution?

The K-Series –
technically different in every way

Although the K-Series differed from the A-Series in every way – *every* way, not just many details – I ought to summarise, briefly, the main features of the engine which was to rule the roost at Longbridge from 1989 to 2005, when the company finally called in the administrators and the plant (which had, by that time, been sold to the Chinese) was progressively shipped of to the Far East.

The following comparison should emphasise that there was no carryover of design from one generation to the other:

	A-Series	K-Series
Layout	4-cylinder	4-cylinder, later a V6 version was added
Sizes (1951–2000)	803cc to 1,275cc	1,120cc to 1,796cc (4-cyl) 1,997cc to 2,497cc (V6)
Cylinder block	Cast iron	Cast aluminium
Cylinder head	Cast iron, five inlet ports	Cast aluminium, eight ports and exhaust ports (four-cylinder engine)
Valve gear	Overhead valves, two per cylinder, side-mounted camshaft	Twin overhead camshaft (except for 1,120cc and one version of 1,396cc, which had a single overhead camshaft)
Valves/cylinder	Two	Four (except two for single-camshaft head)
Camshaft drive	By chain	By toothed belt
Crankshaft	Three main bearings	Five main bearings (four with V6 engine)
Fuelling	SU carburettor	KIF carburettor, or Bosch-Rover fuel injection system

The K-Series, in other words, was entirely different from the old A-Series, this being obvious to anyone looking at the new engine for the first time. Not only was it built in a 'sandwich' manner – there were light alloy castings for the cam cover, the cam carrier, the cylinder head, the cylinder block, the main bearing 'ladder' and the sump pan itself – but all these were squeezed together by 16in-long bolts clamping the top to the bottom. The water capacity, by design, was strictly limited (and would become even more limited as larger-capacity four-cylinder types were developed), this becoming something of a regular problem in later years as engines overheated, and cylinder head gasket failures became commonplace.

To put this engine into historical perspective, the very basics of the cylinder design stemmed from work done on ECV1, ECV2 and ECV3 at BL Technology at Gaydon in the late 1970s and early 1980s, where their four-valve technology and 'clean burn' experience stemmed from what Geoff Johnson's team had already achieved, or suggested, at Longbridge.

In the early 1980s, Roland Bertodo had become director of product strategy, and in 1984 a member of his team, Sivert Hiljemark, became director of power train engineering and brought the technical specification of the new K-Series to maturity.

It then took a long time – a *long* time – to progress any further, during which work occasionally had to be halted entirely while efforts were made to finalise other projects like the larger M16 four-cylinder engine, and to learn everything which needed to be known about Honda's 2.5-litre V6. By 1988 many prototypes had already been built, by 1989 no fewer than 72 specially-modified Montegos had been equipped with K-Series engines, and when the engine was eventually shown to the specialist media the assembly lines had begun to roll.

At this time Rover suggested that they were already equipped to build up to 5,000 K-Series engines every week in East Works, and that they would marry all of them to a Peugeot-derived 'end-on' front-wheel-drive transmission, or to a still unspecified automatic

This cutaway drawing shows that the K-Series, which finally made its debut in 1989, was totally different from the A-Series that it would finally replace. Even so, bitter experience has shown that it was never as reliable as the gallant A-Series had become over the years.

transmission. By definition this meant that A-Series output was bound to be seriously reduced, and the space still available for it in East Works markedly degraded.

Death by a thousand cuts?

With the new K-Series established, and other new-generation Rover Group engines also being launched, these gradually, but inexorably, took over from the A-Series. At Longbridge, the balance steadily moved over – from simple, cast-iron, overhead-valve technology to twin-cam, aluminium block and head, through-bolt construction.

Purely to set the record straight, here is how A-Series users gradually fell by the wayside between the late 1980s and the early 1990s:

Metro – launched 1980, last made with A-Series engine in 1991, re-engined with K-Series, later renamed Rover 100, and finally dropped in 1997.
Maestro – launched 1983, dropped in 1994.
Montego – launched 1984, dropped in 1994.

As far as the ageing but now sadly underused manufacturing plant in East Works at Longbridge was concerned, the first big hiccup therefore came before the end of 1989, when production of new-generation K-Series engines was getting under way just a few metres away under the same cavernous shed roof of what had

originally been the wartime 'shadow factory'. Then, after that, K-Series 200s and 400s sold better and better, demand for the old-fashioned Maestros and Montegos began to fall away, and in the end the arrival of the new-generation, Honda-based Rover 600 put a stop to them too.

In just 20 years the fall-off in demand for A-Series-engined cars had been catastrophic. In the 1970s, when A-Series manufacturing had been at its peak, there were periods when more than 10,000 A-Series power units were being built every week. Now, with only the Mini still using this engine, the old facilities were merely ticking over, with only 400 engines needing to be produced every week.

Even in 1994, however, diehard Mini enthusiasts, it seemed, were sure that their beloved old engine would survive yet again. Having bought Rover in that year, BMW speedily concluded that there was a future for the Mini brand and unleashed Rover to start thinking.

Would there be a new model, still with the A-Series engine? Unhappily – and this confounds all the legends which have been spread around – there would not. Even when chopped-and-widened prototypes – the Minki cars were perfect examples – were built, they used K-Series engines of one type or another. Then, when the first serious sketches were made of a new-generation Mini, these were not even drawn up with an engine in mind, but with merely a rather spacious and empty engine bay up front.

So now it really was the end . . . or was it?

CHAPTER 11

October 2000, and final retirement

Wednesday 4 October 2000 is a date that no Mini enthusiast is ever likely to forget; neither is it a date an A-Series watcher should forget. It was the fateful day when the last classic Mini of all rolled off the assembly lines at Longbridge, and when the use of the dear old A-Series engine finally came to an end.

Although MG-Rover, as the 'Phoenix Four's' company (see next chapter) had come to be named, was proud to note just how many Minis had been built since 1959 – officially the figure was no fewer than 5,378,776 – no one troubled to work out just how many A-Series engines had actually been built in all, over the years. It is only in recent times that it has been concluded that around 13.5 million were produced in the UK for use in BMC/British Leyland products, though many thousands more were manufactured by BMC/British Leyland subsidiaries in 'Empire' countries like South Africa and Australia. If you add in all the sales, quite unquantifiable for all the usual reasons, also made to British specialist manufacturers, along with a number of engines produced for spares or as replacement units, the total – the grand total, that is – must be more than 14 million, perhaps even approaching 15 million.

The long goodbye

As already noted in the previous chapter, A-Series usage had been gradually and persistently eroding since the late 1980s, especially after the new-generation K-Series had been introduced in 1989. The last 'new' user of the A-Series had been the Austin Montego, the medium-size front-wheel-drive range launched in 1984, after which production of various models using the engine gradually began to fall away in the 1990s.

First to go was the Metro, where the K-Series took over in 1990, when the model name was officially changed to Rover Metro, but it was not for another four years that the steady-selling (though hardly exciting) Maestro and Montego front-wheel-drive family cars also bowed out in favour of K-Series/Honda-inspired cars, where the engines were supplied from Honda plants in Swindon or overseas.

From 1994, therefore, this meant that it was only the Mini that still used the A-Series. Even at that time, the classic Mini (which was selling at only about 20,000 cars a year – about 400 cars a week) was only generating enough activity to keep the Mini engine facilities in East Works ticking over. Eric Bareham, who had been retired for many years when the opportunity came to tour East Works in the 1990s, was rather depressed to see one modest A-Series assembly facility tucked into one corner of that massive plant – but mightily impressed by the detailing, and the equipment, which went into the manufacture of K-Series engines.

Even so, it was a far cry from the heady days of the 1960s and 1970s when one in every two cars being assembled at Longbridge was a Mini, and most of the rest were 1100s and 1300s.

More shocks, however, were still to come. No sooner had BMW taken control of the Rover Group in 1994 than the German company made an in-depth study of all the company's brands and their reputations. To their astonishment, BMW discovered that Rover had virtually abandoned the Mini brand to its fate, especially as there had always been a lack of investment capital to rejuvenate, or replace, the existing models. Before 1994 Rover's policy was to keep the existing Mini going just as long as there were people to buy it, and while the existing specification could meet the legislative requirements of countries in which it was still on sale. Yet no Mini-replacement programme had been put in place. Various projects had been talked about over the years, but none had got very far.

Even so, BMW apparently identified the Mini brand as priceless, one to be rated at the same level as other world-famous icons such as Coca-Cola, McDonalds or Nike: 'When they asked us about the Mini,' project engineer Chris Lee told me, 'they were pretty horrified when we said, "When we can't keep it legal, we're going to let it run down."'

BMW marketing experts concluded that no one at Rover appeared to understand how valuable the Mini brand could still be for them, and it was this inertia, no question, which prolonged the life of the 'classic' Mini and its iconic A-Series engine for several more years.

Even so, it was almost from that moment that BMW decided on a strategy that would revive the fortunes of the Mini and rejuvenate the brand completely. There would be two interrelated strands to this strategy. Not only would work go ahead at Longbridge to generate an all-new Mini (which BMW would eventually call the MINI, and which would appear in 2000), but in the interim the existing 'classic' type would be given one final, substantial makeover.

In the next two years Rover was encouraged to have a good, long look at the existing Mini, and to bring forward a package of low-investment improvements for inclusion – effectively those which had already been schemed up and tested, in private, on a piecemeal basis. The result was a thoroughly updated Mini that went on sale in October 1996, and which kept the famous old model alive for another four years. Just 65,695 such cars would be built, all of them being A-Series powered. Many of them were exported, particularly to Japan.

Under the bonnet there was one final, and very significant, update to the venerable A-Series. For this final iteration of the legendary Issigonis car, the familiar 1,275cc engine was fitted with dual-point fuel injection (there would be one injector close to each of the siamesed inlet ports), while the traditional-type Lucas distributor was at last eliminated in favour of a Rover MEMS2J electronic engine management system. By this time, too, the compression ratio had been pushed up to 10.5:1, but peak power was still limited to just

63bhp, at 5,000rpm. (Compare this, by the way, with the 34bhp produced by the original 848cc Mini engine in 1959 – 49bhp/litre, instead of 40bhp/litre, which was an improvement, but not a startling one.)

One bonus connected with multi-point injection was that peak torque was now developed at only 3,000rpm (it had been developed at 3,900rpm on the previous model), and this more broad-shouldered output allowed a much higher final-drive ratio of 2.76:1 to be specified. The good news, therefore, was that high-speed cruising was more relaxed and economical than before; but the bad news was that the little car's acceleration was not up to the standards of the previous model.

From this point, incidentally, automatic transmission was no longer available – not only because it would not have been credible with such high gearing, but because demand for this neat and compact four-speed system had been eroding for some years: Automotive Products of Leamington Spa, who always manufactured this transmission, had thrown down a gauntlet to Rover, telling them that it was no longer economically feasible for them to keep on building such transmissions (it was never confirmed, but it was thought that this had fallen to no more than 2,000 units a year – just 40 every week), and that the lines were to be closed down.

Visually, too, there was another very important change made under the bonnet – the water-cooling radiator had finally been moved to the front of the engine bay, and immediately behind the grille, instead of living in the left-side of that bay, close to the inner wheel-arch. Nothing new here, you might say, for Mini-watchers had noticed front-radiator prototypes running around at Longbridge for at least 20 years, but it was not until the need to reduce noise levels – new drive-by regulations set a limit of only 74dB instead of a previously-allowed 77dB, which doesn't sound much but actually meant halving noise levels – and the space-saving elimination of the forward-facing electrical distributor, that this was done.

It was a significant packaging update. The new aluminium radiator, plus a thermostatically-controlled, electric-driven cooling fan, cooling hoses and a separate plastic expansion tank, cost considerably more than the old-type radiator (which, incidentally, was still retained for cars to be sent to Japan, where the new regulations did not apply), but certainly did a great job. The familiar whirring noise of multi-blade side-mounted fans was henceforth banished to the nostalgia cupboard, and the

Once BMW had decided to go ahead with a new-generation Mini, the classic type began to approach retirement. Here, in August 1998, John Cooper poses between one of the last of the classic A-Series-engined types and an early prototype of the much larger, new-generation models.

The end of an era – pop star Lulu drives the very last A-Series car, a Mini-Cooper, off the line at Longbridge in October 2000. The A-Series engine had been in existence for a full half-century, a quite remarkable career.

electric fan only cut in when water temperatures rose above a high, pre-set, level.

The use of a larger, 65Amp alternator was visually quite obvious, along with the latest type of poly-vee belt drive for that and the water pump. Tucked out of sight, but equally important in this comprehensive update, was an enhanced catalytic converter (in the exhaust system) and an extra rear silencer box.

The most obvious visual improvements to the car were to what an estate agent might call the 'fixtures and fittings'. A truly stylish fascia/instrument panel (wood on the Mini-Cooper) was dominated by the MGF-type steering wheel (complete with built-in airbag), the seating was improved, and the steering column was now collapsible and had new control stalks.

Even so, it was asking a lot for modern whiz-bang journalist/testers to be kind to the Mini when it had been around for so many years, especially when it was powered by such a (to them) old-fashioned engine. When *Autocar* tested a Mini-Cooper in 1997 they only felt able to award it three out of five stars, and described it as having 'prehistoric dynamics, but still great fun'. With the standard 63bhp engine it proved to be capable of just 88mph, with 0–60mph acceleration in 13.3 seconds, both of these figures being slightly down on the factory's own claims.

Even so, the testers discovered that: 'As ever there's a bouncy ride from the all-round independent suspension . . . but find a smooth, sweeping corner and suddenly it makes sense. Four-wheel-drifts are unheard of in contemporary front-wheel-drive cars, but the Mini is fabulous at pulling them off. Thanks to those tyres [175/50-13in Sport Pack, of course], the Cooper will round corners at perplexingly high speeds with an intimate, if crude, feel through the steering . . .'

On the other hand, the new marketing approach had not gone unnoticed: 'Today the Mini is even more of a fashion statement than it was in the '60s. Rover admits as much and is set to exploit this with a mesmerising list of options . . .

'In strictly objective terms the Mini has to be written off as a car from another era. But as an object of basic desire it's still up there with the best of them.'

The final A-Series-engined cars

Well before the end of the century, though, it was clear that the classic Mini was now living on borrowed time – and so was the A-Series engine. In a way, this situation

mirrored that of the famous MG MGB sports car, which carried on using the ancient B-Series engine for years after British Leyland had abandoned it to its fate.

In spite of the lavish launch of October 1996, annual Mini sales continued to slip – from 16,938 in 1997, to 14,311 in 1998 and 11,738 in 1999: in every case, far more were going to export (to Japan in particular), and less than half stayed in the UK. It was almost as if the Mini was a forgotten car at home. Tooling facilities for the manufacture of the Mini engine, still being made in East Works, gradually became decrepit, and were regularly maintained on the 'sticky tape and sealing wax' principle – the miracle being that the final version of the engine was as capable, and as neatly packaged, as any previous version.

There was even more bad news. By this time, Rover's current owners, BMW, had pushed ahead with sponsorship of an all-new next-generation MINI (the capital letters were important to BMW, if not to motoring enthusiasts), and had previewed it at the Frankfurt Motor Show in September 1997, letting it be known that it would go on sale in 2000 and that the classic Mini would finally be dropped to make way for it. It was made plain that there would be no place for the A-Series in the new-type MINI.

The fact that BMW eventually tired of the Rover Group's continuing loss-making and walked away from its problems in March 2000, subsequently selling the company to John Towers' Phoenix consortium (comprising himself, Nick Stephenson, John Edwards and Peter Beale, consequently nicknamed 'the Phoenix Four' by the media) for just £10, and that all MINI activity was subsequently transferred to BMW's Cowley plant – renamed BMW Oxford – made little difference to this process. Rover shortly became MG-Rover, and with plans being made to transfer Rover 75 model assembly from Cowley to Longbridge, which would complicate the factory's assembly process, the Mini was finally doomed.

Signalled weeks in advance, the end finally came on the morning of Wednesday 4 October 2000, when a temporary 'stage' was set up inside the south end of CAB1, where the very last Mini of all (and, by definition, the very last A-Series-powered car of all) – a Cooper Sport in coral red, with a white roof – was ceremonially driven off the final assembly line by singer and pop star Lulu. Looking lissom, vivacious, and hamming it up for the gathered photographers in true showbiz style, Lulu made no secret of the fact that she had been born a year before

Almost the very last of the A-Series pedigree – a Mini of 1999–2000 poses across the river from London's Millennium Dome.

Nice registration – actually used by Michael Cooper on his own personal machines for many years, this particular car having no less than 110bhp from its 1,275cc A-Series engine.

design work on the A-Series had even begun!

MG-Rover managing director Kevin Howe made much of the occasion ('We're paying tribute to a motoring legend, and it's not without a tear in our eyes . . .'), which was also stage-managed to show that the Rover 75, which was posed alongside the last Mini, was about to start production at Longbridge.

In spite of the hype surrounding the demise of this appealing little car, however, there was no doubt that its time had come, as sales had almost dried up. Even after a price reduction of about £900 in 2000, it took time for the last 2,000 stocked Minis to find retail customers. In the meantime, BMW had previewed its own all-new MINI, though sales of that model were not likely to begin until mid-2001.

Now there was no going back, and no possibility of revival. Rover announced that no fewer than 5,378,776 Minis of all types had been built since 1959, and that this, the last Mini of all, would eventually be handed over to the British Motor Industry Heritage Trust at Gaydon for safekeeping. Finally registered X411 JOP, it went to

The very last Mini – and, by the same token, the very last A-Series car – was produced in October 2000, and was immediately handed over to the British Motor Industry Heritage Trust for safekeeping, where it lives to this day. In this posed shot, the last car (red) and 'Old Number One' Mini are the stars. Bob Dover (left, CEO of the BMIHT) and Nick Stephenson (deputy chairman of MG-Rover) do the ceremonial honours.

Gaydon in December 2000, when the handing-over of keys ceremony was made with the last car alongside one of the very oldest surviving Morris Mini Minors of all (621 AOK, originally built on 8 May 1959) – and it now lives on, in a glass case, in the BMIHT museum.

This, though, was not the end. To quote Winston Churchill, after Britain's wartime triumph in the battle of Alamein in 1942: 'This is not the end. It is not even the beginning of the end. But it is, perhaps, the end of the beginning.' Although new-car assembly had ended, the Mini's reputation continued to grow. Every time the new MINI made the news, a damp-eyed writer would invariably refer to the original car. Mini one-make Clubs continued to grow, as did the restoration business that followed the loss of the production car. One thing was for sure – that the legend of the A-Series engine was also secure.

When the Mini was finally laid to rest, most of the design team had gone ahead, but Jack Daniels (Alec Issigonis' faithful interpreter and 'pencil man') was still alive, mentally alert at 88 years of age, and proud to recall some of the highlights of this fabulous machine's career:

'I'm both proud and sad. I never thought the car would last 41 years, but everyone has had one, from royalty downwards.'

Perhaps it was as well that BMW's new-generation MINI bore no technical relationship to the classic Mini, for Alec Issigonis would have hated that. Quite simply, his Mini was irreplaceable.

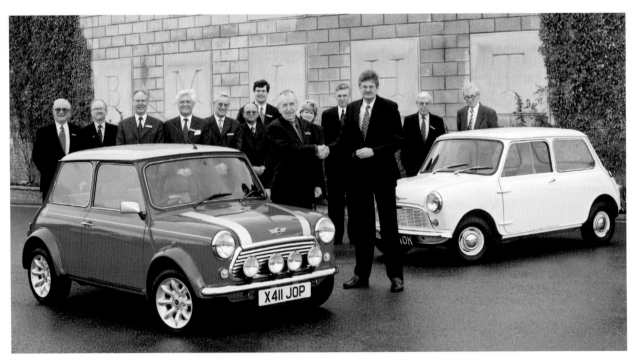

CHAPTER 12

Longbridge factories – now demolished

I f I am to give one heartfelt, and single, piece of advice to those who once revered the Longbridge site as the centre of the Austin, then the BMC, empire it is this – don't pay it a visit today. The state to which this one-time colossus of British car manufacture has descended is depressing, yet so typical of what has happened to the industry as a whole in recent years. Not only did 'the Phoenix Four' sell out almost all of the Longbridge 'estate' before MG-Rover's finances collapsed in 2005, but much of that old factory, and a considerable area of what became known as 'Chinese territory', latterly owned by the SAIC, has now been demolished. Two phrases now apply – 'devastated wasteland' or, more diplomatically, 'work in progress'.

If you study the aerial shot published on page 167, you will see a complex which covered more than two miles from north to south, one that was mainly bordered by the main Birmingham–Cheltenham railway line and straddled the main A38 trunk road from Birmingham towards the M5 motorway. But that was in the late 1960s.

As far as the history of the A-Series engine is concerned, the only remaining buildings with any relevance to the story I have now told are the two massive CABs (Car Assembly Buildings), the first of which was commissioned in 1951, just in time to accommodate the launch of the all-new Austin A30, while the second (CAB2) was built to accommodate the new front-wheel-drive Austin/Morris 1100. In half a century (1951 to 2000), millions of A-Series engines were fitted to cars assembled in those buildings.

For the sake of rounding off the story, let us take a look at the situation as it stands today (2011). Much of the historic old site has been owned by a property development company, St Modwen, since the early

2000s, and much of it has been ruthlessly prepared (*ie* bulldozed) ready for new non-automotive buildings to be erected. West Works, the vast complex on the other side of the A38 from the main Longbridge complex, where body pressings had been stamped and where complete shells (including those of the A30/A35, Mini and Metro ranges) had been assembled, has been completely demolished and levelled. More than half of that entire site was built and commissioned in 1978, in order to construct the then heavily-robotised Mini Metro body assembly facilities. Accordingly, it only had a working life of about 25 years, and has now disappeared for ever.

The massive transporter bridge over the A38 road, which channelled the brand-new bodies to the CABs for final assembly, has also been taken away. Soon after MG-Rover had abruptly ceased operations in 2005, a strong and somewhat scurrilous rumour built up that many of the bodyshells on their way from one factory block to the other were still trapped, stationary, on that bridge, but this was apparently an urban myth.

North Works, the site of the first major expansion of Austin activity in 1916–17 – expansion, that is, from the original 'South' Works – was a cramped site constrained by the A38 main road, by the mainline railway and by the spur railway which led past West Works on its way to Halesowen and beyond. Because it had reached the limit of expansion, and was looking old, it had had nowhere to go for many years. Originally it was set up as a vast machine shop and foundry, but it came to concentrate on engine manufacture from 1928. It was here that the A-Series originally went into production in 1951–52, but after that process was transferred to East Works in the 1960s (see below) North Works became underused. This factory has also been completely levelled, and its site is being redeveloped. New buildings abound, this area being further advanced than other sections of the St Modwen 'estate'.

South Works was the title eventually bestowed on the original Austin factory, the purchase of which I detailed in Chapter 1 and in the panel on page 15 ('Longbridge, the original factory'). It was here that the very first Austin cars were produced from 1906 onwards, and the shell of the complex remained at the heart of BMC/British Leyland/ Rover Group manufacturing operations until the end, after many extensions and revisions had been made over the years. Until the first CAB unit was completed in 1951, in post-war years this was also where final assembly of many Austin cars and trucks had been taking place.

Like North Works, South Works was constrained by roads and railways on three sides – by the B4120 road towards Barnt Green and Redditch, by the mainline railway, and by the spur railway – but until the 1950s there was always a large and originally undeveloped area to the south of that, where small aircraft could, and did, take off and land. Unsurprisingly, this area was always known as the 'Flying Ground', and it was to prove invaluable to Austin after the Second World War, when the company, directed so forcefully by Leonard Lord, needed to erect new assembly plants. It was here that the two most modern plants – CAB1 and CAB2 – along with other ancillary buildings, a large administrative building ('The Kremlin' as it was whimsically known, for it housed Len Lord and his closest colleagues), a new styling building (the 'Elephant House') and a big extension to the engineering block were all located.

To help house the colossal number of cars then being produced every week, a multi-storey car park for short-term storage was also added, close to the exits of CAB1 and CAB2, though as production numbers fell this was demolished by MG-Rover in 2001.

No sooner had MG-Rover gone into receivership in 2005 than St Modwen unveiled plans for redeveloping part of this Longbridge estate (for they had bought the freehold some time beforehand), the result being that the whole of the original (and historic) South Works was demolished, flattened and prepared for redevelopment like the majority of the other areas.

Almost all of the buildings erected by BMC on the old 'Flying Ground' in the 1950s and 1960s, however, had remained in the ownership of MG-Rover, and have survived (a view of the site, from Google Earth, is

enlightening). These, of course, include the CABs, and in recent years they have come to form the core of what Longbridge's modern owners, SAIC of China, are using to relaunch the MG brand in the UK, though the potential output they quote is still pathetically small.

As I have previously commented, the title applied to the 'East Works' part of Longbridge is really a misnomer, for it was located to the south of South Works! Confused? Austin staff were not, but everyone else seems to have been. Hemmed in by the main Birmingham–Cheltenham railway line on its eastern boundary, and by a local road on the western side, this was a massive half-mile-long complex, the last major expansion ever applied to Longbridge. Originally set up in 1936–37, the main building measured 1,500ft by 400ft, but much more was added over time. At first it set out to manufacture and assemble military aircraft engines, and then, from 1938–39, complete military aircraft such as the Fairey Battle, the Short Stirling bomber, the Hawker Hurricane and, latterly, the legendary Avro Lancaster bomber. In the original scheme of things this site was government-owned and financed, with Austin being paid a handsome fee for running the operations.

An important adjunct, a building known as the 'Flight Shed' for entirely logical reasons (for it was on the edge of the 'Flying Ground', where aircraft were made available for flight), was erected close by. In later years it was used to build transmissions for cars like the Marina, and as of 2010–11 it was still standing, though ownership was due to revert to St Modwen during the year.

After the Second World War, Austin's contract to run East Works (it was also known as 'Cofton Hackett', after the nearby village) for the government was suspended, the State took it back, and for a time it was occupied with the building of parts for prefabricated houses. From 1950, however, it came back into Austin's orbit, and was soon completely re-equipped to produce what became known as the Jeep-type Austin Champ 4x4 military vehicle, and thousands of four-cylinder and eight-cylinder Rolls-Royce diesel engines. Truck assembly eventually found a home there too. Eventually it would become a massive BMC power-house for the manufacture of engines and transmissions – it was, for instance, the location of all E4 and E6 engine assembly in the UK, as used in Allegro, Maxi and 2200 models.

It was in this period that it also became the second, and permanent, home for the manufacture of A-Series engines, which had outgrown their original premises. As already noted, the move from North Works came in 1962–63, as part of the vast 1100/1300 programme, after which A-Series engines were built in East Works, at a gradually diminishing rate, until 2000, a period of almost 40 years. The replacement for the A-Series – the overhead-cam K-Series four-cylinder and V6-cylinder types which powered so many Rover and Land Rover models in the 1990s and 2000s – also took shape here.

During and after BMW's ownership of the Rover Group in the 1994–2000 period, East Works was decisively split into two manufacturing areas – power train (ie engines) and front-wheel-drive transmission plants. However, after the 'divorce' from BMW in 2000, and as the German company gradually turned its new-generation MINI into more of a 'German' rather than a 'British' design, the complex rapidly became underused. Along with other areas at Longbridge, St Modwen came to own the site, and after the collapse of MG-Rover in 2005 it was progressively levelled.

By 2010–11 the huge site was completely flat, but brochures show that substantial plans for redevelopment by St Modwen were already in place. The story is that when the Pope visited Birmingham in September 2010, and celebrated Mass in nearby Cofton Park, the flattened area which had once been such an important part of the Longbridge estate was used to park thousands of coaches and cars used by those who attended the service.

Afterlife

Once A-Series manufacture closed down completely in 2000, MG-Rover rapidly erased any evidence that such a magnificent little power unit had ever been built there, and it soon became clear that today's classic car enthusiasts would have to rely on the usual parts supply operation and on the reclamation of existing castings and forgings.

Although Unipart still held the contract to service all BMC/British Leyland cars of the period, this was not a simple project. With grateful thanks, therefore, I quote the ex-Rover Group PR person Ian Elliott, who probably knows more about this than any other historian:

'The standard procedure was always for the Parts operation to project their likely "10 year" requirements and place an "all-time buy" order before the plant was dismantled. In October 2000 I suspect the Parts situation was a little complicated, as I believe MG-Rover were already looking to terminate the Unipart contract and begin the process of moving the parts business to Caterpillar, which eventually branded it X-Part.'

In recent years ambitious A-Series tuners have continued to work away at getting more and more power for motorsport purposes, with Mini Spares of Potter's Bar, North London, (skilfully aided and abetted by Keith Calver) being typical of the companies that have managed to enlarge the 1,275cc unit to 1.4-litres, or even marginally more, and to achieve well over 130bhp – all without making major changes to the original Weslake-style combustion chamber. Where the limits of tuning, caused by event regulations, do not apply, there have been continual advances in technology, whether it be in new materials, lubricants or electronics.

What this means – and every A-Series user and enthusiast will be delighted to remember this – is that this magnificent little engine reached its 60th birthday in 2011 with no sign of it finally disappearing from the scene. By any motor industry standards, it must be one of the most successful engines ever put on sale in the UK, and as far as Austin, BMC or British Leyland is concerned, it was an engine which was absolutely essential to their long-term existence.

Will any other engine ever come along to beat that?

Production Figures

Miraculously, production figures for almost every British A-Series user at Austin, BMC and British Leyland are known, and are listed here. Unhappily, however, no one can say, and no written records exist to tell us, how many engines were provided to the many small and independent concerns which also used the A-Series engine; nor does the number of diesel-engined types (as used in the Mini Tractor) seem to be known. In some cases, too, the figures provided are on a 'best guess' basis.

The author, on the other hand, is quietly confident that, in terms of numbers built, no other British-made engine has ever beaten the achievements of the A-Series.

Model	Production (approx/if known)
Austin A30/A35	577,871
Austin A-40 Farina	342,180
Austin Allegro	494,295
Austin Maestro	300,000 (estimated)
Austin Montego	26,841
Austin-Healey Sprite/Midget	281,885
BMC 1100/1300 (all badges)	2,151,007
Mini (all badges, domestic, including Mini-Cooper)	5,378,776
Mini Metro (all badges)	1,516,165
Morris Minor/1100	1,267,954
Morris Marina/Ital	808,381
Total	*13,200,000 (approx)*

Competition cars included:

'Works' rally cars, including Austin A35s and A40s, Morris Minor 1000s, Mini-Coopers, Mini-Cooper Ss, Sprites, Midgets, etc.

'Works' racing cars including Mini-Coopers, Mini-Cooper Ss, Sprites, Midgets, etc.

Single-seater racing cars in Formula Junior and Formula Three – Cooper, and several other makes.

Special record-breaking cars from Abingdon, badged as Austin-Healey or MG types.

Customer types:

(Figures estimated)

Arkley	900
Dutton	300
Gilbern	100
Lotus Seven	200
Mini Marcos	700
Midas	350
Rochdale	250
Turner	300
Unipower	75

Index

Author's note: There are so many references to Austin, BMC and Leonard Lord in this book, whose actions, decisions, and spirit pervade this book, that I have made no attempt to provide separate index references for them.